Easy *1-2-3*® for Small Business

Sandra Cook Jerome, C.P.A.

COMPUTE! Books

Radnor, PA

Editor: Robert Bixby

Printed in the United States of America

10 9 8 7 6 5 4 3 2 1

Jerome, Sandra
   Easy 1-2-3 for small business / Sandra Cook Jerome.
     p.   cm.
   ISBN 0-87455-205-2
   1. Lotus 1-2-3 (Computer program) 2. Business—Data processing.
3. Small business—Data processing. 4. Electronic spreadsheets.
I. Title.
HF5548.4.L67J47   1989
658.15′028′55369—dc20   89-43125

COMPUTE! Books, Post Office Box 5406, Greensboro, North Carolina 27403, (919) 275-9809, is a Capital Cities/ABC, Inc. company and is not associated with any manufacturer of personal computers.

Contents

Foreword

No book is better suited to the small business user than this one. Look in the table of contents for the task you want to accomplish with *Lotus 1-2-3* and you'll find it. Turn to the page and follow the simple, step-by-step instructions. The result? A working inventory control program or a working check writing program, complete with macros. Whatever you need, just look it up and follow the simple instructions to have that handy business tool working for you.

If, on the other hand, you want to learn *1-2-3* from the ground up in order to construct a complete package of business applications, you have the option of working your way through the book from front to back. Use the author's carefully programmed instruction method to learn *Lotus 1-2-3* to create business programs that make operating any small business easier.

Author Sandra Cook Jerome, experienced writer, C.P.A., and teacher, has developed these exercises while educating managers and owners of small business in the use of *1-2-3*. She's answered hundreds of questions about creating spreadsheets that come from real-world business people facing real-life challenges. Let her expertise and experience work for you.

Learning *1-2-3* can be that easy. Acquiring the applications necessary to running a small business can be that quick and trouble-free. Give it a try.

1
Introduction

Lotus 1-2-3 is one of the most powerful tools available to the small business owner today. *1-2-3* transforms information that was once kept in your accountant's columnar pad into dazzling reports, what-if forecasts, and graphic presentations. The power of *1-2-3* can be overwhelming if you just want to print estimates for your customers, keep track of checks and invoices, or do a weekly payroll.

Easy 1-2-3 for Small Business contains the spreadsheets you'll need every day and straight-forward instructions to transform each into a dazzling report. You can also change each spreadsheet to accommodate the special circumstances of your company or client.

How This Book Can Help You

Although an understanding of *1-2-3* is helpful when using this book, it isn't necessary since each spreadsheet includes easy-to-follow, step-by-step instructions. The spreadsheets are created with a minimal number of commands and functions. You'll get the maximum value from reports, given the information you enter. For example, from the inventory spreadsheet you can print four different reports.

This book isn't intended to be a complete reference to *1-2-3*. The difficulty of using *1-2-3* originates from the complexity and power of the software. By using this book to create the spreadsheets you need to operate your business, you can learn the commands and functions most commonly used in a business environment. By ignoring the complicated scientific and statistical functions, you can easily become proficient with *1-2-3*.

How to Use the Instructions

Two basic tasks are involved in the creation of each spreadsheet:

• Press a key
• Type some numbers or letters

When a function key or command letter is to be pressed, the instructions appear like this: enter

/File **S**ave

and press Enter.

The word *enter* (lowercase) here means to press a keyboard key. For these instructions you would press the first letters of the commands, *F* and *S*, or highlight the command and press Enter. If you need to type a heading or amount, the instructions are to type

Easy Company

and press Enter. The word *type* means to type data into a cell. When you're finished entering or typing something, you'll frequently be instructed to press Enter. In this case, the word *Enter* (with the initial capital) means to press the Enter key (also known as the Return key on some keyboards). Any time you need to enter a cell range, the exact range is specified. It's usually easier to highlight the range with the arrow keys, but the complete range is given for clarity.

What's Included

Most of the spreadsheet instructions are in a *building blocks* style. You create the basic spreadsheet, enter your information, and print reports. From this basic spreadsheet you can add features to provide more information and reports. The purpose of this format is to help you move the data in and out quickly without becoming involved in complicated macros and formulas. Later, when time permits, you can add the macros, lookup tables, and databases without having to enter duplicate information.

Chapter 2 is a guide to worksheet basics. If this is your first time using 1-2-3, this chapter can be your reference guide to commands and functions. Release 2.2 and 3 basics are at the end of Chapter 2 and include file linking, search and replace of a range, the Undo feature, printing with Allways, macro learn, using multiple worksheets, and the new graph features.

Chapter 3, "Financial Reports," is a comprehensive group of financial reports for tax, creditor, management, and investor purposes. You can create each report in the simplest format and customize it later with features such as ratios or graphs. Then you can print the reports and graphs in various formats, depending upon your requirements. This chapter also includes instructions for comparative financial statements and for writing a business plan.

Chapter 4, "Daily Recordkeeping," contains the spreadsheets you need to operate the daily functions of your business. Each spreadsheet holds the data—checks, deposits, and invoices—in a simple form. From the basic spreadsheets, you can obtain numerous reports and summaries of the information in various formats. For example, from the check register you can print a distribution report, expense budget analysis, or account transaction report. From the invoice spreadsheet, you can create sales summaries, commission reports, or accounts receivable statements. The job estimating spreadsheet keeps a record of job costs and estimated profits. You can print the estimate, final invoice, and job cost record from this spreadsheet.

Chapter 5, "Account Balances," contains the spreadsheets to support the account balances in your balance sheet, such as inventory, accounts receivable, accounts payable, and fixed assets. The accounts payable spreadsheet includes a checkwriter option to print your accounts payable checks. The inventory spreadsheet contains four reports, including a *stock out* report for ordering parts and a retail price list for your customers. The fixed asset section provides you with listings of equipment for tax or loan purposes. Each piece of equipment has its own record of cost, accumulated depreciation, and current balance. Sorting instructions are given to create the listings by date, description, or ID number.

Chapter 6, "Payroll," contains two spreadsheets: one to calculate your payroll and another to store the payroll data and employee earnings records. From this data you can create payroll reports covering situations such as employees with overtime, employees with earnings exceeding a certain amount, or a complete earnings record for specific dates. Although this is the most difficult chapter, once you've mastered the instructions, changing for each tax year or adding your state payroll tax tables should be easy. If you have Release 3, the two spreadsheets are kept in one file as a group of multiple worksheets.

Chapter 7, "Other Managing Reports," contains a collection of spreadsheets helpful in analyzing and managing your business. Included is a tax estimator for tax planning, a loan amortization spreadsheet for comparing interest rates and terms, and a volume profit analysis for determining the break-even point and forecasting variable costs and profit.

Appendix A, "*Lotus 1-2-3* Commands," contains the command menu structure.

Appendix B, "Function Keys and Cursor Movements," explains what each function key does and how to move the cursor around the spreadsheet.

Appendix C, "New Commands for Release 2.2," shows the commands and function keys that were added in Release 2.2.

Appendix D, "New Commands for Release 3.3," contains the new commands, functions keys, and cursor movements for Release 3.

Release Changes

All of the spreadsheets in this book work with Release 2.01, 2.2, or 3. At the end of Chapter 2 you'll find the new commands and functions contained in Releases 2.2 and 3. Briefly, the new releases enable

- File linking
- Search and replace of a range
- Use of an Undo key

If you have Release 3, you can

- Stack worksheets in a three dimensional format
- Use a new depreciation function and macro command

With Release 2.2, you can

- Use the add-in Allways to create professional-quality reports

Release 3 requires a minimum of

- An 80286 microprocessor
- 1MB of memory
- A hard disk drive

If you have Release 3, you can link the invoicing and inventory files in Chapters 4 and 5. In addition, you can include the payroll spreadsheets in Chapter 6 in one file and view employee earnings records and the current payroll at the same time. In Chapter 5, you can use the new depreciation function to calculate depreciation according to recent tax law changes, allowing a change from double declining balance method to straight-line when the straight-line method results in a larger deduction. If you have Release 2.2, you can enhance the business plan in Chapter 3, the volume profit analysis in Chapter 7, and create the macro with the macro learn feature at the end of Chapter 4.

Please note: From time to time you will notice that your menus differ slightly from those shown or discussed in this book. This occurs because of variations between releases of *1-2-3*. All spreadsheets in this book work with Release 2.01, 2.2, and 3.

Summary

If you're familiar with *1-2-3*, go straight to the chapter that contains the spreadsheets you need. If you've never used the program, you'll want to read "Worksheet Basics" in Chapter 2. If you're upgrading to Releases 2.2 and 3, turn to the end of Chapter 2 to read an introduction to using the new features. Some of the new features are used at the end of each chapter: file linking is used in Chapter 5, printing with *Allways* in Chapter 7, multiple spreadsheets in Chapter 6, search and replace in Chapter 7, macro learn in Chapter 4, and the Undo feature in Chapter 7. None of the spreadsheets require the new releases. If you don't have the new releases, this book should be helpful in understanding their potential and deciding whether to upgrade and which release to choose.

2
Worksheet Basics

Installing 1-2-3

Lotus 1-2-3 is provided with an install program that simplifies installation. In fact, the program installs *1-2-3* customized for your system as you answer a series of prompts for monitor type, printer manufacturer, and whether you use a hard or floppy drive.

There are advantages in having a hard disk drive while using *Lotus 1-2-3*, including having the PrintGraph, Install, and Translate programs all in one place. Release 3 requires a hard drive. With a hard drive, the easiest procedure for installing *1-2-3* is to make a subdirectory for it and copy all the diskettes that came with the program into this directory. From the DOS prompt type

MD Lotus

and press Enter. Then type

CD \Lotus

and press Enter. Put the first diskette in floppy drive A and type

copy a:*.*

and press Enter. When this disk is finished copying, copy the rest of the disks using the same command. Type

Install

and follow the prompts in the install program.

To install in a floppy system, follow the instructions in your *Lotus 1-2-3* manual. If you have Release 2.2 or 3, you need to initialize the program. Put your System Disk in the A drive, type

A:

and press Enter. Type

Init

for Release 2.2 and 3 to initialize to program. Type

Install

and follow the prompts to install the program.

The Worksheet Screen

Bring up the spreadsheet screen by typing *123* at the DOS prompt. The startup screen will have *columns* lettered *A–H* across the top of the screen and numbers for the *rows* running down the left side. The intersection of these columns and rows are called *cells*, where information is stored. For example, cell B4 is the intersection of the second column across and the fourth row down. Cell D3 is the intersection of the fourth column across and the third row down. The cursor will start in cell A1 and you can move it down or across with the arrow keys. What you type on the keyboard will appear in a space above the columns. When you press the Enter key, it will move into the cell on which the cursor is resting.

There are three major areas in the spreadsheet:

• The control panel
• The worksheet area
• The status line

The control panel. The control panel has three lines. The first line shows the cell address, cell format, protection status, column width, and the value or label in that cell. On the first line in the far right corner is a READY mode indicator that switches from *READY* to *EDIT, ERROR, MENU, POINT, VALUE, LABEL, HELP, FIND, FILES, NAMES, STAT,* or *WAIT.* The most common indicators are

Figure 2-1. Worksheet Screen

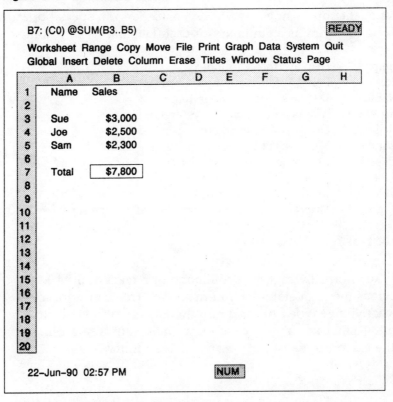

READY and WAIT. The READY indicator means you can enter your information. WAIT means *1-2-3* is calculating and can't accept input at the moment.

The second line is the *command menu* displayed when you press the slash key (/).

The third line is the *submenu*. It changes as you move the cursor to the right and left, highlighting a new menu item.

The last line of the screen is the *status line*, which includes the date and time in the bottom left corner of the screen and various indicators on the bottom right. The most common indicators you'll find in the bottom right corner are *CALC, NUM,* and *CIRC*. CALC means you need to press the F9 key to recalculate the formulas. NUM is displayed when you press the Num Lock key, and CIRC stands for circular reference. When you see CIRC, you've inserted formulas into two cells that depend on each other. Use the Worksheet Status command to find the problem cells.

Function Keys

The keys at the top or side of your keyboard perform special operations. The following is a summary of each key and its function:

F1	Help	Displays the help index
F2	Edit	Enables edit mode for current cell
F3	Name	Displays a list of range names
F4	Absolute	Inserts an absolute ($) reference
F5	GoTo	Quick movement to the specified cell
F6	Window	Moves back and forth between windows
F7	Query	Repeats a Data Query Extract or Find command
F8	Table	Repeats a Data Table command
F9	Calc	Recalculates the formulas
F10	Graph	Displays the current graph or redraws a graph

Cancel or Erase
Esc

The Esc key normally cancels a command and takes you back to the previous menu or status. If you make an error and want to erase what you've typed so far, press the Esc key. If you've already pressed the Enter key and want to erase the contents of a cell, move the cursor to the cell you want to clear. Enter

/Range Erase

and press Enter to accept the range as the current cell.

Moving the Cursor

Use the arrow keys to move from cell to cell. Other helpful keys to know are:

Home	Moves to upper left corner (A1)
PageUp	Moves up one page
PageDown	Moves down one page

Quitting and Saving the Spreadsheet

If you need to quit before completing the spreadsheet and want to save the file, enter

/File Save

1-2-3 will then ask for a filename. Type any name that will be easy for you to remember and press Enter. A filename can be up to eight characters in length but cannnot include any symbols such as + = . * / ? (> % or leave any blank spaces. To quit without saving, enter

/**Q**uit **Y**es

and you should be returned to the DOS prompt. Just type *123* to go back into the spreadsheet.

Other File Commands

Besides the File Save command explained earlier, these are the other file commands:

Retrieve	Load a file
Combine	Bring in all or part of another file
Xtract	Save only a portion of a file
Erase	Delete a worksheet, print, or graph file
List	List all files
Import	Bring another type of file into *1-2-3*
Directory	Change the current directory for files

Entering Numbers and Letters

Each cell can contain a number, letters or words, a formula, a date, or the time. To enter numbers, type the amount with or without the comma. If you see a row of asterisks (*****) instead of the number, use the Worksheet Column Set-Width command to increase the width of the cell. Words can be longer than the cell size as long as the cells to the right of it are empty. Use the following symbols to align the word in the cell:

'	Left side of the cell
"	Right side of the cell
^	Center

The backslash (\ ) prefix repeats the character. Enter \ = for a cell filled with double underscores. The double vertical bar (||) prefix prevents printing the cell contents. Enter || \015 to enter a printer setup command for condensed print for an Epson printer. If a letter or word begins with a number, such as a phone number, preface it with one of the symbols above. Otherwise 555-1212 will result in 1212 being subtracted from 555. Enter ^555-1212 to center the phone number in the cell.

Entering Formulas

To enter a formula, start with a cell reference prefaced with operators such as + ($ or − and enter operators such as + − / or *. The following are examples of simple formulas:

Add	+A1+A2
Subtract	+A1−A2
Multiply	(A1*A2) or +A1*.065
Divide	+A1/A2

Formulas also use functions to simplify calculations. Rather than entering +A1+A2+A3+A4+A5 to total a column, type

@SUM(A1.A5)

and press Enter. You can enter the cell range of A1 to A5 as A1.A5 or A1. .A5.

The following is a summary of the most used functions in business. It isn't a full listing since *1-2-3* contains many scientific and statistical functions. For a complete function list, see the *Lotus 1-2-3* manual.

@SUM	Totals a range of cells: @SUM(A1,A5).
@DSUM	Totals a field in a database: @DSUM(input range, offset, criterion range).
@DATE	Enters the date as a value: @DATE(90,04,30) for 4/30/90.
@TIME	Enters the time as a value: @TIME(22,15,0) for 10:15 p.m..
@IF	If-then-else function: @IF(A1<2,"LESS","MORE"). If cell A1 is less than 2 then *LESS* is displayed; otherwise *MORE* is displayed.
@HLOOKUP	Looks up a value in a table horizontally: @HLOOKUP(value to look up, table range, row number starting with 0).
@VLOOKUP	Looks up a value in a table vertically: @VLOOKUP(value to look up, table range, column number starting with 0).

Entering the Date or Time

To enter the date and time, use the @DATE and @TIME functions listed above and use the Range Format Date or Time command to format them into a readable format.

Entering a Menu Command

When you press the slash key (/), different menu options such as *Worksheet, Range, Copy, File, Print, Graph, Data, System,* and *Quit* appear across the top of the screen. To select a command, press the first letter of the option, then the first letter of the next submenu item until you've executed the desired command. You can also select a menu item by moving the right- and left-arrow keys until the option is highlighted and then pressing Enter. All the instructions in this book will be invoked by entering the first letter.

Commands

All the *1-2-3* commands are listed in the appendix but the following is a summary of the commands most commonly used in business.

Widening and Decreasing a Column
/Worksheet Column Set-Width

To increase a column to ten spaces in width, move the cursor to the column and enter

/**W**orksheet **C**olumn **S**et-Width

Then respond to the prompt *Enter column width:* with

10

and press Enter. To decrease a column to two spaces, move the cursor to the column and enter

/**W**orksheet **C**olumn **S**et-Width

then respond to the prompt *Enter column width:* with

2

and press Enter.

Inserting a Row or Column
/Worksheet Insert Row (Column)

To insert a row, move the cursor below where you want the row. Enter

/Worksheet Insert Row

and press Enter. To insert multiple rows, just use the up arrow to move up as many rows as you need. To insert a column, move the cursor to the right of where you want the column to appear. Enter

/Worksheet Insert Column

and press Enter. To insert multiple columns, use the right arrow to move right as many columns as you need.

Copying Cells
/Copy

To copy from A3 to B3, enter

/Copy

and respond to the prompt *Enter range to copy FROM:* with

A3

and press Enter. Respond to the prompt *Enter range to copy TO:* with

B3

and press Enter.

Absolute and relative copying. If cell A3, copied above, contained a formula, the formula would adjust to the new column. For example, a formula in A3 of *@SUM(A1.A2)* would read *@SUM(B1.B2)* after being copied to column B, which is *relative* to column B. If copied to C3, the same formula would read *@SUM(C1.C2)*, adjusting to column C. If you don't want the column to change, preface the column with an absolute ($) sign before copying:

@SUM($A1.$A2)

Or if you don't want the row to change, preface the row with the absolute sign ($):

@SUM(A$1.A$2)

Or preface both to keep the whole range unchanged:

@SUM($A$1.$A$2)

You can use the F2 (edit) key with the F4 (absolute) key to insert these absolute signs in a range.

Moving Cells
/Move

Moving a cell erases that cell and places the contents in the new location. To move from A1 to B1, enter

/Move

and respond to the prompt *Enter range to move FROM:* with

A1

and press Enter. Respond to the prompt *Enter range to move to:* with

B1

and press Enter.

Formatting
/Range Format
and /Worksheet Global Format

There are two ways to format, the Range Format command or the Worksheet Global Format command. To format just one cell or range of cells such as A1 through A3 to currency, enter

/Range Format Currency

and respond to the prompt *Enter number of decimal places:* with

2

for two decimal places; press Enter. Respond to the prompt *Enter range to format:* with

A1.A3

and press Enter. To format a date in A1, enter

/Range **F**ormat **D**ate **4**

and respond to the prompt *Enter range to format:* with

A1

and press Enter. If the complete spreadsheet will be in currency with two decimal places, enter

/Worksheet **G**lobal **F**ormat

and respond to the prompt *Enter number of decimal places:* with

2

and press Enter. There are many different ways to format the spreadsheet although the most common in business is currency. Enter

/Range **F**ormat

and use the arrow keys to highlight each option and the explanation below.

Printing the Spreadsheet
/Print Printer Range Align Go Quit

To print the spreadsheet enter

/Print **P**rinter **R**ange

and respond to the prompt *Enter print range:* with the range of the area you want to print; press Enter. Roll the paper up to the top of the form and begin the printing job by entering

Align Go Quit

The spreadsheet might be too wide to print on an 80-column printer without going to a second page. If you have a condensed print switch available on your printer, set it to condensed and from the print menu enter

Options Margins Right

and enter

135

for the new right margin. If your printer doesn't have a switch but accepts a condensed print code, enter from the options menu

Setup

For Epson printers, the string for condensed is \ *015.* Look in the *Lotus 1-2-3* appendix for your specific printer code. Enter

Quit

to quit the options menu. To start the print job, enter

Align Go Quit

Sorting the Spreadsheet
/Data Sort Primary Go
The database feature of *1-2-3* sorts data either in ascending or descending order. There are four basic steps to sort data:

• Enter the range to sort: Data Range.
• Select the row or column to sort on: Primary Key.
• Choose Ascending or Descending order.
• Go: begin the sort.

Always save the spreadsheet before beginning a sort. When entering the *Data Range*, specify only the data you want to sort, not the headings or blank lines below the data. Be sure to include all the columns and rows that correspond to the data. For example, if you have an address list you want to sort alphabetically by name, include in the range the address, city, and zip also. The column or row that will control the sort is the *Primary Key*. The Primary Key in the address list sort would be the column containing the last name. In Figure 2-2 below, the Data Range would be A4.E7. The Primary Key for a sort by name would be A4. You can specify an optional Secondary Key such as the first name column if you have many rows with the same last name. The command Reset cancels any ranges and keys you had previously entered and Quit returns you to the previous menu.

Figure 2-2. Database Search

	A	B	C	D	E	F	G	H
1		DATABASE RANGE		A3.E7				
2								
3	Name	Address	City	State	Zip			
4	Jones	343 South	Seattle	WA	98001			
5	Smith	265 West	Seattle	WA	98007			
6	Allen	454 North	Seattle	WA	98001			
7	Brant	467 East	Seattle	WA	98008			
8								
9						CRITERION RANGE F10.F11		
10		OUTPUT RANGE		A12.E50		Zip		
11						98001		
12	Name	Address	City	State	Zip			
13	Jones	343 South	Seattle	WA	98001			
14	Allen	454 North	Seattle	WA	98001			
15								
16								
17								
18								
19								
20								

Searching for Data
/Data Query

1-2-3 has the ability to search though data for items that meet a certain criterion. You can use the database feature of *1-2-3* if you need a special listing items from a database, such as customers with a certain zip code. The steps to execute a search are:

• Type the criterion headings.
• Type the criterion to search.
• Type the headings for the output area of the listing.
• Enter Criterion Range: Data Query Criterion.
• Enter the range to search: Input.
• Enter the range to put the listing: Output.
• Do the search and listing: Extract.

Search criterion. Before entering the search criterion range, you need to type the heading and criterion to search. In Figure 2-2, the criterion range is the field heading Zip and the zip code to be searched. The input range is where the data to be searched is located and includes the heading line. The output range is where you want your listing and the heading line. Be sure to leave enough room in the output listing range for all the records or you'll get an error message that there are too many records for the output range. You have the choice to Extract all records that match, Find and highlight each record that matches, Delete the records that match, or eliminate duplicate records with the Unique command.

Using the query key (F7). Use the F7 function key any time you change the field and criterion searched. If you change the zip in Figure 2-2 to 98007, you don't need to enter the input, criterion, and output ranges again. Press

F7

and the search will start again.

Figure 2-3 Simple Graph

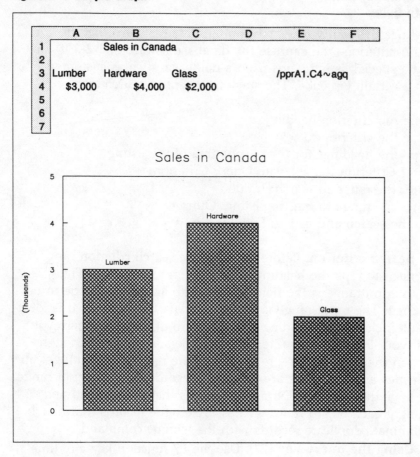

Creating Graphs

Sometimes a graph enables you to see your data much better than amounts listed side by side. There are three basic steps in creating a graph:

• Select the graph type.
• Define the range.
• Enter View to display the graph.

There are more commands that create titles, legends, color display, grids, and custom scaling. To create the simple bar graph in

Figure 2-3, enter the amounts from Figure 2-3 in columns A, B, and C and enter the following steps:

- **Graph Type Bar**
- **A** range: A4.C4
- **O**ptions Data-Labels-A
- **A** range: A3.C3 **C**enter **Q**uit
- **T**itles **F**irst line \B1 Quit
- **V**iew and press any key to return to the graph menu
- Save for printing later with PrintGraph

Viewing the Graph from the Spreadsheet
F10

It's possible to make changes to data in the spreadsheet and have the graph redrawn. Change the amount of lumber to $7,000 and press F10, and the new graph will reflect the change. Press any key to bring back the spreadsheet, change the value back to $3,000, and press F10 again to see the original graph.

Naming a Graph
/Graph Name Create

When you use the File Save command later to save the file, the graph settings are also saved. If you have different graphs in this file, you'll need to name each one. Enter

/Graph **N**ame **C**reate

and respond to the prompt *Enter graph name:* with

SALESCAN

and press Enter.

Printing a Graph

There's no option on the graph menu to print the graph. Sometimes you can produce a satisfactory graph with the Shift-PrintScreen key combination, but you can print a more sophisticated graph with the PrintGraph program. First save the graph in a graph picture file. Enter

/Graph **S**ave

and, when asked for a graph filename, type

SALESCAN

and press Enter. To quit the graph menu, enter

Quit

To exit *1-2-3* enter

/**Q**uit **Y**es

and at the DOS prompt type

LOTUS

and press Enter. This displays the *Lotus Access System menu*, which contains the PrintGraph program. Move the arrow key to highlight PrintGraph and press Enter. The PrintGraph menu displays the Image-Select and Settings options. Highlight the Settings option and press Enter. Check the printer type directory setups, and make any necessary changes. If all are correct, press Esc, highlight Image-Select, and press Enter. After the available graph filenames are displayed, select Salescan, and press Enter. Then enter

Align **G**o

and the graph will print. After printing, highlight the Exit option and press Enter.

Creating Macros

A *macro* is simply a range of cells on the spreadsheet that holds the keystrokes necessary to execute commands. The most common way to use a macro is to store print commands for printing different parts of a worksheet. The basic steps for creating macros are:

• Type the commands in a cell.
• Name the cell range with the Alt key and a letter.
• Execute the macro.

If you wanted to create a macro that would print the sales figures in Figure 2-3 whenever you press the Alt-P key combination, you'd type the following in any empty cell such as E3:

'/pprA1.C4˜agq

Naming a Macro
/Range Name Create

You need to name each macro range before you can execute it. To name the macro, enter

/Range Name Create

and respond to the prompt *Enter name:* with

\P

and press Enter. Respond to the prompt *Enter range:* with

E3

and press Enter. To execute the macro, type Alt-P (hold down the Alt key and type *P*). The commands typed in E3 will execute.

Release 2.2 and 3 Features

Releases 2.2 and 3 come with some excellent new features to save time and enhance worksheets. The features you'll use the most in a business environment include:

• File Linking
• Range Search and Replace
• Undo feature
• Allways printing add-in (Release 2.2 only)
• New graph features
• Macro Learn feature
• Using multiple worksheets (Release 3 only)

File Linking

To link a file you simply enter a formula that refers to another file. The structure of the formula should be

+<<file1.wk1>>B5

If this formula were in cell B5 of file2.wk1 then the amount in cell B5 of file1.wk1 would display in cell b5 of file2.wk1. If you have Release 3, you can link formulas or multiple cell locations. An example of a complex link is

+<<file1.wk3>>B5.B10+<<file2.wk3>>B5.B10

If this formula was in cell B11 of file3.wk3, then the total of the range B5 through B10 of both files would display. If your files aren't in the default directory, then precede the filenames with the directory location.

Search and Replace
/Range Search

This new command searches for labels and cell references and has
the option to replace with a new label or reference. For example, if
your worksheet has headings of Jan 89, Feb 89, and Mar 89 and
across row 1 you want to replace them with Jan 90, Feb 90, and
Mar 90, then enter

/Range Search

and respond to the prompt *Enter the range to search:* with

A1.C1

Respond to the prompt *String to search for:* with

89

and press Enter. Answer

Both

to Formulas or Labels. Enter

Replace

and respond to the prompt *Replacement string:* with

90

and press Enter. Enter

Replace

to replace the first find and continue. This enables you to make
sure you want it replaced before continuing. You can also use this
to replace a cell reference such as +*B6* with +*B5* in each formula
throughout a worksheet.

Undo Feature

The undo feature is enabled automatically after loading *1-2-3*. If not, enter

/**W**orksheet, **G**lobal, **D**efault, **O**ther, **U**ndo, **E**nable, **U**pdate

If you accidentally delete a range, move some cells to the wrong place, or format incorrectly, just press Alt-F4 and the previous command will be undone.

Publishing with Allways, Release 2.2 Only

Allways is an add-in program included with Release 2.2 that enables you to create professional-quality reports. Allways also has the ability to print graphs within *1-2-3* without using the Print-Graph program. To load Allways in Release 2.2 enter

/**A**dd-in **A**ttach

and press Enter when the filename ALLWAYS.ADN is highlighted. If no add-in files appear, you need to install Allways first. Use the instructions for setting up Allways in your *1-2-3* reference manual. After pressing the highlighted ALLWAYS.ADN file, you have the option to assign a key to load Allways each time you use *1-2-3*. Select 7 to make Alt-F7 the key combination that loads Allways. Press Esc twice. Now you'll be able to toggle between your spreadsheet and Allways.

Enter some information in your spreadsheet or load the Allways sample file—press Alt-F7 and Allways will load. Your spreadsheet might have a different appearance, depending on your monitor type. Press the slash (/) to see the Allways commands.

Changing the font. Move the cursor to the cell you want to change and enter

/**F**ormat **F**ont

and highlight the font, such as Triumvirate 14 for a larger print. Press Enter to accept the current cell or type a range for an area of cells.

Making a box. To make a box around a group of cells, enter

/**F**ormat **L**ine **O**utline

and type the range of cells you want the box to enclose.

Shading a box. To shade inside of a box, enter

/Format Shade

and select Light, Dark, Solid, or Clear for the type of shading. Enter the range of the box that was outlined.

Making and erasing a line. To make a line below a group of cells, enter

/Format Line Bottom

and type the range of cells under which you want the line. You can also select a line to the right, left, top, or on all sides. If you need to erase all or a portion of the line, select Clear.

Loading a graph. To load a graph into the spreadsheet, enter

/Graph Add

and respond to the prompt *Name of .PIC file:* with the name of your graph created in *1-2-3.* If you haven't saved the graph yet, return to *1-2-3* by pressing the Alt-F7 and save the graph from the graph menu. The next prompt is for the range to insert the graph; respond with a range for the graph and press Enter. Enter

Quit

to quit the Allways graph menu.

Printing with Allways. To print your spreadsheet in Allways format, enter

/Print Range Set

and respond to the prompt *Enter print range:* with the full range. Be sure to include the range of your boxes and any graphs you've added. Enter

Go

and the spreadsheet and any graphs will print.

You also save these when you save your *1-2-3* file. Press Alt-F7 to return to *1-2-3*, enter

/File Save

and press Enter when the filename is automatically displayed. The software will check to see if you want to write over your previous file, so enter

Replace

You'll now have three types of files:

FILENAME.WK1   *1-2-3* file
FILENAME.PIC   Graph file
FILENAME.ALL   Allways file

Graph Enhancements with Release 2.2 and 3

Both Releases 2.2 and 3 feature enhancements that simplify entering Legends, Format, and Data-Labels on graphs. You can now specify the range that contains legends for all data ranges instead of one range at a time. Enter

/Graph Options Legends Range

and type the range for the legends.

You can format the entire graph instead of one range at a time. Enter

/Graph Options Format Graph

to set the format for all ranges. You can now assign Data-Labels as a group. Enter

/Graph Options Data-Labels Group

and specify the group range. If your data is located in consecutive columns and rows, you can assign all data ranges at once with the Group command. Enter

/Graph Group

and specify the range and whether to use columns or rows as data ranges.

Graph options with Release 3 only. Release 3 adds some enhancements not found in prior releases. The main features are:

• /Graph Type: New graph types; Stock market and Mixed.
• /Graph Options Advanced: Add colors, fonts, patterns.
• /Worksheet Window Graph: See the graph in a window.
• F10: New Quick Graph without entering ranges.

Printing a graph with Release 3. Release 3 of *1-2-3* allows you to print your graph directly from the print menu without using the PrintGraph program. To print a graph, enter

/Print **P**rinter **I**mage **C**urrent **A**lign **G**o **Q**uit

or you can print a Named-Graph instead of the Current graph.

Macro Learn Feature

Macro Learn Feature Release 2.2. There are three steps to using the macro learn feature:

• Enter /Worksheet Learn Range: to select where you want the macro.
• Press Alt-F5 and perform the tasks you want to record.
• Press Alt-F5 and Enter to record the macro.

When you've followed these steps, the macro will appear in the range you specified in the Worksheet Learn Range command. To create a printing macro that executes with the Alt-P key combination, you need to name the macro range before you execute it. To name the macro, enter

/Range **N**ame **C**reate

and respond to the prompt *Enter name:* with

\P

and press Enter. Respond to the prompt *Enter range:* with the range specified in the Worksheet Learn Range command. To execute the macro, press Alt-P.

Macro Learn Feature Release 3. There are six steps to using the macro learn feature:

• Press Alt-F2 Erase previous macros in buffer.
• Perform the tasks you want to record.
• Press Alt-F2 Copy to save the macro.
• Press Tab and left arrow to highlight macro.
• Press Enter.
• Specify range to which macro should be copied and press Enter.

When you've followed these steps, the macro will appear in the range you specified in the Alt-F2 Copy command. To create a printing macro that executes with Alt-P, you need to name the macro range before you can execute it. To name the macro, enter

/Range **N**ame **C**reate

and respond to the prompt *Enter name:* with

\P

and press Enter. Respond to the prompt *Enter range:* with the range specified by the Alt F2 Copy command. To execute the macro, press Alt-P.

Creating Three-Dimensional Spreadsheets with Release 3

You can keep data in separate worksheets in the same file with Release 3. To open a new worksheet behind the current one, enter

/Worksheet **I**nsert **S**heet **A**fter **1**

and press Enter. The first worksheet is sheet A and the new sheet is B. To view both of these together, enter

/Worksheet **W**indows **P**erspective

Press Ctrl-PageDown and Ctrl-PageUp to move between the worksheets. To change the column widths in sheet B to match A, move the cursor to sheet A with the Ctrl-PageDown and enter

/Worksheet Global Group Enable

The group command will make any additional sheets in the file match sheet A. The cells in worksheet A are prefaced with an *A:* and worksheet B with a *B:*. For example, to copy from sheet A to sheet B, enter

/Copy

and respond to the prompt *Enter range to copy FROM:* with

A:A6

and press Enter. Respond to the prompt *Enter range to copy TO:* with

B:A6

and press Enter.

Working with Multiple Files (Release 3 Only)

Rather than opening another worksheet in the current file, you might want to open a saved file and display both it and the current file in 3-D perspective.

To open a second file, enter

File Open After

and respond to the prompt *Enter name of file to open:* with your saved filename. You can also create a new and separate file in memory and on the disk by using the command

File New After

and responding to the prompt *Enter name of file to create:* with your new filename. You can link the files with formulas or copy cells from one file to another.

To view both of the files at the same time, enter

/**W**orksheet **W**indows **P**erspective

and press Ctrl-PageDown and Ctrl-PageUp to move between the files. A filename indicator is in the bottom left corner of the screen to let you know in which file you're currently working.

To delete one of the files from memory, enter

/**W**orksheet **D**delete **F**ile

and enter the name of the file you want to remove from the screen. Don't use the File Delete command since this will erase the file from your disk.

To see which files are currently in memory, enter

/**F**ile **L**ist **A**ctive

and *1-2-3* will list the name, size, and date of all active files.

3
Financial Reports

In this chapter, you will create some spreadsheets necessary for loan applications, management decisions, and tax purposes. Each spreadsheet is in correct form—just substitute your account names and balances. There are two major financial reports required today for most businesses: the *balance sheet* and the *income statement*. From the information in these two statements, you can create other reports such as

• Comparative Balance Sheet
• Comparative Income Statement
• Current Ratio
• Acid-Test Ratio
• Accounts Receivable Turnover
• Merchandise Turnover
• Funds Statement
• Cash Flow Statement
• Projected Income Statement
• Pro-Forma Cash Flow

Lotus 1-2-3 also graphs some financial ratios. Each report will use a previous spreadsheet for its basis, enabling you to save the time of entering duplicate information. All the spreadsheets are in a simple format and should take about thirty minutes to create, once you're familiar with worksheet basics. At the end of the chapter are instructions on how to write a business plan with the reports you've created.

The Balance Sheet
There are three major categories in the balance sheet:

• Assets
• Liabilities
• Owner's capital

Figure 3-1. Balance Sheet

	A	B	C
1	Easy Company		
2	Balance Sheet		
3	December 31, 1989		
4			
5	Assets		
6			
7	Current Assets:		
8	Cash	$500.00	
9	Notes Receivable	$1,000.00	
10	Accounts Receivable Net	$11,700.00	
11	Inventory	$15,000.00	
12	Prepaid Insurance	$400.00	
13	Prepaid Other	$50.00	
14			
15	Total current assets	$28,650.00	
16			
17	Fixed Assets:		
18	Office Equipment	$2,000.00	
19	Less–Accumulated depreciation	($480.00)	
20	Shop Equipment	$5,000.00	
21	Less–Accumulated depreciation	($1,500.00)	
22	Buildings	$80,000.00	
23	Less–Accumulated depreciation	($35,000.00)	
24	Land	$30,000.00	
25			
26	Total fixed assets	$80,020.00	
27			
28	Total Assets	$108,670.00	
29		==========	
30	Liabilities and Capital		
31			
32	Current Liabilities:		
33	Notes payable–Bank	$500.00	
34	Accounts payable–Trade	$7,500.00	
35	Payroll taxes payable	$420.00	
36	Sales taxes payable	$400.00	
37	Total current liabilities	$8,820.00	
38			
39	Owner's Equity		
40			
41	Sam Easy, Capital Jan 1	$96,345.00	
42	Profit or Loss	$25,000.00	
43	Less Draws	($21,495.00)	
44	Sam Easy, Capital December 31	$99,850.00	
45			
46	Total liabilities and capital	$108,670.00	
47		==========	

Assets are the items such as cash, inventories, prepaid expenses, and equipment owned by the company. *Liabilities* are debts owed by the company to banks and vendors. The difference between assets and liabilities is the owner's *capital*. Since the assets must equal the combined total of the owner's liabilities and capital, the report is called a *balance sheet*. The example shown in Figure 3-1 is in *report* form with the assets listed above the liabilities and capital. Normally a balance sheet would have three columns for balances, subtotals, and totals, but this single-column format simplifies the conversion to comparative statements later in the chapter. It is also possible to switch this report form to the *account* form in Figure 3-2, page 41, with the assets on the left and the liabilities and owner's capital on the right. The last step will be an optional switch to this format. You will be given step-by-step instructions for creating, saving, and printing these balance sheets.

Creating the Balance Sheet

What follows is a brief review of the material from Chapter 2. If you're a *1-2-3* newcomer, you should read Chapter 2. Bring up the spreadsheet screen by typing *123* at the DOS prompt. The startup screen will have columns lettered A–H across the top of the screen and numbers for the rows going down the left side. The intersections of these columns and rows are called *cells*, where information is stored. For example, cell B4 is the intersection of the second column over *(B)* and the fourth row down (4). Cell D3 is the intersection of the fourth column over *(D)* and the third row down (3). The cursor will start in cell A1 and you can move it down or across with the arrow keys. What you type on the keyboard will appear on the line above the columns. It will move into the cell on which the cursor is resting when you press the Enter key.

Entering a Menu Command

When you press the slash key (/), different menu options such as Worksheet, Range, Copy, File, Print, Graph, Data, System, and Quit appear across the top of the screen. To select a command, press the first letter of the option, then the first letter of the next submenu item until the command is completed. You can also select a menu item by moving the right- and left-arrow keys until the option is highlighted and then pressing Enter. All the instructions in this chapter will be done by entering the first letter.

Cancel or Erase
Esc

The Esc key normally cancels a command and takes you back to the previous menu or status. If you make an error and want to erase what you've typed so far, press the Esc key. If you've already pressed the Enter key and want to erase the contents of a cell, move the cursor to the cell you want to clear. Press

/Range Erase

and press Enter to accept the range as the current cell.

Moving the Cursor

Use the arrow keys to move from cell to cell. Other helpful keys to
know are:

F5 (Goto)   Moves to any cell location
Home   Moves to upper left corner (A1)
PageUp   Moves up one page
PageDown   Moves down one page

Quitting and Saving the Spreadsheet

If you need to quit before completing the spreadsheet and want to
save the file, enter

/File Save

1-2-3 will then ask for a filename. Type

BalSht

and press Enter. A filename can be up to eight characters, but you
should stick to letters and numbers. Don't include any symbols
such as + = . * / ? (> % or leave any blank spaces.
    To quit without saving, enter

/Quit Yes

and you should be back at the DOS prompt. Just enter *123* to go
back into the spreadsheet.

Widening the Column
/Worksheet Column Set-Width

Since columns A and B must be wide enough to hold long account
names and balances, use the Set-Column Width command. To increase column A, move the cursor to A1 and enter

/Worksheet Column Set-Width

Respond to the prompt *Enter column width:* with

30

and press Enter. To increase column B, move the cursor to B1 and enter

/Worksheet Column Set-Width

Respond to the prompt *Enter column width:* with

12

and press Enter.

Entering the Headings Centered

Move the cursor to A1 and type

^Easy Company

or your company's name and press Enter. The ^ centers the text in the cell. Move the cursor to A2, type

^Balance Sheet

and press Enter. Move the cursor to A3, type

^December 31, 1989

and press Enter. Move the cursor to A5. Type

^Assets

and press Enter.

   Enter the remaining titles in cells A7 through A46 from Figure 3-1 or your own set of accounts. They don't need to be centered. Precede any account that starts with a number, such as *1st Bank Cash Account,* with a single quotation mark prefix: *'1st Bank Cash Account.* Otherwise, 1-2-3 sees *1st Bank* as a number and will return an error message.

Entering Formulas

Some of the cells hold formulas that add or subtract the information in other cells. Cell B28 adds total current assets to total fixed assets to obtain total assets. Move the cursor to B28 and type

+B15+B26

and press Enter. Move the cursor to B15, type

@SUM(B8.B13)

and press Enter.

The @SUM is a function that enables some timesaving. Instead of entering B15 *+B8+B9+B10+B11+B12+B13*, the @SUM function totals every cell from B8 through B13. To enter the remaining formulas, move the cursor to each cell and enter the corresponding formula:

```
B26    @SUM(B18.B24)
B37    @SUM(B33.B36)
B44    @SUM(B41.B43)
B46    +B37+B44
```

Formatting the Spreadsheet to Currency
/Range Format Currency

You need to format Column B to currency. Since you only want this column to be in currency, use the Range command instead of the Worksheet Global Format command. Enter

/Range Format Currency

and respond to the prompt *Enter number of decimal places:* with

2

and press Enter. Respond to the prompt *Enter range to format:* with

B8.B46

and press Enter.

Entering the Repeating Underline (\ =)

Cells B29 and B47 contain an accented underline created with the equal sign. To enter the repeating underline, move the cursor to B29 and enter

\ =

and repeat for cell B47.

Saving the Spreadsheet
/File Save

Since you can use this balance sheet each month or period, save the spreadsheet without data. To save the file, enter

/File Save

1-2-3 will then ask for a filename. Type

BalSht

and press Enter. If you've already saved the spreadsheet, press Enter when the filename *Balsht* is automatically displayed. The software will check to see whether you want to write over your previous file, so enter

Replace

to replace the file.

Retrieving a Spreadsheet File
/File Retrieve

To retrieve the balance sheet you've just saved, enter

/File Retrieve

Then type

BalSht

and press Enter.

How to Use the Balance Sheet

Enter the data in column B from Figure 3-1 or your own accounts. When entering amounts, don't use the comma or dollar sign. When entering a negative amount in parentheses as shown in Figure 3-1, precede the amount with a minus sign. Enter cell B19 as −480.00. If you see a row of asterisks instead of the amount you entered, that's an indication the column isn't wide enough to hold that amount. Use the Worksheet Column-Set command, /WCS, to increase the size of the column.

Saving the Completed Worksheet
/File Save

Save the new worksheet containing this period's data in a new file separate from the previous BalSht file. Enter

/File Save

Then type

BS1289

for *Balance Sheet December 1989* (or use any name that will be easy for you to remember) and press Enter. It's a good idea to save the file before printing.

Printing the Worksheet
/Print Printer Range Align Go Quit

You can print the balance sheet now. The print command allows printing to a file or printer. Roll the paper to the perforation or top of form and enter

/Print Printer Range

Respond to the prompt *Enter print range:* with

A1.B47

and press Enter. To begin the printing job, enter

Align Go Quit

If it doesn't print but flashes an error message, make sure the printer is turned on, online, and properly connected. Press Esc to clear the error and try again. If it still doesn't print, press Esc again and Quit the print menu. Try to print the screen by pressing the Shift-PrintScreen to test if the printer and cabling are correct. If it prints the screen, then possibly your printer isn't installed properly with the *Lotus 1-2-3* software. Try installing your printer per the software manual instructions. If your printer fails the Shift-PrintScreen test, then you have a problem with the printer, computer, or cabling. Check the troubleshooting sections in your computer and printer manuals.

Figure 3-2. Balance Sheet in Account Form

	A	B	C	D	E
1	Easy Company				
2	Balance Sheet				
3	December 31, 1989				
4					
5	Assets			Liabilities and Capital	
6					
7	Current Assets:			Current Liabilities:	
8	Cash	$500.00		Notes payable–Bank	$500.00
9	Notes Receivable	$1,000.00		Accounts payable–Trade	$7,500.00
10	Accounts Receivable Net	$11,700.00		Payroll taxes payable	$420.00
11	Inventory	$15,000.00		Sales taxes payable	$400.00
12	Prepaid Insurance	$400.00		Total current liabilities	$8,820.00
13	Prepaid Other	$50.00			
14				Owner's Equity	
15	Total current assets	$28,650.00			
16				Sam Easy, Capital Jan 1	$96,345.00
17	Fixed Assets:			Profit or Loss	$25,000.00
18	Office Equipment	$2,000.00		Less Draws	($21,495.00)
19	Less–Accumulated depreciation	($480.00)		Sam Easy, Capital December	$99,850.00
20	Shop Equipment	$5,000.00			
21	Less–Accumulated depreciation	($1,500.00)		Total liabilities and capital	$108,670.00
22	Buildings	$80,000.00			=========
23	Less–Accumulated depreciation	($35,000.00)			
24	Land	$30,000.00			
25					
26	Total fixed assets	$80,020.00			
27					
28	Total Assets	$108,670.00			
29		=========			

Saving the Worksheet with Replace
/File Save Replace

After printing the balance sheet save this spreadsheet one more time to keep the printing instructions in the file. Enter

/File Save

and press Enter when the filename *BS1289* is automatically displayed. The software will check to see if you want to write over your previous file, so enter

Replace

to replace the file.

Optional Change from Report Form to Account Form
/Move

It's possible to change the layout of the balance sheet from the current report form with the assets above the liabilities to an account form with the assets on the left and liabilities on the right. If you have a wide carriage printer or the capability to print in condensed mode, then you might prefer the account form. Make sure you've saved the file before attempting this move command. Enter

/Move

Respond to the prompt *Enter range to move FROM:* with

A30.B47

and press Enter. Then respond to the prompt *Enter range to move TO:* with

D5

Next you'll need to widen column D to 30 and column E to 12 with the command /WCS. Move to D1 and enter

/Worksheet Column Set-Width

Respond to the prompt *Enter column width:* with

30

and press Enter. Move to E1 and enter

/Worksheet **C**olumn **S**et-Width

Respond to the prompt *Enter column width:* with

12

and press Enter. Be sure to save this file to a different name if you want both the report and account format available.

When printing the account format, respond to the prompt *Enter Print range:* with A1.E31 and press Enter. This spreadsheet is too wide to print on most 80-column printers without going to a second page. If you have a condensed print switch available on your printer, set the switch to condensed, then turn the printer off and on to register the change to the printer. From the print menu, enter

Options **M**argins **R**ight

and enter

135

for the new right margin. If your printer doesn't have a switch but accepts a condensed print code, press Esc and enter from the options menu

Setup

For Epson printers, the setup string for condensed is \ *015*. Look in the *Lotus 1-2-3* appendix for your specific printer code. Enter

Quit

to quit options menu. To begin the printing job, enter

Align **G**o **Q**uit

The Income Statement

There are two major categories in the income statement: *gross profit* and *expenses*. Gross Profit is the gross sales or receipts less any returns, allowances, and the cost of goods sold. The cost of goods sold is the price you paid for the item, plus any costs associated with getting your product to the customer or manufacturing it. Expenses are the costs of doing business, such as advertising and rent. The format of this income statement is similar to the tax form *Schedule C: Profit or Loss from Business,* as required by the Internal Revenue Service. This spreadsheet resembles the balance sheet in the column size, heading, and format. To save time you can retrieve the file *BalSht* and Range Erase the account titles and formulas. Otherwise follow the instructions below to begin a fresh spreadsheet.

Figure 3-3. Income Statement

	A	B	C
1	Easy Company		
2	Income Statement		
3	December 31, 1989		
4			
5	Income:		
6	Gross receipts or sales	$175,000.00	
7	Less Returns and allowances	($350.00)	
8	Total receipts or sales	$174,650.00	
9			
10	Less Cost of Goods Sold	($63,000.00)	
11	Total Gross Profit	$111,650.00	
12		===========	
13	Expenses:		
14	Advertising	$3,500.00	
15	Bad debts	$400.00	
16	Bank Service Charges	$180.00	
17	Car and Truck Expenses	$2,200.00	
18	Commissions	$4,000.00	
19	Depreciation	$2,700.00	
20	Dues and publications	$30.00	
21	Employee benefits	$500.00	
22	Freight	$200.00	
23	Insurance	$4,000.00	
24	Interest	$5,000.00	
25	Laundry and Cleaning		
26	Legal and professional	$1,500.00	
27	Office Expenses	$320.00	
28	Pension and Profit Sharing		
29	Repairs	$50.00	
30	Supplies	$580.00	
31	Taxes	$1,200.00	
32	Travel	$40.00	
33	Meals and Entertainment	$200.00	
34	Utilities and Telephone	$5,000.00	
35	Wages	$55,040.00	
36	Other Expenses	$10.00	
37			
38	Total Expenses	$86,650.00	
39			
40	Net Profit or (Loss)	$25,000.00	
41		===========	
42			

Creating the Income Statement

Bring up the spreadsheet screen by typing *123* at the DOS prompt. (For further information on calling up and operating the spreadsheet, see Chapter 2.) If you need to quit before completing the spreadsheet and want to save the file, enter

/File Save

1-2-3 will then ask for a filename. Type

IncSt

and press Enter. To quit without saving, enter

/Quit Yes

and you should be back at the DOS prompt. Just enter *123* to go back into the spreadsheet.

Widening the Column
/Worksheet Column Set-Width

Since column A must be wide enough to hold long account names, use the Set-Column Width command. To increase column A, move the cursor to A1 and enter

/Worksheet Column Set-Width

Then respond to the prompt *Enter the column width:* with

30

and press Enter. It's necessary to widen column B to 12 spaces. This can be also be done by using a Set-Column Width command. Move the cursor to B1 and enter

/Worksheet Column Set-Width

Respond to the prompt *Enter the column width:* with

12

and press Enter.

Entering the Headings Centered

^

Move the cursor to A1 and type

^Easy Company

or your company name and press Enter. The ^ key centers the text in the cell. Move the cursor to A2, type

^Income Statement

and press Enter. Move the cursor to A3, type

^December 31, 1989

and press Enter. Move the cursor to A5 and type

Income:

Press Enter. Insert the remaining titles from Figure 3-3 into cells A6 through A40, or use your own set of accounts. Precede any account that starts with a number, such as *2nd Mortgage Interest*, with a single quotation mark prefix: *'2nd Mortgage Interest.*

Entering Formulas

Some of the cells hold formulas that add or subtract the information in other cells. Cell B8 adds the negative returns and allowances to the gross receipts or sales to arrive at gross profit. To enter the formula, move the cursor to B8, type

+B6+B7

and press Enter. Move the cursor to B11, type

+B8+B10

and press Enter. Move the cursor to B38, type

@SUM(B14.B36)

and press Enter. To enter the remaining formula, move the cursor to B40 and type

+B11−B38

Press Enter.

Formatting the Spreadsheet to Currency
/Range Format Currency

You need to format Column B to currency. Since you only want this column to be in currency, use the Range command instead of the Worksheet Global Format command. Enter

/Range Format Currency

Respond to the prompt *Enter number of decimal places:* with

2

and press Enter. Respond to the prompt *Enter range to format:* with

B6.B40

and then press Enter.

Entering the Repeating Underline
\ =

Cells B12 and B41 contain an accented underline created with the equal sign. To enter the repeating underline, move the cursor to B12 and enter

\ =

Repeat for cell B41.

Saving the Spreadsheet
/File Save

Since you can use this income statement each month or period, save the spreadsheet without data. To save the file, enter

/File Save

1-2-3 will then ask for a filename. Type

IncSt

and press Enter. If you've already saved the file, the name *Incst* will automatically display. Enter

Replace

to replace the file.

How to Use the Income Statement

Enter the data in column B from Figure 3.3 or your own accounts. When entering amounts, don't include the comma or dollar sign. When entering a negative amount as shown in Figure 3-3 in parentheses, precede the amount with a minus sign. Enter cell B7 as −350.00. If you see a row of asterisks instead of the amount you entered, the column isn't wide enough to hold that many numbers. Use the Worksheet Column-Set command (/WCS) to increase the size of the column.

Saving the Completed Worksheet
/File Save

Save the new worksheet containing this period's data in a new file separate from the previous Incst file. Enter

/File **S**ave

then type

IS1289

for Income Statement December 1989, or any name that's easy for you to remember, and press Enter.

Printing the Worksheet
/Print Printer Range Align Go Quit

You can print the income statement now. The print command allows printing to a file or printer. Roll the paper to the perforation or top of form and enter

/Print Printer Range

Respond to the prompt *Enter print range:* with

A1.B41

and press Enter. To begin the printing job, enter

Align Go Quit

Saving the Worksheet with Replace
/File Save Replace

After printing the income statement, save this spreadsheet one more time to keep the printing instructions in the file. Enter

/File Save

and press Enter when the filename *IS1289* is automatically displayed. The software will check to see if you want to write over your previous file, so enter

Replace

to replace the file.

Figure 3-4. Comparative Balance Sheet

	A	B	C	D	E
1	Easy Company				
2	Comparative Balance Sheet				
3	December 31, 1988 and December 31, 1989				
4				Amount of	Percentage
5	Assets	1989	1988	Increase	
6				or (Decrease)	
7	Current Assets:				
8	Cash	$500.00	$200.00	$300.00	150%
9	Notes Receivable	$1,000.00	$1,500.00	($500.00)	-33%
10	Accounts Receivable Net	$11,700.00	$11,600.00	$100.00	1%
11	Inventory	$15,000.00	$12,000.00	$3,000.00	25%
12	Prepaid Insurance	$400.00	$200.00	$200.00	100%
13	Prepaid Other	$50.00	$25.00	$25.00	100%
14					
15	Total current assets	$28,650.00	$25,525.00	$3,125.00	12%
16					
17	Fixed Assets:				
18	Office Equipment	$2,000.00	$2,000.00	$0.00	0%
19	Less–Accumulated depreciation	($480.00)	($80.00)	($400.00)	500%
20	Shop Equipment	$5,000.00	$5,000.00	$0.00	0%
21	Less–Accumulated depreciation	($1,500.00)	($1,200.00)	($300.00)	25%
22	Buildings	$80,000.00	$80,000.00	$0.00	0%
23	Less–Accumulated depreciation	($35,000.00)	($33,000.00)	($2,000.00)	6%
24	Land	$30,000.00	$30,000.00	$0.00	0%
25					
26	Total fixed assets	$80,020.00	$82,720.00	($2,700.00)	-3%
27					
28	Total Assets	$108,670.00	$108,245.00	$425.00	0%
29		=========	=========	=========	=====
30	Liabilities and Capital				
31					
32	Current Liabilities:				
33	Notes payable–Bank	$500.00	$5,000.00	($4,500.00)	-90%
34	Accounts payable–Trade	$7,500.00	$6,000.00	$1,500.00	25%
35	Payroll taxes payable	$420.00	$600.00	($180.00)	-30%
36	Sales taxes payable	$400.00	$300.00	$100.00	33%
37	Total current liabilities	$8,820.00	$11,900.00	($3,080.00)	-26%
38					
39	Owner's Equity				
40					
41	Sam Easy, Capital Jan 1	$96,345.00	$91,350.00	$4,995.00	5%
42	Profit or Loss	$25,000.00	$16,560.00	$8,440.00	51%
43	Less Draws	($21,495.00)	($11,565.00)	($9,930.00)	86%
44	Sam Easy, Capital December 31	$99,850.00	$96,345.00	$3,505.00	4%
45					
46	Total liabilities and capital	$108,670.00	$108,245.00	$425.00	0%
47		=========	=========	=========	=====

The Comparative Balance Sheet

The Balance Sheet and Income Statement can now be easily converted to *comparative statements*, which are commonly used to analyze a company's performance and status compared with a previous period. Since simply arranging the two periods side by side can make it difficult to grasp significant changes, two more columns are added to figure the increase or decrease in an account balance and the percentage of this change.

Looking at Figure 3-4, you can see that on row 33, *Notes payable-Bank* is $4,500 less in 1989 than in 1988; this is shown as a decrease, in parentheses. The percentage of decrease, 90 percent, is also shown with a minus sign. To substitute your company's balances, you'll need the account balances for a prior period, usually the previous year.

Retrieving a Spreadsheet File
/File Retrieve

After entering *123* at the DOS prompt, to retrieve the previous balance sheet file enter

/File Retrieve

Then type

BS1289

and press Enter.

Widening All the Columns
/Worksheet Global Column-Width

You need to widen columns C, D, and E to hold the longer account balances and formatting. This can be accomplished with the Global command. This command won't affect column A since it was widened with the Worksheet Column Set-Width command, which overrides any Global column widths. Enter

/Worksheet Global Column-Width

Respond to the prompt *Enter global width:* with

12

and press Enter.

Editing the Cell Contents
F2

Change both cell A2 and A3 to their new titles. Move the cursor to A2 and press F2. Then use the left-arrow key to move the cursor to the *B* in *Balance Sheet* and type

Comparative

Press the space bar and then Enter. Move the cursor to A3 and press F2. Use the left arrow to move the cursor to the *D* in *December* and type *December 31, 1988 and.* Press the space bar and press Enter.

Entering the Headings Centered
^

Move the cursor to B5 and type

^1989

Press Enter. The ^ centers the date in the cell. Move the cursor to C5, type

^1988

and press Enter. Move the cursor to D4, type

Amount of

and press Enter. Move the cursor to D5, D6, and E4 and enter the remaining titles from Figure 3-4.

Entering Formulas

Columns D and E hold formulas that subtract and divide information in other cells. Column D subtracts column C (1988) from column B (1989) to find the amount of increase or decrease in 1989. Move the cursor to D8 and type

+B8−C8

Press Enter. Column E divides column D by column C to get a percentage of the increase or decrease. Move the cursor to E8 and type

+D8/C8

Press Enter. It is normal to have an ERR display in column E, since there is no information in column C yet to divide.

Formatting the Columns
/Range Format Currency

Format columns C and D to currency. Since you only need these two columns to be in currency, use the Range command instead of the Worksheet Global Format command. Enter

/Range Format Currency

Respond to the prompt *Enter the number of decimal places:* with

2

and press Enter. Respond to the prompt *Enter range to format:* with

C8.D46

and press Enter. Format column E to percentage. Enter

/Range Format Percent

Respond to the prompt *Enter the number of decimal places:* with

0

and press Enter. Respond to the prompt *Enter range to format:* with

E8.E46

and press Enter.

Copying Formulas
/Copy
Copy the formula in cell B15, which adds B8 through B13, to cells
C15, D15, and E15 to eliminate the need for entering the formula
again. To copy the formula enter

/Copy

Respond to the prompt *Enter range to copy FROM:* with

B15

and press Enter. Respond to the prompt *Enter range to copy TO:*
with

C15

and press Enter. Move the cursor to C15 and you'll see that the
formula reads @SUM(C8.C13) instead of @SUM(B8.B13). This is
because the copy command copies cells relative to their new destination. Continue copying the formulas and underscores as follows:

B26	to	C26
B28	to	C28
B37	to	C37
B44	to	C44
B46	to	C46
D8	to	D9.D46
E8	to	E9.E46
B29	to	C29.E29
B47	to	C47.E47

Erasing the Contents of a Cell
There's an option available to suppress the zeros in a spreadsheet,
but you need some of the zeros in column D for comparison. To
erase only the cells that contain unwanted zeros and ERR symbols
such as D14 and E14, enter

/Range Erase

As the range, type

D14.E14

and press Enter. Repeat for the following cells, which need to be erased:

D16.E17
D25.E25
D27.E27
D30.E32
D38.E40
D45.E45

Saving the Spreadsheet
/File Save

Since you can use this comparative balance sheet again, save the spreadsheet without data. To save the file, enter

/File Save

1-2-3 will then ask for a filename. Type

CBalSht

and press Enter.

How to Use the Comparative Balance Sheet

Enter the data in column C from Figure 3-4 or your own accounts. When entering amounts, don't enter the comma or dollar sign. Numbers in parentheses should be entered with a minus sign; for example, ($500.00) should be entered as −*500.00.* If you see a row of asterisks instead of the amount you entered, that's an indicator the column isn't wide enough to hold that many numbers. Use the Worksheet Column-Set command, /WCS, to increase the size of the column.

Saving the Completed Worksheet
/File Save

Save the new worksheet containing this period's data in a new file separate from the previous *CBalSht* file. Enter

/File Save

Then type

CBS1289

for *Comparative Balance Sheet December 1989* (or any name that's easy for you to remember) and press Enter.

Printing the Worksheet
/Print Printer Range Align Go Quit

You can print the comparative balance sheet now. The print command allows printing to a file or printer. Roll the paper to the perforation or top of form and enter

/Print Printer Range

Respond to the prompt *Enter print range:* with

A1.E47

and press Enter. To begin the printing job, enter

Align Go Quit

This spreadsheet is too wide to print on most 80-column printers without going to a second page. If you have a condensed print switch available on your printer, set it to condensed and from the print menu enter

Options Margins Right

and enter

135

for the new right margin. If your printer doesn't have a switch but accepts a condensed print code, enter from the options menu

Setup

For Epson printers, the string for condensed is \ *015*. Look in the *Lotus 1-2-3* appendix for your specific printer code. Enter

Quit

to quit the options menu. To start the print job, enter

Align Go Quit

Saving the Worksheet with Replace
/File Save Replace

After printing the comparative balance sheet, save this spreadsheet one more time to keep the printing instructions in the file. Enter

/File Save

and press Enter when the filename *CBS1289* is automatically displayed. The software will check to see if you want to write over your previous file, so enter

Replace

to replace the file.

The Comparative Income Statement

You can also convert the Income Statement to a comparative statement. As a management tool, the comparative income statement is usually more significant for evaluating operations.

Figure 3-5. Comparative Income Statement

	A	B	C	D	E
1	Easy Company				
2	Comparative Income Statement				
3	December 31, 1988 and December 31, 1989			Amount of	Percentage
4				Increase	
5	Income:	1989	1988	or (Decrease)	
6					
7	Gross receipts or sales	$175,000.00	$160,000.00	$15,000.00	9%
8	Less Returns and allowances	($350.00)	($200.00)	($150.00)	75%
9	Total receipts or sales	$174,650.00	$159,800.00	$14,850.00	9%
10					
11	Less Cost of Goods Sold	($63,000.00)	($55,000.00)	($8,000.00)	15%
12	Total Gross Profit	$111,650.00	$104,800.00	$6,850.00	7%
13		=========	=========	=========	========
14	Expenses:				
15					
16	Advertising	$3,500.00	$3,000.00	$500.00	17%
17	Bad debts	$400.00	$1,500.00	($1,100.00)	–73%
18	Bank Service Charges	$180.00	$230.00	($50.00)	–22%
19	Car and Truck Expenses	$2,200.00	$2,100.00	$100.00	5%
20	Commissions	$4,000.00	$3,500.00	$500.00	14%
21	Depreciation	$2,700.00	$2,600.00	$100.00	4%
22	Dues and publications	$30.00	$50.00	($20.00)	–40%
23	Employee benefits	$500.00	$600.00	($100.00)	–17%
24	Freight	$200.00	$300.00	($100.00)	–33%
25	Insurance	$4,000.00	$3,500.00	$500.00	14%
26	Interest	$5,000.00	$4,800.00	$200.00	4%
27	Laundry and Cleaning		$20.00	($20.00)	–100%
28	Legal and professional	$1,500.00	$2,500.00	($1,000.00)	–40%
29	Office Expenses	$320.00	$200.00	$120.00	60%
30	Pension and Profit Sharing			$0.00	
31	Repairs	$50.00	$690.00	($640.00)	–93%
32	Supplies	$580.00	$700.00	($120.00)	–17%
33	Taxes	$1,200.00	$1,000.00	$200.00	20%
34	Travel	$40.00	$700.00	($660.00)	–94%
35	Meals and Entertainment	$200.00	$400.00	($200.00)	–50%
36	Utilities and Telephone	$5,000.00	$5,000.00	$0.00	0%
37	Wages	$55,040.00	$54,845.00	$195.00	0%
38	Other Expenses	$10.00	$5.00	$5.00	100%
39					
40	Total Expenses	$86,650.00	$88,240.00	($1,590.00)	–2%
41					
42	Net Profit or (Loss)	$25,000.00	$16,560.00	$8,440.00	51%
43		=========	=========	=========	========
44					

Retrieving a Spreadsheet File
/File Retrieve

After entering *123* at the DOS prompt, to retrieve the previous income statement file enter

/File Retrieve

Then type

IS1289

and press Enter.

Widening All the Columns
/Worksheet Global Column-Width

You need to widen columns C, D, and E to hold the longer account balances and formatting. This can be accomplished using the Global command. Column A won't be affected by this command since it was widened with the Worksheet Column Set-Width command, which overrides any Global column widths. Enter

/Worksheet Global Column-Width

and respond to the prompt *Enter global width:* with

12

and press Enter.

Editing the Cell Contents
F2

Edit both cell A2 and A3 and change them to their new titles. Move the cursor to A2 and press F2. Then use the left-arrow key to move the cursor to the *I* in *Income Statement.* Type

Comparative

then press the space bar, and press Enter. Move the cursor to A3 and press F2. Use the left-arrow key to move the cursor to the *D* in *December.* Type *December 31, 1988 and;* press the space bar and press Enter.

Entering the Headings Centered

^

Move the cursor to B5, type

^1989

and press Enter. The ^ centers the date in the cell. Move the cursor to C5, type

^1988

and press Enter. Move the cursor to D3 and type

Amount of

Press Enter. Then move the cursor to D4, D5, and E3 and enter the remaining titles.

Inserting a Row
/Worksheet Insert Row

Insert two rows to make the spreadsheet easier to read. Move the cursor to cell A6, enter

/Worksheet Insert Row

and press Enter. Move to A15 and enter

/Worksheet Insert Row

Press Enter.

Entering Formulas

Columns D and E hold formulas that subtract and divide information in other cells. Column D subtracts column C (1988) from column B (1989) to find the amount of increase or decrease in 1989. Move the cursor to D7, type

+B7−C7

and press Enter.

Column E divides column D by column C to get a percentage of increase or decrease. Move the cursor to E7 and type

+D7/C7

Press Enter. It's normal to see an ERR symbol since there is no information in column C by which to divide.

Formatting the Columns
/Range Format Currency

Format columns C and D to currency. Since you only need these two columns to be in currency, use the Range command instead of the Worksheet Global Format command. Enter

/Range Format Currency

Respond to the prompt *Enter number of decimal places:* with

2

and press Enter. Respond to the prompt *Enter range to format:* with

C7.D42
and then press Enter.
Format column E to percentage. Enter

/Range Format Percent

and respond to the prompt *Enter the number of decimal places:* with

0

Press Enter. Respond to the prompt *Enter range to format:* with

E7.E42

and press Enter.

Copying Formulas
/Copy

Copy the formula in cell B9, which adds B7 and B8 to cell C9 to eliminate the need for entering the formula again. To copy, enter

/Copy

and respond to the prompt *Enter range to copy FROM:* with

B9

Press Enter. Respond to the prompt *Enter range to copy TO:* with

C9

and press Enter. Move the cursor to C9, and you'll see the formula reads C7 + C8 instead of B7 + B8. This is because the copy command copies cells relative to their new destination. Continue copying the formulas and underscores as follows:

B12	to	C12
B40	to	C40
B42	to	C42
D7	to	D8.D42
E7	to	E8.E42
B13	to	C13.E13
B43	to	C43.E43

Erasing the Contents of a Cell

There's an option available to suppress the zeros in a spreadsheet, but you'll need some of the zeros in column D for comparison. To erase only the cells that contain unwanted zeros and ERR symbols, such as D10 and E10, enter

/Range Erase

and respond to *Enter range to erase:* with

D10.E10

Press Enter. Repeat for the following cells that need to be erased:

D14.E15
E30
D39.E39
D41.E41

Saving the Spreadsheet
/File Save

Since you can use this comparative income statement again, save the spreadsheet without data. To save the file, enter

/File Save

1-2-3 will then ask for a filename. Type

CIncSt

and press Enter.

How to Use the Comparative Income Statement

Enter the data in column C from Figure 3-5 or your own accounts. When entering amounts, don't enter the comma or dollar sign. Enter values within parentheses as negative numbers without the parentheses. If you see a row of asterisks instead of the amount you entered, the column isn't wide enough to hold that amount. Use the Worksheet Column-Set command, /WCS, to increase the size of the column.

Saving the Completed Worksheet
/File Save

Save the new worksheet containing this period's data in a new file separate from the previous *CIncSt* file. Enter

/File Save

Then type in

CIS1289

for "Comparative Income Statement December 1989," or any name that will be easy for you to remember.

Printing the Worksheet
/Print Printer Range Align Go Quit

You can print the comparative income statement now. The print
command allows printing to a file or the printer. Roll the paper to
the perforation or top of form. Enter

/Print Printer Range

and respond to the prompt *Enter print range:* with

A1.E43

Press Enter.
   To begin the printing job, enter

Align Go Quit

   This spreadsheet is too wide to print on most 80-column printers without going to a second page. If you have a condensed print
switch available on your printer, set it to condensed. From the print
menu, enter

Options Margins Right

for options, margins, right; enter

135

for the new right margin. If your printer doesn't have a switch but
accepts a condensed print code, enter from the options menu

Setup

For Epson printers, the string for condensed mode printing is
\ *015*. Look in the *Lotus 1-2-3* appendix for your specific printer
code. Enter

Quit

to quit the options menu; then to begin the condensed print job, enter

Align Go Quit

Saving the Worksheet with Replace
/File Save Replace

After printing the comparative balance sheet, save this spreadsheet one more time to keep the printing instructions in the file. Enter

/File Save

and press Enter when the filename *CIS1289* is automatically displayed. The software will check to see if you want to write over your previous file, so enter

Replace

to replace the file.

Financial Statement Ratios

Five of the most common financial statement ratios are

• Working capital
• Current ratio
• Acid-test ratio
• Turnover of accounts receivable
• Merchandise turnover

The first three are based strictly on the comparative balance sheet you've already completed; the remaining two require you to enter the sales and cost-of-sales information from your comparative income statement. If you haven't completed comparative statements yet, just ignore the instructions for cells C49 through C58, and this will produce ratios for the current period only.

Figure 3-6. Financial Statement Ratios

40	A	B	C	D	E
41	Sam Easy, Capital Jan 1	$96,345.00	$91,350.00	$4,995.00	5%
42	Profit or Loss	$25,000.00	$16,560.00	$8,440.00	51%
43	Less Draws	($21,495.00)	($11,565.00)	($9,930.00)	86%
44	Sam Easy, Capital December 31	$99,850.00	$96,345.00	$3,505.00	4%
45					
46	Total liabilities and capital	$108,670.00	$108,245.00	$425.00	0%
47		=========	=========	=========	=========
48					
49	Financial Statement Ratios	1989	1988		
50					
51	Working Capital	$19,830.00	$13,625.00		
52	Current Ratio	3.25	2.14		
53	Acid–Test Ratio	1.50	1.12		
54	Turnover of Accounts Receivable	14.93	13.78		
55	Merchandise Turnover	4.20	4.58		
56					
57	Net sales	$174,650.00	$159,800.00		
58	Cost of Sales	$63,000.00	$55,000.00		
59					

Working Capital

Working capital is the excess of your company's current assets after subtracting the current liabilities. Your company needs sufficient working capital to meet current debts, carry adequate inventory, and extend credit to your customers. Measurement of working capital is an important analyzing tool.

The formula for working capital is:

Current Assets − Current Liabilities

You can enter these ratios on the bottom of your completed comparative balance sheet.

Retrieving a Spreadsheet File
/File Retrieve

After entering *123* at the DOS prompt, you can retrieve the previous comparative balance sheet file by entering

/File Retrieve

then typing in

CBS1289

and pressing Enter. Move the cursor to A49, type

Financial Statement Ratios

and press Enter. Move the cursor to B49, type

^1989

and press Enter. Move the cursor to C49, type

^1988

and press Enter. Move the cursor to A51, type

Working Capital

and press Enter. Move the cursor to B51 and enter the following formula:

+B15−B37

Press Enter. This will subtract current liabilities in cell B37 from current assets in cell B15.

Formatting the Cell to Currency
/Range Format Currency

Format cell B51 to currency before copying the formula to C51. Since you only need this cell to be in the currency format, use the Range Format command instead of the Worksheet Global Format command. Move the cursor to cell B15 and enter

/Range Format Currency

Respond to the prompt *Enter the number of decimal places:* with

2

and press Enter. Respond to the prompt *Enter range to format:* with

B51

or just press Enter, since your cursor is on cell B51.

Copying Formulas
/Copy

Copy the formula in cell B51 to cells C51 to eliminate the need for entering the formula again. To copy, enter

/Copy

and respond to the prompt *Enter range to copy FROM:* with

B51

and press Enter. Respond to the prompt *Enter range to copy TO:* with

C51

Press Enter.

Current Ratio

Bankers and creditors use the *current ratio* to assess your company's ability to pay debts as they become due. The formula for the current ratio is:

Current Assets
Current Liabilities

The result is stated as a ratio to 1. In Figure 3-6 the current ratio for 1989 is 3.25 to 1. A good ratio is at least 2 to 1, depending on the type of business. If your company is service-oriented, such as a painting contracting business, then a ratio of 1 to 1 can be good. Conversely, if you have a manufacturing business that requires extensive inventories, 3 to 1 might be the standard. The best way to judge is to find out from trade publications or your banker what is considered favorable for your type of industry.

To enter the current ratio, move the cursor to A52, type

Current Ratio

and press Enter. Move the cursor to B52, type

+B15/B37

and press Enter. This will divide the current assets in cell B15 by the current liabilities in cell B37. You'll need to format the cell to a fixed number of decimal places since the result is too long for this ratio.

Formatting the Cell to Fixed
/Range Format Fixed

You need to format the remaining three ratios to a fixed number of decimal places. To format these cells to two decimal places, enter

/Range Format Fixed

Respond to the prompt *Enter number of decimal places:* with

2

and press Enter. Respond to the prompt *Enter range to format:* with

B52.B55

and press Enter.

Acid-Test Ratio

A tougher test of liquidity is the *acid-test ratio* or *quick ratio*. This ratio consists of the product of dividing only certain liquid assets by current liabilities. The test gives a better evaluation of your company's ability to meet current debts and obligations. The formula is:

Cash + Notes receivable + Accounts receivable
Current liabilities

To enter this ratio, move the cursor to A53, type

Acid-Test Ratio

and press Enter. Move the cursor to B53, type

@SUM(B8.B10)/B37

and press Enter. An acid-test ratio of 1 to 1 is normally considered adequate.

Turnover of Accounts Receivable

This ratio is a tool to compare how efficiently your company uses working capital. A quick turnover of accounts receivable allows a smaller investment of capital in that account, enabling you to use those resources for other assets. The formula for the turnover of accounts receivable is:

Net Sales

Year-end accounts receivable

Now, you will obtain two amounts from the comparative income statement. Enter net sales and cost of sales for both 1988 and 1989 into this spreadsheet. Type into each of the cells the following or your own values:

B57   174650.00
C57   159800.00
B58   63000.00
C58   55000.00

and press Enter. In A57 and A58 you can enter the titles *Net sales* and *Cost of sales* for clarity. Move the cursor to A54, type

Turnover of Accounts Receivable

and press Enter. Move cursor to B54, type

+B57/B10

and press Enter. This divides net sales by the accounts receivable balance on the balance sheet above. The result of 14.93 (in Figure 3-6) means that the accounts receivable balance has a turnover of almost 15 times for the year. The most exact calculation of the accounts receivable turnover would use an average of the accounts receivable balance for the year and net charge sales. Since most balance sheets provide neither, the simpler calculation method is normally acceptable.

Merchandise Turnover

This ratio is only applicable to businesses that have inventory. Similar to the accounts receivable turnover, this ratio measures efficient use of assets. The formula for merchandise turnover is:

Cost of Goods Sold

Inventory

To enter this ratio, move the cursor to A55, type

Merchandise Turnover

and press Enter. Move the cursor to B55 and type

+B58/B11

Press Enter. This divides the cost of sales that was obtained from the income statement by the inventory balance. A more accurate ratio would use average inventory for the year, but since that information isn't available on most balance sheets, this method is acceptable.

Copying Formulas
/Copy

Copy the formulas in cells B52 though B55 to cells C52 though C55 to eliminate the need for entering the formulas again for 1988. To copy, enter

/Copy

Respond to the prompt *Enter range to copy FROM:* with

B52.B55

and press Enter. Respond to the prompt *Enter range to copy TO:* with

C52

and press Enter. Since you formatted column B before copying, the results in column C should already be properly formatted. You might want to format the net sales and cost of sales figures in B57 through C58 if you plan to print them in your final spreadsheet.

Formatting a Cell to Currency
/Range Format Currency

To format a cell to currency, enter

/Range Format Currency

Respond to the prompt *Enter number of decimal places:* with

2

and press Enter. Respond to the prompt *Enter range to format:* with

B57.C58

and then press Enter.

Printing the Spreadsheet
/Print Printer Range Align Go Quit

You can print the financial statement ratios now. Roll the paper to the perforation or top of form and enter

/Print Printer Range

Respond to the prompt *Enter print range:* with

A49.C58

and press Enter. To begin the printing job, enter

Align Go Quit

Saving the Spreadsheet
/File Save

Since this comparative balance sheet now has ratios, save the spreadsheet with the ratios in a file separate from the file *CBS1289.* Enter

/File Save

1-2-3 will then respond with *CSB1289* for a filename, so type

FSRATIO

and press Enter.

Graphing the Ratios

Sometimes a graph enables you to see changes much better than simple values listed side by side would allow. You can create two graphs from these ratios, one for comparing working capital and the other for displaying current and acid-test ratios. Your computer will need the ability to display graphics in order to view the graph on your monitor. If a graphic mode isn't possible, you'll still be able to print the graph you've created if you have a graphics printer.

Figure 3-7. Working Capital Graph

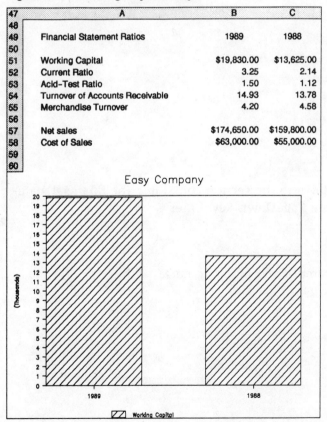

	A	B	C
47			
48			
49	Financial Statement Ratios	1989	1988
50			
51	Working Capital	$19,830.00	$13,625.00
52	Current Ratio	3.25	2.14
53	Acid-Test Ratio	1.50	1.12
54	Turnover of Accounts Receivable	14.93	13.78
55	Merchandise Turnover	4.20	4.58
56			
57	Net sales	$174,650.00	$159,800.00
58	Cost of Sales	$63,000.00	$55,000.00
59			
60			

Working Capital Graph

There are three basic steps involved in creating a graph:

- Select the graph type.
- Define the range.
- Enter View to display the graph.

There are more commands that create titles, legends, color displays, grids, and custom scaling. To create the simple working capital graph shown, load the file that created the financial statement ratios above.

Retrieving a Spreadsheet File
/File Retrieve

After entering *123* at the DOS prompt, you can retrieve the previous financial statement ratios file by entering

/File Retrieve

Then type in

FSRATIO

and press Enter.

Creating the Graph
/Graph

Move the cursor down to the section containing the financial statement ratios with the PageDown key. Enter

/Graph Type Bar A

Respond to the prompt *Enter first data range:* with

B51.C51

and press Enter. Press

X

for the *x*-axis range and respond to the prompt *Enter X axis range:* with

B49.C49

and press Enter. This will enter the dates along the bottom of the graph. Enter

Options **T**itles **F**irst line

and type

Easy Company

and press Enter. Enter

Legend **A**

for the A range. Respond to the prompt *Enter legend for A range:* with

Working Capital

and press Enter. Enter

Quit **V**iew

to quit the options menu and view the graph.

If you hear a beep and see a blank screen, then possibly your computer system or software setup isn't ready for graphics. After viewing the graph, press any key to bring back the graph menu. Enter

Quit

to quit the graph menu and bring back the spreadsheet.

Viewing the Graph from the Spreadsheet
F10

It's possible to make changes to data in the spreadsheet and have the graph redrawn. Change the year to 1990 and press F10, and the new graph will reflect the change. Press any key to bring back the spreadsheet; then change the year back to 1989 and press F10 again to see the original graph.

Naming the Graph

When you use the File Save command later to save the *FSRatio* file, the graph settings will also be saved. Since there will be at least two different graphs in this file, you'll need to name each one. Enter

/Graph **N**ame **C**reate

and respond to the prompt *Enter graph name:* with

WorkingCapital

Press Enter.

Saving the Spreadsheet with Replace
/File Save Replace

After finishing the graph settings, enter

Quit

to quit the graph menu. Now save this spreadsheet one more time to keep the graph instructions in the file. Enter

/**F**ile **S**ave

and press Enter when the filename *FSRatio* is automatically displayed. The software will check to see if you want to write over your previous file, so enter

Replace

to replace the file.

Printing the Graph

There's no option on the graph menu to print the graph. Sometimes you can produce a satisfactory graph with the Shift-PrintScreen keys, but you can print a more sophisticated graph with the PrintGraph program. First save the graph in a graph picture file. Enter

/Graph **S**ave

When asked for a graph filename, type

WorkCap

and press Enter. To quit the graph menu, enter

Quit

Then to exit *1-2-3*, enter

/Quit **Y**es

then at the DOS prompt type

LOTUS

and press Enter. This displays the Lotus Access System menu, which contains the PrintGraph program. Move the arrow key to highlight PrintGraph and press Enter. The PrintGraph menu displays the Image-Select and Settings options. Highlight the Settings option and press Enter. Check the printer type and directory setups, and make any necessary changes. If all are correct, press Esc, highlight Image-Select, and press Enter. After the available graph filenames are displayed, select *WorkCap* and press Enter. Then enter

Align **G**o

and the graph will print. After printing, highlight the Exit option and press Enter.

Financial Ratios Graph

You can graph up to six different ranges on one graph. The working capital graph only graphed one range. The following graph will include two ranges, grouping the ranges by year.

Figure 3-8. Financial Ratios Graph

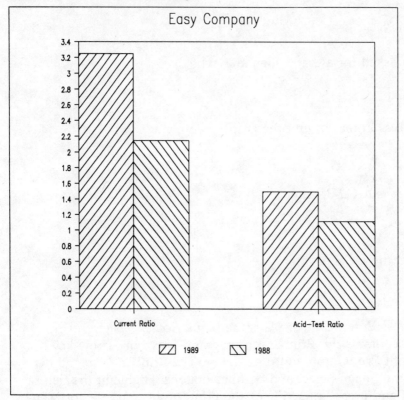

Retrieving a Spreadsheet File
/File Retrieve

Enter *123* at the DOS prompt. To retrieve the previous financial statement ratios file, enter

/**F**ile **R**etrieve

Then type in

FSRATIO

and press Enter.

Creating the Graph
/Graph

Move the cursor down to the section containing the financial statement ratios with the PageDown key. To clear the previous graph, enter

/**G**raph **R**eset **G**raph

Then enter

Type **B**ar **A**

for the A range, and respond to the prompt *Enter first data range:* with

B52.B53

Press Enter. To enter the *B* range, press

B

and respond to the prompt *Enter second data range:* with

C52.C53

and press Enter. Then enter

X

for the *x*-axis range. Respond to the prompt *Enter X axis range:* with

A52.A53

and press Enter. This will enter the titles *Current Ratio* and *Acid-Test Ratio* along the bottom of the graph. Enter

Option **T**itles **F**irst line

and type

\ **A1**

and press Enter. For the *A* range, enter

Legend **A**

and respond to the prompt *Enter legend for A range:* with

1989

Press Enter. For the *B* range, enter

Legend **B**

and respond to the prompt *Enter legend for B range:* with

1988

and press Enter.
     To quit the options menu and view the graph, enter

Quit **V**iew

After viewing the graph, press any key to return to the graph menu. Press **Q** to Quit.

Naming the Graph

When you use the File Save command later to save the *FSRatio* file, the graph settings will also be saved. Since there will be at least two different graphs in this file, you'll need to name each one. Enter

/Graph Name Create

and respond to the prompt *Enter graph name:* with

CurrAcid

Press Enter.

Saving the Spreadsheet with Replace
/File Save Replace

After finishing the graph settings, enter

Quit

to quit the graph menu. Now save this spreadsheet one more time to keep the instructions for both graphs in the file. Enter

/File Save

and press Enter when the filename *FSRatio* is automatically displayed. The software will check to see if you want to write over your previous file, so enter

Replace

to replace the file.

Saving the Graph for Printing

Save the graph in a graph picture file. Enter

/Graph Save

and, when asked for a graph filename, type

CurrAcid

and press Enter.

Printing the Graph

To quit the graph menu, enter

Quit

To exit *1-2-3*, you would enter

/Quit Yes

then at the DOS prompt type

LOTUS

and press Enter. This displays the Lotus Access System menu, which contains the PrintGraph program. Move the arrow key to highlight PrintGraph and press Enter. The PrintGraph menu displays the Image-Select and Settings options. Highlight the Settings option and press Enter. Check the printer type and directory setups, and make any necessary changes. If all are correct, press Esc, highlight Image-Select, and press Enter. After the available graph filenames are displayed, select **CurrAcid** and press Enter. Then enter

Align Go

and the graph will print. After printing, highlight the Exit option and press Enter.

Funds Statement and Cash Flow Statement

Often simple financial reports such as comparative balance sheets and income statements don't fully explain changes that have happened during the year. The Easy Company had a profit of $25,000 but working capital only increased by $6,205 and cash by only $300. Two additional reports will explain these changes—the *Funds Statement* and *Cash Flow Statement*. You can produce both reports from the comparative balance sheet and income statement completed earlier in the chapter.

The Funds Statement

The purpose of the funds statement is to find the difference in working capital and identify the source of the increase or decrease. A normal source of increase occurs when the company makes a profit. Borrowing money and selling assets are other sources of increased working capital. Easy Company had only one source of funds: a profit increased by adding back the noncash depreciation expense. Any expenses that aren't paid in cash, such as depreciation and accruals, are added back to the source of working capital. You could cause a decrease in funds by purchasing fixed assets, paying long term liabilities, or sending dividends or draws to owners and investors. Easy Company had one decrease of funds caused by the draws paid to the owner. Write down these amounts after retrieving the comparative balance sheet since you'll eventually delete these cells.

Figure 3-9. Funds Statement

	A	B	C	D	E
1	Easy Company				
2	Funds Statement for the Year Ended				
3	December 31, 1989				
4				Amount of	Percentage
5	Working Capital Changes	1989	1988	Increase	
6				or (Decrease)	
7	Current Assets:				
8	Cash	$500.00	$200.00	$300.00	150%
9	Notes Receivable	$1,000.00	$1,500.00	($500.00)	–33%
10	Accounts Receivable Net	$11,700.00	$11,600.00	$100.00	1%
11	Inventory	$15,000.00	$12,000.00	$3,000.00	25%
12	Prepaid Insurance	$400.00	$200.00	$200.00	100%
13	Prepaid Other	$50.00	$25.00	$25.00	100%
14					
15	Total current assets	$28,650.00	$25,525.00	$3,125.00	12%
16					
17		==========	==========	==========	=======
18					
19	Current Liabilities:				
20	Notes payable–Bank	$500.00	$5,000.00	($4,500.00)	–90%
21	Accounts payable–Trade	$7,500.00	$6,000.00	$1,500.00	25%
22	Payroll taxes payable	$420.00	$600.00	($180.00)	–30%
23	Sales taxes payable	$400.00	$300.00	$100.00	33%
24	Total current liabilities	$8,820.00	$11,900.00	($3,080.00)	–26%
25					
26		==========	==========	==========	=======
27					
28	Net Increase in Working Capital	$19,830.00	$13,625.00	$6,205.00	38%
29				==========	
30	Flow of Funds				
31					
32	Sources of new working capital:				
33	Current operations:				
34	Net Income per income statement	$25,000.00			
35	Add:depreciation	$2,700.00			
36	Total new working capital		$27,700.00		
37					
38	Uses of working capital				
39	Draw paid to owner	$21,495.00			
40					
41	Total working capital used		$21,495.00		
42					
43	Net Increase in Working Capital			$6,205.00	
44				==========	

Retrieving a Spreadsheet File
/File Retrieve

After entering *123* at the DOS prompt, you can retrieve the previous comparative balance sheet file by entering

/File Retrieve

then typing in

CBS1289

and pressing Enter. Write down the following three amounts from the 1989 balance sheet, since you'll delete these cells later.

B42	Profit or Loss 1989	$25,000.00
B43	Draws 1989	21,495.00
D19, D21, D23	Depreciation	2,700.00

Entering the Headings Centered
^

Move the cursor to A2 and type

^Funds Statement for the Year Ended

or your company name and press Enter. The ^ centers the text in the cell. Move the cursor to A5, type

^Working Capital Changes

and press Enter.

Editing the Cell Contents
F2

Edit cell A3 to give it a new title. Move the cursor to A3, press F2, then use the left-arrow key to move the cursor to the *D* in *December 31, 1988*. Press the Del key until only the *December 31, 1989* remains.

Deleting a Row
/Worksheet Delete Row

This funds statement is only concerned with current assets and liabilities, so you need to delete all other information. To delete the necessary rows, enter

/Worksheet Delete Row

and respond to the prompt *Enter row delete range:* with

A16.A28

Press Enter. You need only specify column A, since the command deletes the whole row. Continue the deletion of the rows by entering

/Worksheet Delete Row

Respond to the prompt *Enter row delete range:* with

A18

and press Enter. Then enter

/Worksheet Delete Row

and respond to the prompt *Enter row delete range:* with

A26.A33

and press Enter. If you've made a mistake and deleted the wrong rows, just retrieve the file CBS1289 and try again. After deleting the rows, don't save this file as *CBS1289.*

Entering Formulas

Cells B28 and C28 subtract *Total current assets* from *Total current liabilities* to obtain *working capital.* Move the cursor to B28, type

+B15−B24

and press Enter. Move the cursor to C36, type

@SUM(B34.B35)

and press Enter. Use the @SUM function here if you need to insert some rows later to account for all sources of working capital.

To enter the remaining two formulas, move the cursor to each cell and enter the corresponding formula:

C41   @SUM(B39.B40)
D43   +C36−C41

Entering Titles and Data

Move the cursor to A28, type

Net Increase in Working Capital

and press Enter. Move the cursor to A30, type

^Flow of Funds

and press Enter. Enter the remaining titles shown in cells A32 through A43 from Figure 3-9. Enter the following amounts in the following cells:

B34   25000
B35   2700
B39   21495

Press Enter.

Copying Formulas
/Copy

Copy the formula in cell B28 to cells C28, D28, and E28 to eliminate the need for entering the formula again. To copy, Enter

/Copy

and respond to the prompt *Enter range to copy FROM:* with

B28

Press Enter. Respond to the prompt *Enter range to copy TO:* with

C28.E28

and press Enter.

Formatting the Spreadsheet to Currency
/Worksheet Global Format Currency

Since you'll need to format most of the new spreadsheet to currency, use the Global Format command. Enter

/Worksheet Global Format Currency

Respond to the prompt *Enter number of decimal places:* with

2

and press Enter.

Formatting One Cell to Percentage
/Range Format Percent

Format cell E28 to percentage. Since you only need this cell to be in percentage, use the Range command. Enter

/Range Format Percent

Respond to the prompt *Enter number of decimal places:* with

0

and press Enter. Respond to the prompt *Enter range to format:* with

E28

and press Enter.

Entering the Repeating Underline
\ =

Cells D29 and D44 contain an accented underline created with the equal sign. To enter the repeating underline, move the cursor to D29 and enter

\ =

Repeat for cell D44.

Saving the Spreadsheet
/File Save

It's a good habit to save the spreadsheet before printing. To save the file, enter

/File Save

1-2-3 will automatically prompt with the filename *CBS1289,* so instead type

Fund1289

and press Enter.

Printing the Worksheet
/Print Printer Range Align Go Quit

You can print the funds statement now. The print command allows printing to a file or printer. Roll the paper to the perforation or top of form, enter

/Print Printer Range

and respond to the prompt *Enter print range:* with

A1.E44

and press Enter. This spreadsheet is too wide to print on most 80-column printers without going to a second page. If you have a condensed print switch available on your printer, set it to condensed and enter from the print menu

Options Margins Right

for options, margins, right. Enter

135

for the new right margin. If your printer doesn't have a switch but accepts a condensed print code, from the print menu enter

Setup

For Epson printers, the string for condensed is \ *015*. Look in the *Lotus 1-2-3* appendix for your specific printer code. Enter

Quit

to quit the options menu. Then to begin the print job, enter

Align Go Quit

Saving the Worksheet with Replace
/File Save Replace

After printing the balance sheet, save this spreadsheet one more time to keep the printing instructions in the file. Enter

/File Save

and press Enter when the filename *Fund1289* is automatically displayed. The software will check to see if you want to write over your previous file, so enter

Replace

to replace the file.

The Cash Flow Statement

Easy Company made a profit of $25,000 in 1989 but cash only increased by $300. Where did the cash go? A simple example of the loss of cash is the inventory account. At the end of 1988 the inventory was $12,000, compared with $15,000 in 1989. Some of the missing cash paid for that extra inventory. But to offset this increase in inventory, Easy Company now owes $1,500 more to trade creditors.

As you can see, finding out where the cash went is complicated if done by hand. The following cash flow statement uses amounts only from the comparative balance sheet. The difficult part is deciding what is a *source*, or increase in cash, and what is a *use*, or decrease in cash. If you simply remember that decreasing assets (selling assets) and increasing liabilities (borrowing money) increases cash, and that increasing assets (buying assets) and decreasing liabilities (paying off loans) uses cash, the rest is simple. Fortunately a cash flow statement on a spreadsheet allows you to move accounts around until the statement balances.

Figure 3-10. Cash Flow Statement

	A	B	C
49	Easy Company		
50	Cash Flow Statement for Year Ended		
51	December 31, 1989		
52			
53	Beginning Cash Balance		$200.00
54			===========
55	Cash Provided by		
56	Operations–net income		$25,000.00
57	Add: Depreciation Expense		$2,700.00
58	Decrease in Notes Receivable		$500.00
59	Increase in Accounts Payable		$1,500.00
60	Increase in Sales Tax Payable		$100.00
61	Less:Increase in Inventory	$3,000.00	
62	Increase in Prepaids	$225.00	
63	Increase in Accounts Receivable	$100.00	
64	Decrease in Notes Payable	$4,500.00	
65	Decrease in P/R Taxes Payable	$180.00	($8,005.00)
66			
67	Cash provided by Operations		$21,795.00
68			
69	Cash was used to:		
70	Draws paid to owner		($21,495.00)
71			
72			
73	Increase in Cash		$300.00
74			
75	Ending Cash Balance		$500.00
76			=========

Retrieving a Spreadsheet File
/File Retrieve

After entering *123* at the DOS prompt, retrieve the previous comparative balance sheet file by entering

/File Retrieve

Then type in

CBS1289

and press Enter.

Entering the Headings Centered
^

Move the cursor to A49, type

^Easy Company

and press Enter. Move the cursor to A50, type

^Cash Flow Statement for the Year Ended

and press Enter. The ^ key centers the text in the cell. Move the cursor to A51, type

^December 31, 1989

and press Enter. Then move the cursor to A53, type

Beginning Cash Balance

and press Enter. Type in the remaining titles shown in cells A55 through A75 from Figure 3-10.

Widening the Column
/Worksheet Column Set-Width

To increase column A, move the cursor to A1 and enter

/Worksheet Column Set-Width

Respond to the prompt *Enter column width:* with

36

and press Enter.

Entering Formulas

Some of the cells get their information from column D in the comparative balance sheet and others contain formulas that add or subtract a column of cells. You need to enter any decrease in an asset or liability with a negative sign before the cell address. After typing the titles in column A, enter the following formulas in columns B and C:

```
C53   +C8
C56   +B42
C57   −D19−D21−D23
C58   −D9
C59   +D34
C60   +D36
B61   +D11
B62   +D12+D13
B63   +D10
B64   −D33
B65   −D35
C65   −@SUM(B61.B65)
C67   @SUM(C56.C65)
C70   +B43
C73   +C67+C70
C75   +C53+C73
```

Formatting the Spreadsheet to Currency
/Worksheet Global Format Currency

Since you need to format most of the new spreadsheet to currency, use the Worksheet Global Format command. Enter

/Worksheet Global Format Currency

Respond to the prompt *Enter number of decimal places:* with

2

and press Enter.

Entering the Repeating Underline
\ =

Cells C54 and C76 contain an accented underline created with the equal sign. To enter the repeating underline, move the cursor to C54 and enter

\ =

Repeat for cell C76.

Cells C66 and C72 contain a single underline also created with the equal sign. To enter the repeating underline, move the cursor to C66 and enter

_

and repeat for cell C72.

Saving the Spreadsheet
/File Save

It's a good habit to save the spreadsheet before printing. To save the file, enter

/File Save

1-2-3 will automatically prompt with the filename *CBS1289,* so instead type

Cash1289

and press Enter.

Printing the Worksheet
/Print Printer Range Align Go Quit

You can print the funds statement now. The print command allows printing to a file or printer. Roll the paper to the perforation or top of form. Enter

/Print Printer Range

and respond to the prompt *Enter print range:* with

A49.C76

and press Enter. To begin the print job, enter

Align **G**o **Q**uit

Saving the Worksheet with Replace
/File Save Replace

After printing the balance sheet, save this spreadsheet one more time to keep the printing instructions in the file. Enter

/File **S**ave

and press Enter when the filename Cash1289 is automatically displayed. The software will check to see if you want to write over your previous file, so enter

Replace

to replace the file.

How to Write a Business Plan

The purpose of a business plan is to apply for a loan or attract investors for your business. You'll need a word processor to complete some of the plan, but you can use *1-2-3* for most of the suggested financial information. The following is a sample table of contents for a business plan (with the items you can create using this book noted):

Table of Contents
1. Introduction
   Use a word processor and state the purpose of the loan, your repayment ability, a description of the business, the qualifications of management, and proposed marketing of your product.
2. Financial Data
   A. Balance Sheet (Figure 3-1 or 3-4)
   B. Income Statement (Figure 3-3 or 3-5)
   C. Financial Statement Ratios and Graph (Figure 3-7)
   D. Volume Profit and Breakeven Analysis (Figure 7-4)
   E. Cash Flow Statement (Figure 3-10) or Funds Statement (Figure 3-9)
   F. Pro Forma Cash Flow (Figure 3-11)
   G. Income Projections (Figure 3-11)

3. Collateral
   A. Fixed Assets (Figure 5-11)
   B. Accounts Receivable Aging (Figure 5-6)
   C. Inventory (Figure 5-1)

Your banker or investors might also ask for your accounts payable (Figure 5-7) or a personal financial statement. To create a personal financial statement, use the balance sheet format and change the account names to personal property items: House, Autos, Stocks and Bonds, and Other Investments, for example.

Figure 3-11. Financial Projections for the Business Plan

	A	B	C	D	E
1	Easy Company				
2	Income Projections				
3	Proposed 1990				
4		JAN	FEB	MAR	APR
5	Income:				
6	Gross receipts or sales	$14,583	$14,583	$14,583	$14,583
7	Less Returns and allowances	($29)	($29)	($29)	($29)
8	Total receipts or sales	$14,554	$14,554	$14,554	$14,554
9					
10	Less Cost of Goods Sold	($5,250)	($5,250)	($5,250)	($5,250)
11	Total Gross Profit	$9,304	$9,304	$9,304	$9,304
12					
13	Expenses:				
14	Advertising	$292	$292	$292	$292
15	Bad debts	$33	$33	$33	$33

	A	B	C	D	E
49	Easy Company				
50	Proforma Cash Flow		1989	JAN	FEB
51	1990				
52					
53	Beginning Cash Balance		$200	$500	$525
54			=========	=======	======
55	Cash Provided by				
56	Operations–net income		$25,000	$2,083	$2,083
57	Add: Depreciation Expense		$2,700	$225	$225
58	Decrease in Notes Receivabale		$500	$42	$42
59	Increase in Accounts Payable		$1,500	$125	$125
60	Increase in Sales Tax Payable		$100	$8	$8
61	Less:Increase in Inventory		($3,000)	($250)	($250)
62	Increase in Prepaids		($225)	($19)	($19)
63	Increase in Accounts Receivable		($100)	($8)	($8)
64	Decrease in Notes Payable		($4,500)	($375)	($375)
65	Decrease in P/R Taxes Payable		($180)	($15)	($15)
66					
67	Cash provided by Operations		$21,795	$1,816	$1,816
68					
69	Cash was used to:				
70	Draws paid to owner		($21,495)	($1,791)	($1,791)
71					
72					
73	Increase in Cash		$300	$25	$25
74					
75	Ending Cash Balance		$500	$525	$550
76			=========	=======	======

Changing the Statements to Financial Projections

You can use the Income Statement (Figure 3-3) and Cash Flow Statement (Figure 3-10) to create the Income Projection and Pro Forma Cash Flow in Figure 3-11. Retrieve your income statement file (IS1289) and change cells A2 and A3 to *Income Projections* and *Proposed 1990*. Enter the months in row 4.

If you plan to have identical amounts for the next year (or to make your forecasting easier), insert 12 columns to the left of column B. The formula in each row would be $N6/12, $N7/12, $N8/12, continuing down the column and copied across the months. Use the printing instructions for the original statement, adjusting the range for your new columns. Save the file with a new filename. Retrieve the cash flow statement file (CASH1289) and change cells A2 and A3 to *Pro Forma Cash Flow* and *1990*. Erase Cells B61 to B65, and enter amount in C61 through C65 preceded by a negative sign. Change the formula in D53 to +C75, to make the beginning balance each month the ending balance from the previous month.

Copy the formula in D53 across the row, change the formula in C67 to @SUM(C56.C65), and enter the months in row 50. Enter the formula *$C56/12* in D56. You can copy the formulas down to row 65 and then across each month, copying each subtotal formula across. Use the printing instructions for the original statement, adjusting the range for your new columns. Finally, save the file with a new filename.

If you have Release 2.2, you can use Allways to print professional quality statements and graphs. See Chapter 2 and Chapter 7 for instructions on using Allways.

4
Daily Recordkeeping

In this chapter, you can create spreadsheets that are helpful in keeping a daily record of your business. Each one will provide you with different reports for your business. From the check register, invoicing, and job estimating spreadsheets you'll be able to produce:

• Check Registers
• Distribution Reports or Posting Summaries
• Expense Budget Analyses
• Account Transaction Reports
• Invoices
• Sales Summaries
• Salesperson Commission Reports
• Accounts Receivable Statements
• Job Estimates for Clients
• Job Cost Records with Estimated Profits

Both the check register and invoice spreadsheets have instructions for the simplest form, and you can upgrade them later in the chapter with macros for maximum input speed. You can use the job estimating spreadsheet for unit or fixed price bidding. As actual costs are incurred, the spreadsheet calculates the estimated profit based on the percentage of completion method.

The Check Register

The basic check register allows you to enter the check number, description, amount, and account number. The current balance is calculated at the top of the screen. You can enter checks and deposits, and then compare the balance with the amount in your checkbook or journal. After completing the basic check register, you can create a database from this information. This query will search for a certain account number and list all the checks or deposits for that account.

The next step in customizing the register will be to "spread" the accounts across the spreadsheet, creating a true cash disbursement journal. You can add a lookup table to find the account name when you enter an account number. You can create a budget for your expense accounts that's updated with each check you enter. The basic check register might be all you need, but if you want a powerful spreadsheet, continue through all the instructions. You can add any of the additional features before or after entering all your checks.

Figure 4-1. Simple Check Register

	A	B	C	D	E
1		Easy Company			
2		Check Register		BalFwd	$3,290.00
3		January 1990		Bal.	$618.98
4					
5	Check#	Description	Amount	Acct#	
6					
7	1000	Toy Co.	$123.00	66	
8	1001	First Bank	$340.00	230	
9	1001	First Bank	$78.32	77	
10	1002	City News	$330.00	50	
11	Dep	Sue Evans	($50.00)	120	
12	1003	MeriMaid	$75.00	66	
13	1004	Sloan Co.	$297.00	86	
14	1005	Joe Fish P/R	$300.00	90	
15	1005	Joe Fish P/R	($47.30)	232	
16	Dep	Cash Sales	($2,305.00)	101	
17	1006	Toy Co	$3,430.00	140	
18	1007	Rotary	$100.00	69	
19					
20					

Creating the Check Register

What follows is a brief review of the material from Chapter 2. If you're a 1-2-3 newcomer, you should read Chapter 2. Bring up the spreadsheet screen by typing 123 at the DOS prompt. The startup screen will have columns lettered A–H across the top of the screen and numbers for the rows going down the left side. The intersection of these columns and rows are called *cells*, where information is stored. For example, cell B4 is the intersection of the second column over (B) and the fourth row down (4). Cell D3 is the intersection of the fourth column over (D) and the third row down (3). The cursor will start in cell A1 and you can move it down or across with the arrow keys. What you type on the keyboard will appear on the line above the columns. It will move into the cell on which the cursor is resting when you press the Enter key.

Entering a Menu Command

When you press the slash key (/), different menu options such as Worksheet, Range, Copy, File, Print, Graph, Data, System, and Quit appear across the top of the screen. To select a command, press the first letter of the option, then the first letter of the next submenu item until you're finished. You can also select a menu item by moving the right- and left-arrow keys until the option is highlighted, and then pressing Enter. All the instructions in this chapter will be done by entering the first letter.

Cancel or Erase
Esc

The Esc key normally cancels a command and takes you back to the previous menu or status. If you make an error and want to erase what you've typed so far, press the Esc key. If you've already pressed the Enter key and want to erase the contents of a cell, move the cursor to the cell you want to clear. Enter

/Range Erase

and press Enter to accept the range as the current cell.

Moving the Cursor

Use the arrow keys to move from cell to cell. Other helpful keys to know are:

F5 (Goto)	Moves to any cell location
Home	Moves to upper left corner (A1)
PageUp	Moves up one page
PageDown	Moves down one page

Quitting and Saving the Spreadsheet

If you need to quit before completing the spreadsheet and want to save the file, enter

/File Save

1-2-3 will then ask for a filename. Type

ChkReg

and press Enter. A filename can be up to eight characters, but you should stick to letters and numbers. Don't include any symbols such as + = . * / ? (> % or leave any blank spaces.

To quit without saving, enter

/Quit Yes

and you should be back at the DOS prompt. Just enter *123* to go back into the spreadsheet.

Widening the Columns
/Worksheet Global Column-Width

Since almost all the columns must be wide enough to hold long amounts, use the Worksheet Global Column-Width command. To increase the columns, enter

/Worksheet Global Column-Width

Then respond to the prompt *Enter column width:* with

11

and press Enter.

Widening the Column
/Worksheet Column Set-Width

Since column B must be wide enough to hold long descriptions, and column A and D shorter for check numbers and account numbers, use the Set-Column Width command. To increase column B, move the cursor to B1 and enter

/**W**orksheet **C**olumn **S**et-Width

Then respond to the prompt *Enter column width:* with

15

and press Enter. To decrease column A, move the cursor to A1 and enter

/**W**orksheet **C**olumn **S**et-Width

Then respond to the prompt *Enter column width:* with

7

and press Enter. To decrease column D, move the cursor to D1 and enter

/**W**orksheet **C**olumn **S**et-Width

Respond to the prompt *Enter column width:* with

6

and press Enter.

Entering the Headings

Move the cursor to B1 and type

^Easy Company

(or your company name) and press Enter. The ^ key centers the text in the cell. Move the cursor to B2, type

^Check Register

and press Enter. Move the cursor to B3, type

^January 1990

and press Enter. You don't need to center the remaining headings. Type the following in the cells below and press Enter:

D2   BalFwd
D3   Bal.
A5   Check#
B5   Description
C5   Amount
D5   Acct#

Entering Formulas

Cell E3 holds a formula that subtracts the total of the checks and deposits from the balance forward in cell E2. Move the cursor to E3, type

+E2−@SUM(C7.C50)

and press Enter.

The @SUM is a function that enables some timesaving. In E3, instead of entering $E2-C7+C8+C9$ through $C50$, the @SUM function totals every cell from C7 through C50.

Formatting the Spreadsheet to Currency
/Range Format Currency

You need to format Column C and cells E2 and E3 to currency. Since you only want this column and two cells to be in currency format, use the Range command instead of the Worksheet Global Format command. Enter

/Range Format Currency

and respond to the prompt *Enter number of decimal places:* with

2

Press Enter. Respond to the prompt *Enter range to format:* with

C7.C50

and press Enter. Then enter

/**Range** Format Currency

and respond to the prompt *Enter number of decimal places:* with

2

and press Enter. Respond to the prompt *Enter range to format:* with

E2.E3

and press Enter.

Saving the Spreadsheet
/File Save

Since you can use this check register each month or period, save
the spreadsheet without data. To save the file, enter

/**File S**ave

1-2-3 will then ask for a filename; type

ChkReg

and press Enter. If you've already saved the spreadsheet earlier,
press Enter when the filename *ChkReg* is automatically displayed.
The software will check to see if you want to write over your previous file, so enter

Replace

to replace the file.

Entering the Data

Enter the checks and deposits in columns A, B, C, and D from Figure 4-1 or your own checkbook. Enter the balance forward in cell
E2. When entering amounts, don't enter the comma or dollar sign.
When entering a deposit as a negative amount, as shown by parentheses in Figure 4-1, precede the amount with a minus sign. Enter
cell C11 as −50.00; this will make deposits add to the balance

rather than being subtracted like checks. If you see a row of asterisks instead of the amount you've entered, the column isn't wide
enough to hold that amount. Use the Worksheet Column-Set command */WCS* to increase the width of the column. Sometimes a
check number is duplicated on the next row, such as number 1001
to First Bank. This is because the payment to First Bank goes to
two accounts. The same is true for payroll check number 1005 to
Joe Fish. His gross wages go to account 90 and the payroll taxes are
a credit to account 232.

Saving the Completed Worksheet
/File Save

Save the new worksheet containing this period's data in a new file
separate from the previous *ChkReg* file. Enter

/File Save

Then type in

CRJan90

for "Check Register January 1990" (or any name that will be easy
for you to remember) and press Enter. It's a good idea to save the
file before printing.

Printing the Worksheet
/Print Printer Range Align Go Quit

You can print the check register now. The print command allows
printing to a file or printer. Roll the paper to the perforation or top
of form and enter

/Print Printer Range

Respond to the prompt *Enter print range:* with

A1.E50

and press Enter. To begin the printing job, enter

Align Go Quit

Saving the Worksheet with Replace
/File Save Replace

After printing the check register, save this spreadsheet one more time to keep the printing instructions in the file. Enter

/**F**ile **S**ave

and press Enter when the filename *CRJan90* automatically displays. The software will check to see if you want to write over your previous file, so enter

Replace

to replace the file.

Figure 4-2. Account Transaction Report

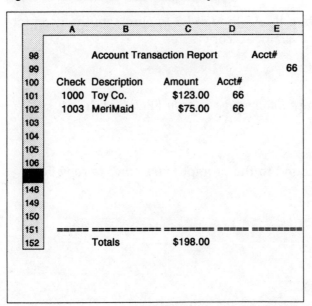

Account Transaction Report

1-2-3 has the ability to search though all the checks and deposits for items that meet a certain criterion. You can use the database feature of *1-2-3* if you need a listing of all checks charged to a certain account. You can create this database at the bottom of the spreadsheet. If you think you'll use more than 50 to 100 checks per month, move to A500 or A1000 instead of A100. To move quickly to the database area, press function key F5 and respond to the prompt *Enter address to go to:* with

A100

and press Enter.

Copying the Headings
/Copy

Copy the headings in cells A5 though E5 to eliminate the need for entering the headings again. To copy enter

/Copy

Respond to the prompt *Enter range to copy FROM:* with

A5.E5

and press Enter. Respond to the prompt *Enter range to copy TO:* with

A100

and press Enter.

Entering the Headings

Type the following headings in the cells below:

B98   Account Transaction Report
E98   Acct#

Entering the Account Number to Be Searched

Cell E99 holds the account number that will be searched each time. You can search account number 140 in this first example. Move the cursor to E99, enter

140

and press Enter.

Setting the Input, Criterion, and Output Ranges

You need to let *1-2-3* know three things before it can do a search: the *input range*, the *criterion range*, and the *output range.*

The input range is where you enter the checks and includes the heading line. The titles from the heading line—Check#, Description, Amount, and Acct#—become the field names. It's easy to forget to include this line in the input, criterion, and output ranges when doing a search.

The criterion range is the field name *Acct#* and any account number for which you want to search. The output range is where you want the result of the search to list. Again, the output range must include the heading line, which becomes the field names. To do the search, enter

/Data **Q**uery **I**nput

and respond to the prompt *Enter Input range:* with

A5.E50

and press Enter. Enter

Criteria

and respond to the prompt *Enter Criteria range:* with

E98.E99

and press Enter. Enter

Output

and respond to the prompt *Enter Output range:* with

A100.D150

and press Enter. To begin the search, enter

Extract **Q**uit

All checks that were charged to account number 140 are listed in the output range of A100 through D150.

Using the Query Key
F7

Use the F7 function key anytime you change the account number to be searched. Search for account number 66 next. Move the cursor to E99, type

66

and press Enter. You don't need to enter the input, criterion, and output ranges again. Press F7 and the search will start again.

Entering Totals and Underscore

To make a totaling line at the bottom of the account transaction report, move the cursor to A151 and enter

\ =

Press Enter. To copy the underscore across the report, enter

/**C**opy

and respond to the prompt *Enter range to copy FROM:* with

A151

Press Enter. Respond to the prompt *Enter range to copy TO:* with

B151.D151

and press Enter.

To enter the formula for the total, move the cursor to C152, type

@DSUM(A5.E50,2,E98.E99)

and press Enter. This sums column 3 (the columns are numbered 0, 1, 2, and 3) in your input range for the account in the database criterion range. To title this sum, move the cursor to B152 and type

Totals

Press Enter.

Formatting the Area to Currency
/Range Format Currency

You need to format Column C to currency. Since you only want this column to be in currency, use the Range command instead of the Worksheet Global Format command. Enter

/Range Format Currency

and respond to the prompt *Enter number of decimal places:* with

2

and press Enter. Respond to the prompt *Enter range to format:* with

C101.C152

and press Enter.

Saving the Worksheet with Replace
/File Save Replace

Before printing it's best to save the file. Enter

/File Save

and press Enter when the filename *CRJan90* is automatically displayed. The software will check to see if you want to write over
your previous file, so enter

Replace

to replace the file.

Printing the Account Transaction Report
/Print Printer Range Align Go Quit

You can print the account transaction report now. The print command allows printing to a file or printer. Roll the paper to the perforation or top of form and enter

/Print Printer Range

Respond to the prompt *Enter print range:* with

A98.E152

and press Enter. To begin the printing job, enter

Align Go Quit

Saving the Worksheet with Replace
/File Save Replace

After printing the transaction report, save this spreadsheet one
more time to keep the printing and data search instructions in the
file. Enter

/File Save

and press Enter when the filename *CRJan90* is automatically displayed. The software will check to see if you want to write over
your previous file, so enter

Replace

to replace the file.

Adding Account Names and Account Distribution

You now have a basic check register that might be sufficient for your company's needs. It's possible to add a few features to make the check register easier to use and to provide you with additional information. One feature displays an account name after entering the account number. Another feature spreads the account number balances across in an account distribution for a posting summary. Finally, you can create a budget for expense account analysis.

Figure 4-3. Account Names for Lookup Table

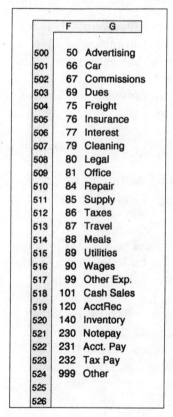

	F	G
500	50	Advertising
501	66	Car
502	67	Commissions
503	69	Dues
504	75	Freight
505	76	Insurance
506	77	Interest
507	79	Cleaning
508	80	Legal
509	81	Office
510	84	Repair
511	85	Supply
512	86	Taxes
513	87	Travel
514	88	Meals
515	89	Utilities
516	90	Wages
517	99	Other Exp.
518	101	Cash Sales
519	120	AcctRec
520	140	Inventory
521	230	Notepay
522	231	Acct. Pay
523	232	Tax Pay
524	999	Other
525		
526		

Creating a Lookup Table

You can create a lookup table in cells F500 through G524 that will hold the account number and corresponding account name. When you enter an account number in column D of the check register, a formula in column E will look up the number and display the name from the table. To enter the table, press the function key F5 and respond to the prompt *Enter address to go to:* with

F500

Press Enter.

Enter the account number and names from Figure 4-3 or use your own accounts. You must enter the account numbers in ascending order for the lookup function to work. Later, you can enter the budget information for an expense budget analysis. To enter the formula for the lookup function, press the function key F5 and answer the prompt *Enter address to go to:* with

E7

Press Enter. Enter the following formula in E7 and press Enter:

@VLOOKUP(D7,$F$500. .$G$524,1)

The account name *Car* will display. This formula tells *1-2-3* to look up vertically the account number in D7 at the table located at F500 through G524, and then use the information in the first column after the account number.

Enter the location of the table with a dollar sign prefix for an absolute location. When you copy this formula down column E, the location of F500 through G524 won't adjust to F501.G525, F502.G526, and so forth, but D7 will adjust to D8, D9, D10, and so on down the column.

Copying Formulas
/Copy

Copy the formula in cell E7 (which contains the lookup formula) down the column to eliminate the need for entering the formula again. To copy, enter

/Copy

and respond to the prompt *Enter range to copy FROM:* with

E7

Press Enter. Respond to the prompt *Enter range to copy TO:* with

E8.E50

and press Enter. Move the cursor to E8 and you'll see that the formula reads *@VLOOKUP(D8,$F$500.$G$524,1)* and *Notepay* is now in that cell. Now when you type a new account number in column D, the account name will display in column E. An *ERR* message will display in the row until an account number is entered. The next steps will create the account distribution.

Saving the Worksheet with Replace
/File Save Replace

It's best to save the spreadsheet often. Enter

/File Save

and press Enter when the filename *CRJan90* is automatically displayed. The software will check to see if you want to write over your previous file, so enter

Replace

to replace the file.

Figure 4-4. Account Names and Distribution Report

	C	D	E	F	G	H	E	J
2		BalFwd	$3,290.00					
3		Bal.	$618.98					
4								
5	Amount	Acct#	Acct. Name		50	66	67	69
6					Advertising	Car	Commission	Dues
7	$123.00	66	Car		$0.00	$123.00	$0.00	$0.00
8	$340.00	230	Notepay		$0.00	$0.00	$0.00	$0.00
9	$78.32	77	Interest		$0.00	$0.00	$0.00	$0.00
10	$330.00	50	Advertising		$330.00	$0.00	$0.00	$0.00
11	($50.00)	120	AcctRec		$0.00	$0.00	$0.00	$0.00
12	$75.00	66	Car		$0.00	$75.00	$0.00	$0.00
13	$297.00	86	Taxes		$0.00	$0.00	$0.00	$0.00
14	$300.00	90	Wages		$0.00	$0.00	$0.00	$0.00
15	($47.30)	232	Tax Pay		$0.00	$0.00	$0.00	$0.00
16	($2,305.00)	101	Cash Sales		$0.00	$0.00	$0.00	$0.00
17	$3,430.00	140	Inventory		$0.00	$0.00	$0.00	$0.00
18	$100.00	69	Dues		$0.00	$0.00	$0.00	$100.00
19			ERR		$0.00	$0.00	$0.00	$0.00
20			ERR		$0.00	$0.00	$0.00	$0.00
49			ERR		$0.00	$0.00	$0.00	$0.00
50			ERR		$0.00	$0.00	$0.00	$0.00
51	========	=====	==========	====	========	======	==========	======
52				Totals	$330.00	$198.00	$0.00	$100.00
53								

Copying the Account Number and Titles with Transpose /Range Transpose

Since you want the account numbers and titles that are listed down a column in the lookup table to move across rows 5 and 6 in the distributions area, use the range transpose command instead of the copy command. Enter

/Range Transpose

and respond to the prompt *Enter range to copy FROM:* with

F500.G524

and press Enter. Respond to the prompt *Enter range to copy TO:* with

G5

and press Enter.

Centering the Account Names
/Range Labels Center

To center the account names in each of the cells in row 6, enter

/Range Label Center

and respond to the prompt *Enter range of labels:* with

G6.AE6

and press Enter.

Entering the Formula to Distribute by Account Number

Move the cursor to G7 and type

@IF($D7=G$5,$C7,0)

and press Enter. This formula means that if the account number in D7 equals the account number in the column heading G5, then display the amount from C7. If not, a zero is entered.

Copying the Formula
/Copy

To copy the formula in cell G7, which determines if the account number matches the column heading, enter

/Copy

Respond to the prompt *Enter range to copy FROM:* with

G7

and press Enter. Respond to the prompt *Enter range to copy TO:* with

G7.AE50

and press Enter. Move the cursor to H8 and you'll see that the formula reads *@IF($D8=H$5,$C8,0)*. This is because the copy command didn't alter any column or row with the absolute ($) symbol prefix, such as columns C and D and row 5. All other columns and rows are relative to their new destination.

Setting the Recalculation to Manual
/Worksheet Global Recalculation Manual

At this point the spreadsheet will become very slow because of the amount of checking it must perform each time a new entry is made. To speed up entry, you can change the spreadsheet to calculate manually. Enter

/Worksheet Global Recalculation Manual

and then press F9 anytime you need to recalculate the spreadsheet. To set the spreadsheet back to automatic recalculation, enter

/Worksheet Global Recalculation Automatic.

Suppress Zero Display
/Worksheet Global Zero Yes

It may be difficult to see the amounts in the account distribution area with the display of zeros. To suppress them, enter

/Worksheet Global Zero Yes

and the zeros will disappear.

Entering Totals and Underscore

To make a totaling line at the bottom of the account distribution area, move the cursor to G51, enter

\ =

and press Enter. To enter the formula for the totals, move the cursor to G52, type

@SUM(G7.G50)

and press Enter.

Copying the Formula and Underscore
/Copy

Copy the formula in cell G52, which adds G7 through G50, to the columns across the distribution report. To copy, enter

/Copy

and respond to the prompt *Enter range to copy FROM:* with

G52

and press Enter. Respond to the prompt *Enter range to copy TO:* with

H52. .AE52

and press Enter. Continue copying the underscore from G51 to H51. .AE51.
   In cell F52 type

Totals

and press Enter.

Formatting the Area to Currency
/Range Format Currency

Enter

/Range Format Currency

and respond to the prompt *Enter number of decimal places:* with

2

and press Enter. Respond to the prompt *Enter range to format:* with

G7.AE52

and press Enter.

Saving the Worksheet with Replace
/File Save Replace

It's best to save the spreadsheet often. Enter

/File Save

and press Enter when the filename *CRJan90* is automatically displayed. The software will check to see if you want to write over your previous file so enter

Replace

to replace the file.

Printing the Worksheet
/Print Printer Range Align Go Quit

You can print the account distribution report or posting summary now. Unfortunately the print commands from the account transaction report are saved and will have to be overridden. Roll the paper to the perforation or top of form and enter

/Print Printer Range

Respond to the prompt *Enter print range:* with

F5.AE52

and press Enter. To begin the printing job, enter

Align Go Quit

This spreadsheet is too wide to print on most 80- and 135-column printers without going to a second or third page. If you have a condensed print switch available on your printer, you'll probably be able to print on only two pages. Set it to condensed and from the print menu enter

Options Margins Right

and enter

135

for the new right margin. If your printer doesn't have a switch but accepts a condensed print code, from the options menu enter

Setup

For Epson printers, the string for condensed is ＼*015*. Look in the *Lotus 1-2-3* appendix for your specific printer code. Enter

Quit

to quit the options menu. Then to start the print job, enter

Align Go Quit

Saving the Worksheet with Replace
/File Save Replace

After printing the account distribution report, save this spreadsheet one more time to keep the printing instructions in the file. Enter

/File Save

and press Enter when the filename *CRJan90* is automatically displayed. The software will check to see if you want to write over your previous file, so enter

Replace

to replace the file.

Figure 4-5. Expense Budget Analysis

	BA	BB	BC	BD	BE
2		Easy Company		January 1990	
3		Expense Budget Analysis			
4					Over (Under)
5	Acct#	Name	Actual	Budget	Variance
6	=====	=========	=========	=========	=========
7	50	Advertising	$330.00	$500.00	($170.00)
8	66	Car	$198.00	$250.00	($52.00)
9	67	Commissions	$0.00	$300.00	($300.00)
10	69	Dues	$100.00	$50.00	$50.00
11	75	Freight	$0.00	$25.00	($25.00)
12	76	Insurance	$0.00	$80.00	($80.00)
13	77	Interest	$78.32	$79.00	($0.68)
14	79	Cleaning	$0.00	$50.00	($50.00)
15	80	Legal	$0.00	$200.00	($200.00)
16	81	Office	$0.00	$150.00	($150.00)
17	84	Repair	$0.00	$30.00	($30.00)
18	85	Supply	$0.00	$20.00	($20.00)
19	86	Taxes	$297.00	$400.00	($103.00)
20	87	Travel	$0.00	$100.00	($100.00)
21	88	Meals	$0.00	$50.00	($50.00)
22	89	Utilities	$0.00	$500.00	($500.00)
23	90	Wages	$300.00	$5,000.00	($4,700.00)
24	99	Other Exp.	$0.00	$20.00	($20.00)
25	=====	=========	=========	=========	=========
26		Totals	$1,303.32	$7,804.00	($6,500.60)

Creating the Expense Budget Analysis

The budget shown in Figure 4-5 uses the account numbers and names already entered in the lookup table, and the balances from the account distribution report. It's a simple task to copy this information to an area set aside for budgeting each month. As you enter each check, the budget is automatically updated. To move the cursor to an unused area away from the main spreadsheet, press the F5 function key and respond to the prompt *Enter address to go to:* with

BB2

and press Enter.

Entering the Headings

After moving to cell BB2, type

Easy Company

and press Enter. Move the cursor to BB3 and type

Expense Budget Analysis

and press Enter. Move the cursor to BD2 and type

+B3

and press Enter. In cells BA5 through BE5 and BE4 enter the following headings:

BA5   Acct#
BB5   Name
BC5   Actual
BD5   Budget
BE5   Variance
BE4   Over (Under)

Copying the Account Numbers and Titles
/Copy

Use the copy command to save time entering the account number and titles in columns BA and BB. Enter

/Copy

and respond to the prompt *Enter range to copy FROM:* with

F500.G517

and press Enter. Respond to the prompt *Enter range to copy TO:* with

BA7

and press Enter. Only the expense accounts that end at G517 are copied since this budget is for expense analysis.

Copying the Account Balances with Transpose
/Range Transpose

Since the balances you want are across a row (G52 through AD52) and need to be copied down a column (BC7 through BC24), you need to use the range transpose command instead of the copy command. First you'll need to edit each cell in row 52 to an absolute reference. Move the cursor to G52 and press first F2, then F4, and then Enter. G52 should change from *@SUM(G7. .G50)* to *@SUM($G$7. .$G$50)*. Press the right arrow to move to H52; press F2, F4, and then Enter. Press the right arrow and continue moving the cursor through cell X52. Make sure all cells from G52 through X52 are now an absolute reference. Enter

/Range Transpose

and respond to the prompt *Enter range to copy FROM:* with

G52.X52

and press Enter. Respond to the prompt *Enter range to copy TO:* with

BC7

Press Enter.

Entering Formulas and Underscore

To make a totaling line at the top and bottom of the expense budget analysis, move the cursor to BA6, enter

\ =

and press Enter. Repeat for BA25. To enter the formula for the totals, move the cursor to BC26 and type

@SUM(BC7.BC24)

Press Enter.

To title this sum, move the cursor to BB26, type

Totals

and press Enter. Column BE will subtract column BD from BC to arrive at the variance between actual and budgeted expenses. To enter the formula, move the cursor to BE7, type

+BC7−BD7

and press Enter.

Copying Formulas
/Copy

Copy the formula in cell BC26 (which adds BC7 through BC24) to cells BD26 and BE26 to eliminate the need for entering the formula again. To copy, enter

/Copy

and respond to the prompt *Enter range to copy FROM:* with

BC26

and press Enter. Respond to the prompt *Enter range to copy TO:* with

BD26.BE26

and press Enter. Continue copying the formula and underscores as follows:

BA6	to	BB6.BE6
BA25	to	BB25.BE25
BE7	to	BE8.BE24

Formatting the Area to Currency
/Range Format Currency

You need to format Columns BC, BD, and BE to currency. Since you only want these columns to be in currency, use the Range command instead of the Worksheet Global Format command. Enter

/Range Format Currency

and respond to the prompt *Enter number of decimal places:* with

2

and press Enter. Respond to the prompt *Enter range to format:* with

BC7.BE26

and press Enter.

Entering the Data

Enter the budget data in column BD from Figure 4-5 or your own accounts. If you see a row of asterisks instead of the amount you entered, the column isn't wide enough to hold that amount. Use the Worksheet Column-Set command (/WCS) to increase the size of the column. Press F9 to recalculate.

Saving the Worksheet with Replace
/File Save Replace

It's a good habit to save before starting a print job. Enter

/File Save

and press Enter when the filename *CrJan90* automatically displays. The software will check to see if you want to write over your previous file, so enter

Replace

to replace the file.

Printing the Expense Budget Analysis
/Print Printer Range Align Go Quit

You can print the expense budget analysis now. The print command allows printing to a file or printer. Roll the paper to the perforation or top of form and enter

/Print Printer Range

Respond to the prompt *Enter print range:* with

BA2.BE26

and press Enter. To begin the printing job, enter

Align Go Quit

Figure 4-6. Macros for Printing Jobs

	BA	BB	BC	BD	BE
50	Printing Macros				
52	Alt C			Alt N	
53	Check Register			Account Number Listing	
54	{calc}/ppr			/ppr	
55	A1.E50~agq			F500.G524~agq	
57	Alt A			Alt E	
58	Account Transaction Report			Expense Budget Analysis	
59	{Query}{calc}			{calc}	
60	/ppr			/ppr	
61	A98.E152~agq			BA2.BE26~agq	
64	Alt D				
65	Distribution Report or Posting Summary				
66	/wgzy~{calc}				
67	/ppomr135~s\015~qr				
68	F5.AE52~agq				

Entering Macros to Print Reports

Each time you save the spreadsheet, only the latest printing instructions are saved. To print the account transaction report, you
have to enter the range again, since the range for the expense budget report is now saved. You can save the printing instructions in
macros that you execute with the combination of the Alt key and a
letter. A *macro* is simply a range of cells on the spreadsheet that
holds the keystrokes necessary to execute commands. You can create five macros to print the following reports:

Alt-C	Check Register
Alt-A	Account Transaction Report
Alt-D	Distribution Report or Posting Summary
Alt-N	Account Number Listing
Alt-E	Expense Budget Analysis

    To move to an unused portion of the spreadsheet, press the F5
function key and respond to the prompt *Enter address to go to:* with

BA50

and press Enter. Type the heading,

Printing Macros

and press Enter. Move the cursor to BA52, type

Alt C

and press Enter. (Be sure to type the word *Alt* followed by the letter *C—do not press the Alt key and C combination.*) Move to BA53,
type

Check Register

and press Enter. Type the information shown in the remaining cells
of Figure 4-6. When entering text into a cell that begins with the
slash, such as the text in BD54, add a single quotation mark (')
prefix.

To Create a Macro
/Range Name Create

You need to name each macro range before you can execute it. To name the check register printing macro, enter

/Range Name Create

respond to the prompt *Enter name:* with

\C

and press Enter. Respond to the prompt *Enter range:* with

BA54.BA55

and press Enter. Repeat for the other four macros.

Name:	Range:
\N	BD54.BD55
\A	BA59.BA61
\E	BD59.BD61
\D	BA66.BA68

To execute the check register–printing macro, hold down the Alt key and simultaneously press the letter C. The macro in cells BA54 and BA55 will recalculate the spreadsheet and then execute the Print Printer Range command. The range A1 through E50 will be typed after the prompt to enter the print range and the tilde symbol (˜) and the Enter key are pressed. Next the Align, Go, and Quit commands will be issued.

How to Use the Check Register

Enter your company name in cell B1. Enter the month and year in B3. Use the Range Erase command to clear any checks you've entered in columns A, B, C, and D starting with row 7. Don't erase the formula in column E. Enter your balance forward in cell E2, and enter your account numbers and names starting in cell F500. Use the instructions under the section head "Copying the Account Number and Titles with Transpose /Range Transpose" to copy your account numbers to rows 5 and 6, starting with column G.

Use the instructions under the section head "Copying the Account Numbers and Titles /Copy" to copy your account numbers to the Expense Budget Analysis starting in BA7. Finally, enter your budget amounts for the month in column BD.

Saving the Worksheet with Replace /File Save Replace

Save the completed worksheet. Enter

/File **S**ave

and press Enter when the filename *CRJan90* automatically displays. The software will check to see if you want to write over your previous file, so enter

Replace

to replace the file.

The Sales Invoice

The basic sales invoice allows you to enter the customer information, quantity, description, and pricing. The invoice spreadsheet will total and tax the items. After completing the basic invoice, you can create a summary section in the spreadsheet to store the invoice totals. From this summary section, sales reports and accounts receivable statements can be generated. The basic sales invoice might be all you need, but if you want a powerful spreadsheet, continue through all the instructions. You can add any of the additional features after entering and storing your invoices in the sales summary.

Figure 4-7. Sales Invoice

	A	B	C	D	E	F	G
1			Easy Company				
2	Inv#	1001	123 Easy Street		Date		02/11/90
3			Everytown, CA 93449				
4			(805) 555-5555				
5							
6			** INVOICE **				
7	Sold To:	Sam Toy		Tax Rate	6.5%		
8		345 West St.					
9		Everytown, CA 93449		Salesperson		Joe First	
10							
11	Quantity	Stock#	Description	Each	Ext.	Tax	Total
12	=====	=====	==========	=====	=====	=====	=====
13	3	150	Rope	$3.00	$9.00	$0.59	$9.59
14	16	140	Ball	$23.00	$368.00	$23.92	$391.92
15							
16							
17							
18							
19							
20							
21	Inv#	Date	Customer	S/P	Sale	Tax	Total
22	=====	=====	==========	=====	=====	=====	=====
23	1001	02/11/90	Sam Toy	Joe First	$377.00	$24.51	$401.51
24							

Creating the Sales Invoice

What follows is a brief review of the material from Chapter 2. If you're a *1-2-3* newcomer, you should read Chapter 2. Bring up the spreadsheet screen by typing *123* at the DOS prompt. The startup screen will have columns lettered A–H across the top of the screen and numbers for the rows going down the left side. The intersection of these columns and rows are called *cells*, where information is stored. For example, cell B4 is the intersection of the second column over (B) and the fourth row down (4). Cell D3 is the intersection of the fourth column over (D) and the third row down (3). The cursor will start in cell A1 and you can move it down or across with the arrow keys. What you type on the keyboard will appear on the line above the columns. It will move into the cell on which the cursor is resting when you press the Enter key.

Entering a Menu Command

When you press the slash key (/), different menu options such as Worksheet, Range, Copy, File, Print, Graph, Data, System, and Quit appear across the top of the screen. To select a command, press the first letter of the option and then the first letter of the next submenu item until you finish. You can also select a menu item by moving the right- and left-arrow keys until the option is highlighted and then pressing Enter. All the instructions in this chapter will be done by entering the first letter.

Cancel or Erase
Esc

The Esc key normally cancels a command and takes you back to the previous menu or status. If you make an error and want to erase what you've typed so far, press the Esc key. If you've already pressed the Enter key and want to erase the contents of a cell, move the cursor to the cell you want to clear. Enter

/Range Erase

and press Enter to accept the range as the current cell.

Moving the Cursor

Use the arrow keys to move from cell to cell. Other helpful keys to know are:

F5 (Goto)   Moves to any cell location
Home   Moves to upper left corner (A1)
PageUp   Moves up one page
PageDown   Moves down one page

Quitting and Saving the Spreadsheet

If you need to quit before completing the spreadsheet and want to save the file, enter

/File Save

1-2-3 will then ask for a filename; type

Invoice

and press Enter. A filename can be up to eight characters, but you should stick to letters and numbers. Don't include any symbols such as + = . * / ? (> % or leave any blank spaces. To quit without saving, enter

/Quit Yes

and you should be back at the DOS prompt. Just enter *123* to go back into the spreadsheet.

Widening the Column
/Worksheet Column Set-Width

Since column C must be wide enough to hold long descriptions, use the Column Set-Width command. To increase column C, move the cursor to C1 and enter

/Worksheet Column Set-Width

Then respond to the prompt *Enter column width:* with

18

and press Enter. Move the cursor to B1 and enter

/Worksheet Column Set-Width

Respond to the prompt *Enter column width:* with

12

and press Enter.

Entering the Headings

Move the cursor to C1 and type

^Easy Company

(or your company name) and press Enter. The ^ key centers the text in the cell. Move the cursor to C2 and type

^123 Easy Street

and press Enter. Move the cursor to C3 and C4, type

^Everytown, CA 93449
^(805) 555-5555

and press Enter. You don't need to center the remaining headings. Type the following in the cells below:

Cell	Entry
A2	Inv#
E2	Date
A7	Sold To:
D7	Tax Rate
E7	.065
C6	** INVOICE **
D9	Salesperson
A11	Quantity
B11	Stock#
C11	Description
D11	Each
E11	Ext.
F11	Tax
G11	Total

Entering Formulas

Cell E13 holds a formula that multiplies each price by the quantity to arrive at an *extended* price. Move the cursor to E13, type

+A13*D13

and press Enter. Column F figures the tax on this extended price. Move the cursor to F13, type

+E13*$E$7

and press Enter. Column G adds the tax to the extended price for an item line total. Move the cursor to G13 and type

+E13+F13

Press Enter.

Copying Formulas
/Copy

Copy the formulas in cells E13, F13, and G13 down the invoice to eliminate the need for entering the formula again. To copy, enter

/Copy

and respond to the prompt *Enter range to copy FROM:* with

E13. .G13

Press Enter. Respond to the prompt *Enter range to copy TO:* with

E14. .G20

and press Enter.

Move the cursor to E14 and you'll see that the formula reads *+A14*D14* instead of *+A13*D13*. This is because the copy command copies cells relative to their new destination unless you put an absolute symbol ($) in front of the cell address.

Formatting the Spreadsheet to Currency
/Range Format Currency

You need to format Columns D, E, F, and G to currency. Since you only want these columns in currency, use the Range command instead of the Worksheet Global Format command. Enter

/Range Format Currency

Respond to the prompt *Enter number of decimal places:* with

2

and press Enter. Respond to the prompt *Enter range to format:* with

D13.G1100

and press Enter. Move the cursor to E7, enter

/Range Format Percent

and respond to the prompt *Enter number of decimal places:* with

1

Press Enter. Then press Enter again to accept the current cell as the range to format.

Entering the Summary Section

Type the headings in cells A21 through G21 from Figure 4-7. Move the cursor to A12, enter

\=

and press Enter. Repeat for cell A22. To copy across the row, enter

/Copy

Respond to the prompt *Enter range to copy FROM:* with

A12

and press Enter. Respond to the prompt *Enter range to copy TO:* with

B12.G12

and press Enter. Repeat for A22, copied to B22 through G22. Enter the following formulas in cells A23 through G23:

```
A23    +B2
B23    +F2
C23    +B7
D23    +F9
E23    @SUM(E13.E20)
F23    @SUM(F13.F20)
G23    +E23+F23
```

Saving the Spreadsheet
/File Save

Since you can use this invoice each time you have a sale, save the spreadsheet without data. To save the file, enter

/File Save

1-2-3 will then ask for a filename. Type

Invoice

and press Enter. If you saved the spreadsheet earlier, press Enter when the filename *Invoice* automatically displays. The software will check to see if you want to write over your previous file, so enter

Replace

to replace the file.

Entering the Data

Make a sample invoice to test the spreadsheet. In cells B7 through B9 enter the customer name and address from Figure 4-7 or from your own files. Remember to put a , before a street address beginning with a number. Enter an invoice number in B2 and a Salesperson in Cell F9. Move the cursor to row 13 and enter a quantity, stock#, description, and price each. The rest will be automatically calculated.

Entering a Date

The date in Cell F2 can easily be entered as a label, *2/11/90*, but you'll need it to be in a valid date format later if you want aged invoices. To enter a date, move the cursor to F2, type

@DATE(90,2,11)

and press Enter. To format the cell to display in a date format, enter

/Range Format **D**ate **4**

and press Enter to accept the current range. Move the cursor to B23, enter

/Range Format **D**ate **4**

and press Enter to accept the current range.

Suppress Zero Display
/Worksheet Global Zero Yes

The invoice looks nicer if you eliminate the unnecessary zeros before printing. To suppress them, enter

/Worksheet Global **Z**ero **Y**es

and the zeros will disappear.

Saving the Worksheet with Replace
/File Save Replace

It's best to save the spreadsheet often. Enter

/File **S**ave

and press Enter when the filename *Invoice* automatically displays. The software will check to see if you want to write over your previous file, so enter

Replace

to replace the file.

Printing the Invoice
/Print Printer Range Align Go Quit

You can print the invoice now. The print command allows printing to a file or printer. Roll the paper to the perforation or top of form and enter

/Print Printer Range

Respond to the prompt *Enter print range:* with

A1.G23

and press Enter. To begin the printing job, enter

Align Go Quit

Figure 4-8. Sales Summary

	A	B	C	D	E	F	G
1003		Easy Company		Month:			
1004		Sales Summary		February 1990			
1005		======	========	=========	=======	=======	=======	======
1006							
1007	Inv#	Date	Customer	S/P	Sale	Tax	Total
1008	1005	02/11/90	Sam Toy	Joe First	$51.00	$3.32	$54.32
1009	1004	02/11/90	Try Inc.	Sue Smith	$384.00	$24.96	$408.96
1010	1003	02/11/90	Sam Toy	Joe First	$13.50	$0.88	$14.38
1011	1002	02/11/90	Gift Co.	Joe First	$34.50	$2.24	$36.74
1012	1001	02/11/90	Sam Toy	Joe First	$377.00	$24.51	$401.51
1013							
1049							
1050							
1051		======	========	=========	=======	=======	=======	======
1052				Totals	$860.00	$55.90	$915.90
1053	Alt R Prints Summary						
1054	/pprA1000.G1052~agq						
1055							

Creating a Sales Summary

After printing the invoice, you might want to save it in a separate
file as SToy1001. Unfortunately each spreadsheet takes up a sub-
stantial amount of disk space, and you might quickly run out of
room by saving every invoice. After printing duplicated copies of
the invoice, it's possible to save only the *summary section* to provide the information you need to print sales reports and account
receivable statements. This summary section will be a database in
an unused area of the invoice spreadsheet. To move quickly to the
database area, press the F5 function key and respond to the prompt
Enter address to go to: with

A1000

Press Enter.

Copying the Headings
/Copy

Copy the headings in cells A21 though G21 to eliminate the need
for entering the headings again. To copy, enter

/Copy

Respond to the prompt *Enter range to copy FROM:*

A21.G21

and press Enter. Respond to the prompt *Enter range to copy TO:*
with

A1007.G1007

and press Enter.

Entering the Headings

Type the following headings in the cells below:

B1003   Easy Company
B1004   Sales Summary
D1003   Month:
D1004   February 1990

Entering the Repeating Underline
\=

Cell A1005 and A1051 contain an underline created with the equal sign. To enter the repeating underline, move the cursor to A1005 and enter

\=

To copy across, enter

/Copy

Respond to the prompt *Enter range to copy FROM:* with

A1005

and press Enter. Respond to the prompt *Enter range to copy TO:* with

B1005.G1005

and press Enter. Repeat for cell A1051 copied to B1051 through G1051.

Entering the Totals Line

You can use the sales summary for a monthly sales journal, posting summary, or sales tax report. To create a totaling line, move the cursor to D1052, type

Totals

and press Enter. Move the cursor to E1052, type

@SUM(E1008.E1050)

and press Enter. To copy the formula to column F and G, enter

/Copy

and respond to the prompt *Enter range to copy FROM:* with

E1052

and press Enter. Respond to the prompt *Enter range to copy TO:* with

F1052.G1052

and press Enter.

Saving the Invoice Summary Line in the Summary Section
/Range Value

After entering and printing an invoice, you can save the summary information on row 23 to the newly created summary section of your spreadsheet. Copy the value of the summary row in the invoice. When you copy a value, the actual amount in the cell is copied rather that the formula. Enter

/Range Value

and respond to the prompt *Enter range to copy FROM:* with

A23.G23

and press Enter. Respond to the prompt *Enter range to copy TO:* with

A1008.G1008

and press Enter.

Clearing the Invoice
/Range Erase

After storing the summary line in the database section, you can clear the invoice. Press the Home key to return to the invoice section. Enter

/Range Erase

and respond to the prompt *Enter range to erase:* with

B2

Press Enter. Repeat for the following cells that need to be erased:

B7.B9
F9
A13.D20

Figure 4-9. Macros

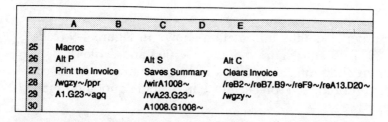

Entering Macros to Print, Save, and Clear Invoices

It's time-consuming to erase the cells each time you enter a new invoice. You'll also be saving printing instructions for the sales report rather than the invoice once the spreadsheet is complete. To avoid having to enter the new print range each time you need to print an invoice, you can save the printing instructions in a macro, which you execute with the combination of the Alt key and a letter. A *macro* is simply a range of cells on the spreadsheet that holds the keystrokes necessary to execute commands. You can create four macros to execute the following jobs:

Alt-P   Print the Invoice.
Alt-S   Save Invoice Summary Line.
Alt-C   Clear the Invoice.
Alt-R   Print Sales Summary.

Move the cursor to A25, type the heading,

Macros

and press Enter. Move the cursor to A26 and type

Alt P

Press Enter. Be sure to type the word *Alt* and letter *P—not the Alt-P key combination.* Move to A27, type

Print the Invoice

and press Enter. Type the information shown in Figure 4-9 (cells A26 through E30) and Figure 4-8 (cells A1053 and A1054).

When entering information in a cell that begins with a slash, such as the entry in A30, precede it with a single quotation mark (') prefix.

To Create a Macro
/Range Name Create

You need to name each macro range before you can execute it. To name the invoice and sales summary macros, enter

/Range Name Create

and respond to the prompt *Enter name:* with

\P

and press Enter. Respond to the prompt *Enter range:* with

A28.A29

and press Enter. Repeat for the other two macros:

/Range Name Create

and respond to the prompts:

Name:	Range:
\S	C28.C30
\C	E28.E29
\R	A1054

You should save prior to executing the macro. Enter

/File Save

and press Enter when the filename *Invoice* automatically displays. The software will check to see if you want to write over your previous file, so enter

Replace

to replace the file.

To execute the print macro, type the Alt-P key combination (hold down the Alt key and simultaneously press the letter *P*). The macro in cells A28 through A29 will suppress the zeros in the invoice and then execute the Print Printer Range command. The range A1 through G23 will be typed after the prompt to enter the print range, and the tilde symbol (˜) executes the Enter key action. Next the Align, Go, and Quit commands are issued.

Saving the Worksheet with Replace
/File Save Replace

After printing the invoice, save this spreadsheet one more time to keep the macro instructions in the file. Enter

/File Save

and press Enter when the filename *Invoice* automatically displays. The software will check to see if you want to write over your previous file, so enter

Replace

to replace the file.

How to Use the Invoice

Use the Range Erase command to erase all practice invoices in cells
A1008 through G1050. Enter your company name in B1003 and
the month in D1004. Enter your company name and address centered (^) starting in G1, using the Alt-C macro to clear the prior
invoice.

   To enter a date in F2, type *@DATE(90,2,11)* for February 11,
1990. Use the edit key (F2) to edit the contents for simplicity. Enter
your tax rate in B7 as .065 or 6.5%. Enter the invoice number in
B2. Enter your customer name and address starting in cell B7.
Move the cursor to row 13 and enter a quantity, stock#, description, and price each.

   The rest will calculate automatically. If you have Release 3, use
the instructions at the end of the inventory spreadsheet in Chapter
5 to create a lookup table. You can "link" the inventory and invoice file to enable the description and price to automatically
display.

Figure 4-10. Statement with Macros

	A	B	C	D	E	F
50			** STATEMENT **			
51						
52			Easy Company			
53			123 Easy Street		Date	02/28/90
54			Everytown, CA 93449			
55			(805) 555-5555			
56	Customer					
57	Sam Toy					
58	345 West St.					
59	Everytown, CA 93449					
60	======	========	=========	=======	======	====== ======
61	Inv#	Date		Sale	Tax	Total
62	1005	02/11/90		$51.00	$3.32	$54.32
63	1003	02/11/90		$13.50	$0.88	$14.38
64	1001	02/11/90		$377.00	$24.51	$401.51
65						
66						
67						
68						
69						
70						
71						
72						
73	Previous Past Due Balance				$230.00	
74	======	========	=========	=======	======	====== ======
75	Terms – Net 10 days				$700.20	
76	Alt B to do Search			Alt A to Print Statement		
77	/dqiA1007.G1050~cA56.A57~			/pprA50.F75~agq		
78	oA61.F72~eq					

Creating the Customer Statement

For practice and to collect some data in the database section, make some more sample invoices. After creating each one, use the Alt-S and Alt-C macros to save the summary line and clear the invoice. After you have as many invoices as in Figure 4-8, you can generate a customer statement using the database commands.

To move to an unused portion of the spreadsheet, press the F5 function key and respond to the prompt *Enter address to go to:* with

C50

and press Enter. Type the heading,

^ STATEMENT **

and press Enter. To copy the company name and address from the invoice form above, enter

/Copy

and respond to the prompt *Enter range to copy FROM:* with

C1.F4

Press Enter. Respond to the prompt *Enter range to copy TO:* with

C52

and press Enter. Edit the date in cell F53 to your normal statement date with the F2 key. Move the cursor to A56, type

Customer

and press Enter. Type the headings in cells A61 through F61, A73, and A75 from Figure 4-10. Leave cell C61 blank. The headings in row 61 and cell A56 must match exactly with those same headings in the sales summary section, cells A1007 through G1007. Don't change Inv# to *Invoice* or Customer to *Customer Name,* or the search won't work properly.

Entering the Repeating Underline

\ =

Cells A60 and A74 contain an accented underline created with the equal sign. To enter the repeating underline, move the cursor to A60, enter

\ =

and repeat for cell A74. To copy across the row, enter

/Copy

and respond to the prompt *Enter range to copy FROM:* with

A60

Press Enter. Respond to the prompt *Enter range to copy TO:* with

B60.F60

and press Enter. Repeat for A74 copied to B74 through F74.

Entering the Customer Name to Search

Cell A57 will hold the customer name you'll search for each time. You can search for *Sam Toy* in this first example. Move the cursor to A57, enter

Sam Toy

and press Enter. You need to type the name exactly as it appears in the customer section of the sales summary.

Setting the Input, Criterion, and Output Ranges

You need to let *1-2-3* know three things before it can do a search: the input range, the criteria range, and the output range.

The *input range* is the sales summary and includes the heading line. The titles from the heading line (Inv#, Date, Customer, S/P, Sale, Tax, and Total) become the field names. The easiest thing to forget when doing a search is to not include this line in the input, criteria, and output ranges.

The *criteria range* is the field name, Customer, and any customer name for which you want to search.

The *output range* is where you want the result of the search to list, or the account receivable statement. Again, the output range must include the heading line for the field names.

To do the search, enter

/Data Query Input

and respond to the prompt *Enter Input range:* with

A1007.G1050

and press Enter. Next, enter

Criterion

and respond to the prompt *Enter Criteria range:* with

A56.A57

and press Enter. Then enter

Output

and respond to the prompt *Enter Output range:* with

A61.F72

and press Enter. To begin the search, enter

Extract Quit

All invoices charged to the customer Sam Toy are listed in the output range of A61 through F72.

Using the Query Key
F7

Use the F7 function key any time you change the customer to be searched. Search for customer name *Gift Co.* (or one you entered) next. Move the cursor to A57, type

Gift Co.

and press Enter. You don't need to enter the input, criterion, and output ranges again. Press F7 and the search will restart.

Entering Totals

To enter the formula for the statement total, move the cursor to F75, type

@SUM(F62.F73)

and press Enter. You can put a previous balance in cell F73 and it will be totaled in this balance.

Entering Macros to Print Reports and Execute Search

To avoid entering the print range and database ranges each time you need to print a statement, you can save the printing and search instructions in a macro executed with an Alt-key combination. You can create two macros to execute the following jobs:

Alt-B   Search for a Customer
Alt-A   Print Accounts Receivable Statement

Type the information in Cells A76 through F78 from Figure 4-10. Be sure to type the word *Alt* and then the letter *B—not the Alt-B key combination.* When entering into a cell text that begins with a slash, such as the text in A77, precede with a single quotation mark (') prefix.

To Create a Macro
/Range Name Create

You need to name each macro range before you can execute it. To name the search and printing macros, enter

/Range Name Create

and respond to the prompt *Enter name:* with

\B

and press Enter. Respond to the prompt *Enter range:* with

A77.A78

and press Enter. Repeat for the other macro:

/Range Name Create

Respond to the prompt *Enter name:* with

\A

and press Enter. Respond to the prompt *Enter range:* with

E77

and press Enter.

To execute the print macro, hold down the Alt key and simultaneously press the letter *A*. The macro in cell F77 executes the Print Printer Range command. The range A50 through F75 is typed after the prompt to enter the print range, and the tilde symbol(˜) activates the Enter key. Next the macro issues the Align, Go, and Quit commands.

Enter the customer, *Sam Toy*, and press the Alt-B key combination. The invoices for Sam Toy will list in cells A62 through F72. You can add an address in cells A58 and A59 before printing and mailing the statement.

How to Use the Customer Statement

Type your company name and address centered (^) starting in G52.
Type your customer name and address starting in A57. Use the
Alt-B and Alt-A macros to search for invoices for this customer and
print a statement.

Figure 4-11. Salesperson Sales and Commission Report

	A	B	C	D	E	F
100			Salesperson Sales and Commission Report			
101						
102	S/P		Month:	February 1990		
103	Joe First		Commission Rate		40%	
104	======	========	=========	=======	=======	============
105	Inv#	Date	Customer	Sale	Commission Due	
106	1005	02/11/90	Sam Toy	$51.00	$20.40	
107	1003	02/11/90	Sam Toy	$13.50	$5.40	
108	1002	02/11/90	Gift Co.	$34.50	$13.80	
109	1001	02/11/90	Sam Toy	$377.00	$150.80	
110-119						
120				=======	============	
121			Totals	$476.00	$190.40	
122						
123	Alt D for Search			Alt E to Print Report		
124	/dqiA1007.G1050~cA102.A103~			/wgzy~/pprA100.E121~agq		
125	oA105.D119~eq					
126						

Saving the Worksheet with Replace
/File Save Replace

After printing the statement, save this spreadsheet one more time
to keep the macro instructions in the file. Enter

/File Save

and press Enter when the filename *Invoice* automatically displays.

The software will check to see if you want to write over your previous file, so enter

Replace

to replace the file.

Creating the Salesperson Sales and Commission Report

You can generate many additional reports from the information in the sales summary, including a salesperson report you can use to calculate commissions. To move to an unused portion of the spreadsheet, press the F5 function key; respond to the prompt *Enter address to go to:* with

B100

and press Enter. Type the heading,

Salesperson Sales and Commission Report

and press Enter. Type the headings in cells A102 through E105 from Figure 4-11.

    The headings in row 105 and cell A102 must match exactly those same headings in the sales summary section, cells A1007 through G1007. Don't change *S/P* to *Salesperson* or *Customer* to *Customer Name,* or the search won't work properly.

Entering the Repeating Underline
\ =

Cells A104 and D120 contain an accented underline created with the equal sign. To enter the repeating underline, move the cursor to A104 and enter

   \ =

Repeat for cell D120. To copy across the row, enter

/**C**opy

and respond to the prompt *Enter range to copy FROM:* with

A104

and press Enter. Respond to the prompt *Enter range to copy TO:* with

B104.F104

and press Enter. Repeat for D120 to E120.

Entering the Salesperson to Search

Cell A103 will hold the salesperson's name for which you're searching each time. You can search for *Joe First* in this first example. Move the cursor to A103, enter

Joe First

and press Enter. You need to type the name exactly as it appears in the S/P section of the sales summary.

Setting the Input, Criteria, and Output Ranges

You need to let *1-2-3* know three things before it can perform a search: the input range, the criteria range, and the output range.

The input range is the sales summary, which includes the heading line. The titles from the heading line of Inv#, Date, Customer, S/P, Sale, Tax, and Total become the field names. The easiest thing to forget when doing a search is to leave this line out of the input, criteria, and output ranges.

The criteria range is the field name, S/P, and any salesperson for whom you want to search. The output range is where you want the result of the search to list or the area of the salesperson sales report. Again, the output range must include the heading line that becomes the field names.

To initiate the search, enter

/Data Query Input

Respond to the prompt *Enter Input range:* with

A1007.G1050

and press Enter. Enter

Criteria

and respond to the prompt *Enter Criteria range:* with

A102.A103

and press Enter. Enter

Output

and respond to the prompt *Enter Output range:* with

A105.D119

and press Enter. Finally enter

Extract Quit

to begin the search. All invoices sold by the salesperson Joe First are listed in the output range of A106 through E120.

Using the Query Key F7

Use the F7 function key any time you change the salesperson for whom you want to search. Move the cursor to A103, type

Sue Smith

and press Enter. You don't need to enter the input, criteria, and output ranges again. Press F7 and the search will restart.

Entering the Commissions and Totals

Move the cursor to E103, type

.40

and press Enter. To format the cell to percent, enter

/Range Format Percent

and respond to the prompt *Enter number of decimal places:* with

0

and press Enter. To accept the current range, press Enter again. Move the cursor to E106, type

+D106*$E$103

and press Enter. To copy the formula, enter

/Copy

and respond to the prompt *Enter range to copy FROM:* with

E106

and press Enter. Respond to the prompt *Enter range to copy TO:* with

E107.E119

and press Enter. To enter the formula for the report totals, move the cursor to C121, type

Totals

and press Enter. Move the cursor to D121, type

@SUM(D106.D119)

and press Enter. To copy to E121, enter

/Copy

and respond to the prompt *Enter range to copy FROM:* with

D121

and press Enter. Respond to the prompt *Enter range to copy TO:* with

E121

and press Enter.

Formatting the Area to Currency
/Range Format Currency

You need to format column E to currency. Enter

/Range Format Currency

Respond to the prompt *Enter number of decimal places:* with

2

and press Enter. Respond to the prompt *Enter range to format:* with

E106.E121

and press Enter.

Entering Macros to Print Reports and Execute Search

To avoid entering the print range and database ranges each time you need to print a salesperson report, you can save the printing and search instructions in a macro, which you execute with the combination of the Alt key and a letter. You can create two macros to execute the following jobs:

Alt-D   Search for a Salesperson
Alt-E   Print Salesperson Report

Type the information in Cells A123 through D125 from Figure 4-11. Be sure to type the word *Alt* and the letter *D—don't press the Alt-D key combination*. When entering information into a cell that begins with a slash, such as the entry in A124, precede it with a single quotation mark (') prefix.

To Create a Macro
/Range Name Create

You need to name each macro range before you can execute it. To name the search and printing macros, enter

/Range Name Create

and respond to the prompt *Enter name:* with

\D

and press Enter. Respond to the prompt *Enter range:* with

A124.A125

and press Enter. Repeat for the other macro:

/Range Name Create

Respond to the prompt *Enter name:* with

\E

and press Enter. Respond to the prompt *Enter range:* with

D124

and press Enter.

To execute the print macro, hold down the Alt key and simultaneously press the letter E. The macro in cell D124 suppresses the zeros and then executes the Print Printer Range command. The range A100 through E121 is typed after the prompt to enter the print range, and the tilde symbol (˜) activates the Enter key. Next, the macro issues the Align, Go, and Quit commands.

Enter the salesperson, *Joe First*, again and press the Alt-D key combination. The invoices for Joe First will list in cells A106 through E120.

Saving the Worksheet with Replace
/File Save Replace

After printing the statement, save this spreadsheet one more time to keep the macro instructions in the file. Enter

/File Save

and press Enter when the filename Invoice automatically displays. The software will check to see if you want to write over your previous file, so enter

Replace

to replace the file.

How to Use the Salesperson Sales and Commission Report

Type the month in D102. Type your commission rate in E103 as .40 or 40%. Enter a salesperson's name in A103, and use the Alt-D and Alt-E macros to search for that salesperson and print the report.

The Job Estimate and Job Cost Record

The spreadsheet contains three areas: estimate, unit price, and job cost record. You can print the estimate for your client, preferably on your printed letterhead or estimate sheets.

The ratios are for unit pricing based on square footage. For example, the framing cost of $12,250 in Figure 4-12 is based on $5.00 per square foot. (Normally you wouldn't print these columns for your clients unless it's customary for your type of bidding.) If you use a fixed price, omit columns F and G from your spreadsheet. After the job is finished, you can edit cell C1 to *Invoice* and then use the estimate for billing your client.

The job cost record at the bottom is a valuable way to know how much profit is earned to date, and the final cost accounting for a job. If you use a percentage of completion method of accounting for tax purposes, keeping this record will aid in estimating your profit. If you've bid the job on a cost-plus contract, this record will be your final billing for the job after adding your profit percentage.

Figure 4-12. Job Estimate and Job Cost Record

	A	B	C	D	E	F	G
1			Estimate				
2							
3		For: Jim C. Sneed		Square Ft.	2,450	Ratios based on	
4		Address: 343 W. South St.				Square Ft.	
5							
6		Item	Labor	Materials	Total	Labor	Material
7		============	=======	=======	======		
8		Permits and Fees	$0	$1,470	$1,470	$0.00	$0.60
9		Site Prep/Concrete	$9,800	$17,150	$26,950	$4.00	$7.00
10		Lumber	$0	$22,050	$22,050		$9.00
11		Framing	$12,250	$0	$12,250	$5.00	
12		Hardware	$0	$8,575	$8,575	$0.00	$3.50
13		Plumbing	$4,900	$5,635	$10,535	$2.00	$2.30
14		Electrical	$3,430	$5,880	$9,310	$1.40	$2.40
15		Tile and Carpet	$1,838	$3,675	$5,513	$0.75	$1.50
16		Heating and Air	$1,225	$4,900	$6,125	$0.50	$2.00
17		Landscaping	$1,838	$613	$2,450	$0.75	$0.25
18		Supervision	$4,900	$0	$4,900	$2.00	$0.00
19							
20							
21							
22		Totals	$40,180	$69,948	$110,128		
23					=======		
24							
25			Job Cost Record				
26		Job 307	Percent Complete		95%		
27							
28		Date Item	Labor	Material	Total		
29		=== ============	=======	=======	=======		
30		3/1 Permit–SD County		$850	$850		
31		3/5 Fees–Vista City		$589	$589		
32		4/3 Site–Wilson Const.	$8,750	$13,240	$21,990		
33		4/7 Good Lumber		$18,909	$18,909		
34		4/9 Freddy Framer	$11,456		$11,456		
35		4/23 Good Supplies		$6,759	$6,759	Alt P	
36		5/3 Sam Electrical	$2,589	$4,582	$7,171	Print Estimate	
37		6/2 Upright Floors	$1,200	$3,100	$4,300	/wgzy	
38		6/3 Cool and Hot Air	$1,100	$3,700	$4,800	/pprB1.E23~agq	
39		6/8 Green Tree Inc.	$1,700	$400	$2,100		
50		=== ============	=======	=======	=======		
51		Totals	$26,795	$52,129	$78,924		
52							
53		Estimated Total Cost	$28,205	$54,873	$83,078		
54		Bid Price	$40,180	$69,948	$110,128		
55							
56		Estimated Profit	$11,975	$15,075	$27,050		

Creating the Job Estimate and Job Cost Record Spreadsheet

What follows is a brief review of the material from Chapter 2. If you're a 1-2-3 newcomer, you should read Chapter 2. Bring up the spreadsheet screen by typing 123 at the DOS prompt. The startup screen will have columns lettered A–H across the top of the screen and numbers for the rows going down the left side. The intersection of these columns and rows are called *cells*, where information is stored. For example, cell B4 is the intersection of the second column over *(B)* and the fourth row down (4). Cell D3 is the intersection of the fourth column over *(D)* and the third row down (3). The cursor will start in cell A1 and you can move it down or across with the arrow keys. What you type on the keyboard will appear on the line above the columns. It will move into the cell on which the cursor is resting when you press the Enter key.

Entering a Menu Command

When you press the slash key (/), different menu options such as Worksheet, Range, Copy, File, Print, Graph, Data, System, and Quit appear across the top of the screen. To select a command, press the first letter of the option, then the first letter of the next submenu item until you're finished. You can also select a menu item by moving the right- and left arrow-keys until the option is highlighted and then pressing Enter. All the instructions in this chapter will be done by entering the first letter.

Cancel or Erase
Esc

The Esc key normally cancels a command and takes you back to the previous menu or status. If you make an error and want to erase what you've typed so far, press the Esc key. If you've already pressed the Enter key and want to erase the contents of a cell, move the cursor to the cell you want to clear. Enter

/Range Erase

and press Enter to accept the range as the current cell.

Moving the Cursor

Use the arrow keys to move from cell to cell. Other helpful keys to know are:

F5 (Goto)	Moves to any cell location
Home	Moves to upper left corner (A1)
PageUp	Moves up one page
PageDown	Moves down one page

Quitting and Saving the Spreadsheet

If you need to quit before completing the spreadsheet and want to save the file, enter

/File Save

1-2-3 will then ask for a filename; type

Jobest

and press Enter. A filename can be up to eight characters, but you should stick to letters and numbers. Don't include any symbols such as + = . * / ? (> % or leave any blank spaces.

   To quit without saving, enter

/Quit Yes

and you should be back at the DOS prompt. Just enter *123* to return to the spreadsheet.

Widening the Column
/Worksheet Column Set-Width

Since column B must be wide enough to hold long descriptions, use the Set-Column Width command. To increase column B, move the cursor to B1 and enter

/Worksheet Column Set-Width

Then respond to the prompt *Enter column width:* with

18

and press Enter.

Decreasing the Column Width
/Worksheet Column Set-Width

Since column A must be shorter for dates, use the Set-Column Width command. Move to A1 and enter

/Worksheet Column Set-Width

Then respond to the prompt *Enter column width:* with

6

and press Enter.

Global Settings

Most of the spreadsheet will be in currency, so the columns need to be wider and formatted for currency. Enter

/Worksheet Global Column-width

Then respond to the prompt *Enter column width:* with

12

and press Enter. Then enter

/Worksheet Global Format Currency

and respond to the prompt *Enter number of decimal places:* with

0

and press Enter.

Entering the Headings

Move the cursor to C1, type

Estimate

and press Enter. Move the cursor to B3, type

For:

and press Enter. Move the cursor to D3, type

Square Ft.

and press Enter. Move the cursor to F3, type

Ratios based on

and press Enter. Move the cursor to B4, type

Address:

and press Enter. Move the cursor to F4, type

Square Ft.

and press Enter. Enter the headings on line 6 from Figure 4-12. Enter the headings on lines 25 through 28 for the job cost record from Figure 4-12.

Entering Formulas

Columns C and D hold a formula that multiplies the unit price by the square footage in cell E3. Column E adds the labor and materials to get the total price. Move the cursor to C8, type

+$E$3*F8

and press Enter. Move the cursor to D8, type

+$E$3*G8

and press Enter.

To total columns C and D, move the cursor to E8 and type

+C8+D8

Press Enter.

To total each column, move the cursor to B22, type

Totals

and press Enter. Move the cursor to C22, type

@SUM(C8.C18)

and press Enter.

The formulas in the job cost record add columns C and D since there are no unit prices. Move the cursor to E30, type

+C30+D30

and press Enter. Move the cursor to A51, type

Totals

and press Enter. Move the cursor to C51, type

@SUM(C30.C49)

and press Enter.

The total estimated cost on line 53 is calculated by figuring the percentage to complete the job and multiplying it by the cost incurred to-date. Move the cursor to C53, type

+C51/$E$26

and press Enter. (ERR will appear in the cell, since no data has been entered.) The bid price on line 54 is from the total line in the estimate above. Move the cursor to C54, type

+C22

and press Enter.

The estimated profit subtracts estimated cost from bid price. Move the cursor to C56, type

+C54−C53

and press Enter. Enter the headings in column A from Figure 4-12 on lines 53, 54, and 56.

Formatting the Spreadsheet
/Range Format

Some of the cells in the spreadsheet won't be in currency. To format the square footage cell, enter

/Range Format Fixed

Respond to the prompt *Enter number of decimal places:* with

0

and press Enter. Respond to the prompt *Enter range to format:* with

E3

and press Enter. To format the completion percentage, enter

/Range Format Percent

Respond to the prompt *Enter number of decimal places:* with

0

and press Enter. Respond to the prompt *Enter range to format:* with

E26

and press Enter. Next enter

/Range Format Currency

and respond to the prompt *Enter number of decimal places:* with

2

and press Enter. Respond to the prompt *Enter range to format:* with

F8.G21

and press Enter.

Saving the Spreadsheet
/File Save

To save the file, enter

/File Save

1-2-3 will then ask for a filename; type

Jobest

and press Enter. If you saved the spreadsheet earlier, press Enter when the filename *Jobest* automatically displays. The software will check to see if you want to write over your previous file, so enter

Replace

to replace the file.

Entering the Repeating Underline
\ =

Cells B7, E23, A29, and A50 contain an accented underline created with the equal sign. To enter the repeating underline, move the cursor to B7 and enter

\ =

Then repeat for cells E23, A29, and A50.

Copying Formulas
/Copy

Copy the formulas in row 8 down to eliminate the need for entering the formula again. To copy, enter

/Copy

Respond to the prompt *Enter range to copy FROM:* with

C8.E8

and press Enter. Respond to the prompt *Enter range to copy TO:* with

C9.E18

and press Enter. Continue copying formulas and underscore as follows:

B7	to	C7.E7
C22	to	D22.E22
A29	to	B29.E29
E30	to	E31.E49
A50	to	C50.E50
C51.C56	to	D51.E56
C54	to	D54.E54

Saving the Worksheet with Replace
/File Save Replace

It's best to save the spreadsheet often. Enter

/File **S**ave

and press Enter when the filename *Jobest* automatically displays. The software will check to see if you want to write over your previous file, so enter

Replace

to replace the file.

How to Use the Job Estimate and Job Cost Spreadsheet

Use the F2 Edit function key to add the name and address to cells B3 and B4. Enter the square feet in cell E3. Enter your unit prices in columns F and G. When entering amounts, don't enter the comma or dollar sign. If you see a row of asterisks instead of the amount you entered, the column isn't wide enough to hold that amount. Use the Worksheet Column-Set command, /WCS, to increase the size of the column. Type the bid items in column B, rows 8 through 18. You can expand the range to include more items by adjusting the formulas in row 22. The totals in row 22 will calculate automatically. Move the cursor to B26 and enter the job number with a single quotation mark (') prefix. This aligns the job number to the left side of the cell. Move the cursor to E26 and enter a percentage as .95 or 95%. Enter the dates in column A as '3/1, with a single or double quotation mark prefix. Enter your actual costs in rows 30 through 49. The totals and profit will calculate automatically.

Saving the Completed Worksheet
/File Save

Save the new worksheet containing this job's data in a new file separate from the previous Jobest file. Enter

/File Save

Then type

Job307

for Job #307 (or any name that's easy for you to remember) and press Enter. It's a good idea to save the file before printing.

Suppress Zero Display
/Worksheet Global Zero Yes

The estimate will look better if you eliminate the zeros before printing. To suppress them, enter

/Worksheet Global Zero Yes

and the zeros will disappear.

Printing the Worksheet
/Print Printer Range Align Go Quit

You can now print the estimate and job cost record. The print command allows printing to a file or printer. To print the estimate, roll the paper to the top of your letterhead or estimate form and enter

/Print Printer Range

Respond to the prompt *Enter print range:* with

B1.E23

and press Enter. To begin the printing job, enter

Align Go

To print the job cost record, enter

Range

to enter a new range and respond to the prompt *Enter print range:* with

A25.E56

and press Enter. To begin the printing job, enter

Align Go

To print the full spreadsheet, enter

Range

to enter a new range and respond to the prompt *Enter print range:* with

A1.G56

Press Enter. To begin the printing job, enter

Align Go Quit

This last spreadsheet is too wide to print on most 80 column printers without going to a second page. If you have a condensed print switch available on your printer, set it to condensed and from the print menu enter

Options **M**argins **R**ight

for options, margins, right. Enter

135

for the new right margin. If your printer doesn't have a switch but accepts a condensed print code, enter from the options menu

Setup

for setup string. For Epson printers, the string for condensed is ╲*015*. Look in the *Lotus 1-2-3* appendix for your specific printer code. Enter

Quit

to quit the options menu. Then to start the print job, enter

Align **G**o **Q**uit

Saving the Worksheet with Replace
/File Save Replace

After printing, save this spreadsheet one more time to keep the printing instructions in the file. Enter

/File **S**ave

and press Enter when the filename *Job307* automatically displays. The software will check to see if you want to write over your previous file, so enter

Replace

to replace the file.

Macro Learn Feature Release 2.2

You can use the macro learn feature of Release 2.2 to create an easy printing macro for the job estimate. There are three steps to using the macro learn feature:

• Enter /Worksheet Learn Range and select where you want the macro.
• Press Alt-F5 and perform the tasks you want to record.
• Press Alt-F5 to finish recording the macro.

When you've followed these steps, the macro will appear in the range specified in the Worksheet Learn Range command.
    To create the printing macros, enter

/Worksheet Learn Range

Respond to the prompt *Enter learn range:* with

G37.G48

and press Enter. Press Alt-F5 to record, then enter the following tasks:

/Worksheet Global Zero Yes /Print Printer Range *B1.E23* (press Enter)
Align Go Quit

and press Enter. Press Alt-F5 to record the macro in G37 and G38. Move the cursor to G37 and G38. The macro is now displayed in those cells. Enter

/Range Name Create

and respond to the prompt *Enter name:* with

\P

and press Enter. Respond to the prompt *Enter range:* with

G37.G48

which is the range specified in the Worksheet Learn Range command.

To execute the macro, hold down the Alt key and type the letter *P* simultaneously. You should type into G35 and G36

Alt P
Print Estimate

to label the macro.

Saving the Worksheet with Replace
/File Save Replace

Save the completed worksheet. Enter

/File Save

and press Enter when the filename *Job307* automatically displays. The software will check to see if you want to write over your previous file, so enter

Replace

to replace the file.

5
Account Balances

In this chapter, you can create spreadsheets that are helpful in maintaining schedules to support the balances of certain asset and liability accounts. Each spreadsheet will provide different reports for your business. From the inventory, accounts receivable, accounts payable, and depreciation spreadsheets you'll be able to produce:

- Inventory Listing in Stock Number Order
- Stock Out Report
- Inventory Listing in Description Order
- Price Listings
- Accounts Receivable Detailed Aging Summary
- Accounts Receivable Detail by Customer
- Accounts Receivable Aging Summary by Customer
- Accounts Payable Listing
- Accounts Payable Checks
- Fixed Asset Depreciation Record
- Listing of Fixed Assets

The inventory listing has instructions for the simplest form, and you can upgrade it later in the chapter with *1-2-3*, Release 3 to link with the invoicing spreadsheet created in Chapter 4. You can also use Release 3 to enhance the Fixed Asset Depreciation Record with the use of the new function @VDB. This function calculates depreciation using the double-declining balance method and automatically switches to straight-line when it's greater than double-declining balance depreciation, as allowed by the new tax laws.

The Inventory Listing

The basic inventory listing allows you to enter the stock number, description, quantity, cost, and vendor. You can calculate the sales price automatically based on a standard markup percentage. The total value of your inventory is calculated based on the quantity on hand multiplied by the cost. After completing the basic inventory listing, you can create a database sort from this information. This query will search for an inventory item with zero quantity for a stock-out report. Almost any type of search can be done: you can search based on items from a certain vender, items with a value more than a certain amount, or even items that start with a certain letter of the alphabet. You can generate many different reports, such as

- A price list without the cost for your customers
- A total listing for your banker
- A listing in description order for taking inventory
- A stock-out report for your purchasing agent.

Figure 5-1. Inventory Listing

	A	B	C	D	E	F	G	H	I
1		Easy Company			Markup				
2		Inventory Listing				40%			
3				Date	07/20/89				
4									
5	Stock#	Description	Quanity	SalePrice		Cost	Value	Vendor	
6	100	Jacks–Blue	2	$5.60		$4.00	$8.00	Justin	
7	110	Jacks–Red	5	$0.70		$0.50	$2.50	Justin	
8	120	Book–Zoo Animal	8	$4.20		$3.00	$24.00	Justin	
9	130	Ball–Red	4	$4.90		$3.50	$14.00	Justin	
10	140	Ball–Blue	21	$0.84		$0.60	$12.60	Moore	
11	150	Rope–Jump	0	$1.05		$0.75	$0.00	Moore	
12	160	Pencils	80	$0.14		$0.10	$8.00	Justin	
13	170	Folders–School	25	$4.90		$3.50	$87.50	Moore	
14	180	Crayons	0	$2.10		$1.50	$0.00	Moore	
15	190	Book–Travels	3	$2.10		$1.50	$4.50	Justin	
16				$0.00			$0.00		
17				$0.00			$0.00		
18				$0.00			$0.00		
19				$0.00			$0.00		
20				$0.00			$0.00		
21				$0.00			$0.00		
22				$0.00			$0.00		
23				$0.00			$0.00		
24				$0.00			$0.00		
25				$0.00			$0.00		
26				$0.00			$0.00		
27	===== ============ ======			======	==========	=======	========	========	
28				Total Value			$161.10		
29	Print Macros								
30	Alt S	Print in Stock# Order			{goto}A6~/dsrd.{end}{down}{end}{right}~PA6~a~g/pprfullinv~agq				
31									
32	Alt D	Print in Description Order			{goto}A6~/dsrd.{end}{down}{end}{right}~PB6~a~g/pprfullinv~agq				
33									
34	Alt V	Print Stock Out Report			/rel3.O3~{goto}K3~+C6<1~{query}/pproutput~agq				
35									
36	Alt P	Print Price List (without cost)			/pprA1.D28~agq				
37									

Creating the Inventory Listing

What follows is a brief review of the material from Chapter 2. If you're a *1-2-3* newcomer, you should read Chapter 2. Bring up the spreadsheet screen by typing *123* at the DOS prompt. The startup screen will have columns lettered A–H across the top of the screen and numbers for the rows going down the left side. The intersection of these columns and rows are called *cells*, where information is stored. For example, cell B4 is the intersection of the second column over (B) and the fourth row down (4). Cell D3 is the intersection of the fourth column over (D) and the third row down (3). The cursor will start in cell A1 and you can move it down or across with the arrow keys. What you type on the keyboard will appear on the line above the columns. It will move into the cell on which the cursor is resting when you press the Enter key.

Entering a Menu Command

When you press the slash key (/), different menu options such as Worksheet, Range, Copy, File, Print, Graph, Data, System, and Quit appear across the top of the screen. To select a command, press the first letter of the option, then the first letter of the next submenu item until you've finished. You can also select a menu item by moving the right- and left-arrow keys until the option is highlighted, and then pressing Enter. All the instructions in this chapter are done by entering the first letter.

Cancel or Erase
Esc

The Esc key normally cancels a command and takes you back to the previous menu or status. If you make an error and want to erase what you've typed so far, press the Esc key. If you've already pressed the Enter key and want to erase the contents of a cell, move the cursor to the cell you want to clear. Enter

/Range Erase

and press Enter to accept the range as the current cell.

Moving the Cursor

Use the arrow keys to move from cell to cell. Other helpful keys to know are:

F5 (Goto)   Moves to any cell location
Home   Moves to upper left corner (A1)
PageUp   Moves up one page
PageDown   Moves down one page

Quitting and Saving the Spreadsheet

If you need to quit before completing the spreadsheet and want to save the file, enter

/File Save

1-2-3 will then ask for a filename; type

Invent

and press Enter. A filename can be up to eight characters, but you should stick to letters and numbers. Don't include any symbols such as + = . * / ? (> % or leave any blank spaces. To quit without saving, enter

/Quit Yes

and you should be back at the DOS prompt. Just enter *123* to return to the spreadsheet.

Widening the Column
/Worksheet Column Set-Width

Since column B must be wide enough to hold long descriptions, use the Set-Column Width command. To increase column B, move the cursor to B1 and enter /Worksheet Column Set-Width. Then respond to the prompt *Enter column width:* with

15

and press Enter.

Entering the Headings

Move the cursor to B1 and type

Easy Company

or your company name and press Enter. Move the cursor to B2, type

Inventory listing

and press Enter. Move the cursor to C3, type

"Date

and press Enter. The double quotation mark aligns the heading with the right side of the cell. Type the following into the cells below and press Enter:

E1   Markup
E2   .40
D3   '7/20/89
A5   Stock#
B5   Description
C5   Quantity
D5   SalePrice
E5   Cost
F5   Value
G5   Vendor
D28   Total Value

Entering Formulas

Cell D6 holds a formula that multiplies the cost by the markup percentage in cell E2 and adds it to the cost. Cell F6 multiplies the quantity by the cost to get the total value. Move the cursor to D6, type

($E$2*E6)+E6

and press Enter. Move the cursor to F6, type

+E6*C6

and press Enter. To total the value column, move the cursor to F28 and type

@SUM(F6.F26)

Formatting the Spreadsheet
/Range Format Currency

You need to format columns D through F to currency. Since you only want these columns to be in currency, use the Range command instead of the Worksheet Global Format command. Enter

/Range Format Currency

Respond to the prompt *Enter number of decimal places:* with

2

and press Enter. Respond to the prompt *Enter range to format:* with

D6.F28

and press Enter. To format the markup percentage, enter

/Range Format Percent

and respond to the prompt *Enter number of decimal places:* with

0

and press Enter. Respond to the prompt *Enter range to format:* with

E2

and press Enter.

Saving the Worksheet with Replace
/File Save Replace

It's best to save the spreadsheet often. Enter

/File Save

and press Enter when the filename *Invent* automatically displays. The software will check to see if you want to write over your previous file, so enter

Replace

to replace the file.

Entering the Repeating Underline
\ =

Cell A27 contains an underline created with the equal sign. To enter the repeating underline, move the cursor to A27 and enter

\ =

Copying Formulas
/Copy

Copy the formulas in row 6 to eliminate the need for entering the formula again. To copy, enter

/Copy

and respond to the prompt **Enter range to copy FROM:** with

D6.F6

and press Enter. Respond to the prompt **Enter range to copy TO:** with

D7.F26

and press Enter. Then enter

/Copy

and respond to the prompt *Enter range to copy FROM:* with

A27

and press Enter. Respond to the prompt *Enter range to copy TO:* with

B27.G27

and press Enter.

Entering the Data

Enter the inventory items in columns A, B, C, E, and G from Figure 5-1 or your inventory. Don't enter anything in columns D and F—the sales price and value calculate automatically. When entering amounts, don't enter the comma or dollar sign. If you see a row of asterisks instead of the amount you entered, the column isn't wide enough to hold that amount. Use the Worksheet Column-Set command, /WCS, to increase the size of the column.

Saving the Worksheet with Replace
/File Save Replace

It's best to save the spreadsheet often. Enter

/File Save

and press Enter when the filename *Invent* automatically displays. The software will check to see if you want to write over your previous file, so enter

Replace

to replace the file.

Printing the Worksheet
/Print Printer Range Align Go Quit

You can print the inventory listing now. The print command allows printing to a file or printer. Roll the paper to the perforation or top of form and enter

/Print Printer Range

and respond to the prompt *Enter print range:* with

A1.G28

and press Enter. To begin the printing job, enter

Align Go Quit

Saving the Worksheet with Replace
/File Save Replace

After printing the inventory listing, save this spreadsheet one more time to keep the printing instructions in the file. Enter

/File Save

and press Enter when the filename *Invent* automatically displays. The software will check to see if you want to write over your previous file, so enter

Replace

to replace the file.

Figure 5-2. Inventory Search

	I	J	K	L	M	N	O
1	Search Criterion						
2	Stock#	Description	Quantity	SalePrice	Cost	Value	Vendor
3			0				
4							
5	Stock#	Description	Quanity	SalePrice	Cost	Value	Vendor
6	180	Crayons	0	$2.10	$1.50	$0.00	Moore
7	150	Rope–Jump	0	$1.05	$0.75	$0.00	Moore
8				$0.00		$0.00	
9				$0.00		$0.00	
10				$0.00		$0.00	
11				$0.00		$0.00	
12				$0.00		$0.00	
13				$0.00		$0.00	
14				$0.00		$0.00	
15				$0.00		$0.00	
16				$0.00		$0.00	
17				$0.00		$0.00	
18				$0.00		$0.00	
19							

Inventory Search

1-2-3 has the ability to search through all the inventory for items
that meet a certain criterion. You can use the database feature of *1-
2-3*, if you need a listing of items from a certain vendor, or all
items with a zero quantity. You can create this database to the right
of the listing. To move quickly to the database area, press the F5
function key and respond to the prompt *Enter address to go to:* with

I1

(letter *I* and number 1) and press Enter. In this cell, type

Search Criterion

and press Enter.

Copying the Headings
/Copy

Copy the headings in cells A5 through G5 to eliminate the need for entering the headings again. To copy, enter

/Copy

Respond to the prompt *Enter range to copy FROM:* with

A5.G5

and press Enter. Respond to the prompt *Enter range to copy TO:"* with

I2

(letter *I* and number 2) and press Enter. Copy the headings in cells A5 through G5 to column I, row 5. To copy, enter

/Copy

and respond to the prompt *Enter range to copy FROM:* with

A5.G5

Press Enter. Respond to the prompt *Enter range to copy TO:* with

I5

and press Enter.

Widening the Column
/Worksheet Column Set-Width

To increase column J, move the cursor to J1 and enter

/Worksheet Column Set-Width

Then respond to the prompt *Enter column width:* with

15

and press Enter.

To Create a Range Name
/Range Name Create

You need to name the range in the inventory listing and search area to simplify searches and printing. To name a range, enter

/Range Name Create

and respond to the prompt *Enter name:* with

Invlist

Press Enter. Respond to the prompt *Enter range:* with

A5.G26

and press Enter. Continue naming the following ranges with the Range Name Create command:

Name	Range
Output	I5.O25
Fullinv	A1.G28

Entering the Criterion to Search

Cell K3 will hold the formula that is the criterion for your first search. Move the cursor to K3, enter

+C6<1

and press Enter. This formula will list any items with a quantity less than one.

Setting the Input, Criteria, and Output Ranges

You need to let *1-2-3* know three things before it can perform a search:

• The input range
• The criteria range
• The output range

The input range is where you entered the inventory and includes the heading line. The titles from the heading line—Stock#,

Description, Quantity, and Vendor—become the field names. The easiest thing to forget when performing a search is to fail to include this line in the input, criteria, and output ranges.

The criteria range consists of the field names, and any certain field for which you want to search.

The output range is where you want the result of the search to be listed. Again, the output range must include the heading line that will contain the field names.

To do the search, enter

/**D**ata **Q**uery **I**nput

and respond to the prompt *Enter Input range:* with

Invlist

and press Enter. Enter

Criteria

and respond to the prompt *Enter Criteria range:* with

I2.O3

and press Enter. Enter

Output

and respond to the prompt *Enter Output range:* with

Output

and press Enter. Enter

Extract Quit

to begin the search. All items with a quantity of zero are listed in the output range of I6 though O25.

Using the Query Key
F7

Use the F7 function key any time you change the field and criterion searched. Search for vendor Moore next. Move the cursor to K3 and erase the formula. Enter

/Range Erase

and press Enter to accept the current range. Move the cursor to O3, type

Moore

and press Enter. You don't need to enter the input, criteria, and output ranges again. Press F7 and the search will start again. Everything you've purchased from the vendor named Moore will be listed.

Printing the Inventory Search
/Print Printer Range Align Go Quit

You can print the inventory search now. The print command allows printing to a file or printer. Roll the paper to the perforation or top of form and enter

/Print Printer Range

Respond to the prompt *Enter print range:* with

Output

and press Enter. To begin the printing job, enter

Align **Go Q**uit

Saving the Worksheet with Replace
/File Save Replace

After printing the search, save this spreadsheet one more time to keep the printing and data search instructions in the file. Enter

/File Save

and press Enter when the filename *Invent* automatically displays. The software will check to see if you want to write over your previous file, so enter

Replace

to replace the file.

Entering Macros to Print Reports

Each time you save the spreadsheet only the latest printing instructions are saved. To print the inventory listing you have to enter the range again, since the range for the search is now saved. You can save the printing instructions in macros that you execute with the combination of the Alt key and a letter. A *macro* is simply a range of cells on the spreadsheet that holds the keystrokes necessary to execute commands. You can create four macros to print the following reports:

Alt-S   Inventory Listing in Stock Number Order
Alt-D   Inventory Listing in Description Order
Alt-V   Stock Out Report
Alt-P   Price List (without cost)

To move to an unused portion of the spreadsheet, press the F5 function key. Respond to the prompt *Enter address to go to:* with

A29

and press Enter. Type the heading

Print Macros

and press Enter. Move the cursor to A30, type

Alt S

and press Enter. Be sure to type the word *Alt* and the letter *S—don't press the Alt-S key combination.* Move to B30 and type

Print in Stock# Order

and press Enter. Type the remaining print macros shown in Figure

189

5-1 in columns A, B, and E through row 36. When entering information into a cell that begins with the slash, such as the data in E34, precede it with single quotation mark (') prefix.

To Create a Macro
/Range Name Create

You need to name each macro range before you can execute it. To name the inventory listing printing, enter

/Range Name Create

Respond to the prompt *Enter name:* with

\S

and press Enter. Respond to the prompt *Enter range:* with

E30

and press Enter. Repeat for the other four macros:

Name	Range
\D	E32
\V	E34
\P	E36

To execute the inventory listing macro, press the Alt-S key combination. The macro in cell E30 enters a data sort command to put the listing in stock-number order and then executes the Print Printer Range command. The range *fullinv* will be typed after the prompt to enter the print range, and the tilde symbol (˜) executes the Enter key. Next the macro issues Align, Go, and Quit commands.

How to Use the Inventory Spreadsheet

Type your company name in cell B1. Type your markup percentage in E2 as .40 or 40%. Enter current date in D3 as '7/03/90 for July 3, 1990. Use the Range Erase command to clear the practice inventory items in columns A, B, C. Don't erase the formulas in columns D and F. Use the Range Erase command to clear the items in columns E and G. On row 6 enter your stock number, description, quantity, cost, and vendor for each item. The sales price and value will calculate automatically. Use the macros Alt-S, Alt-D, Alt-V, and Alt-P to print the various reports.

Saving the Worksheet with Replace
/File Save Replace

After creating the macros, save this spreadsheet one more time to keep the macros' instructions in the file. Enter

/File Save

and press Enter when the filename *Invent* automatically displays. The software will check to see if you want to write over your previous file, so enter

Replace

to replace the file.

Linking the Inventory Listing with Invoicing Using Release 3

Release 3 of *1-2-3* enables you to *link* files together and use information from one file in another. You can use the inventory listing as a lookup table in the invoicing spreadsheet. Once you've made changes and saved the new files in Release 3 of *1-2-3*, the file will have an extension of .WK3 and won't load on previous releases of *1-2-3*. If you're developing a spreadsheet to work on both releases, be sure to keep backup copies of the unchanged versions of the Invoice and Invent files.

Retrieving a Spreadsheet File
/File Retrieve

To retrieve the previous inventory spreadsheet you've just created, enter

/File Retrieve

then type

Invent

and press Enter. You need to sort the inventory list in stock-number order for the lookup table to work. Use the Alt-S macro to sort and print the inventory. If you created this file in a previous release of 1-2-3, you need to save it with Release 3 to create a file with the extension WK3. Do the same for the file Invoice before continuing.

Opening a Second File
/File Open Before

To open the invoice file in front of the inventory file, enter

/File Open Before

Respond to the prompt *Enter name of file to open:* with

Invoice

and press Enter.

Viewing the Spreadsheet in 3-D
/Worksheet Window Perspective

To view both files at the same time, enter

/Worksheet Window Perspective

and press the Home key to go to the top of each spreadsheet. Use Ctrl-PageDown and Ctrl-PageUp to move between the two files.

Linking the Files with a Formula

To link files, you need only enter a formula that refers to another file. Move to the Invoice spreadsheet with the Ctrl-PageDown key combination. You can tell which file you're in by the indicator in the bottom left-hand corner. Move the cursor to C13, the first line in the Invoice file under Description, and type the following formula:

@IF($A13>0,@VLOOKUP($B13,<<INVENT.WK3>>$INVLIST,1)," ")

Press Enter. The formula means if the quantity in A13 is greater than zero, then look up the stock number in Invlist range of the Invent file and insert the description in column 1. If the quantity isn't greater than zero, then a blank (" ") is displayed.

Move the cursor to D13, type

@IF($A13>0,@VLOOKUP($B13,<<INVENT.WK3>>$INVLIST,3)," ")

and press Enter. This formula is the same except it looks to the third column for the sales price. Be sure you've saved the Invent file with the extension of .WK3 for the formula to work. This formula won't work with Release 2.2, because that release only uses one cell in a range during file linking. The range Invlist contains multiple cells.

Copying Formulas
/Copy
Copy the formulas in row 13 down to eliminate the need for entering the formula again. To copy, enter

/Copy

and respond to the prompt *Enter range to copy FROM:* with

C13.D13

Press Enter. Respond to the prompt *Enter range to copy TO:* with

C14.D20

and press Enter. These files will remain linked as long as the formula exists in the Invoice file that refers to the Invent file.

The Accounts Receivable Detailed Aging Summary
The basic accounts receivable summary brings the invoice data from the Invoice file created in Chapter 4 or enables you to enter your invoices directly from your sales information. Formulas in spreadsheets calculate the aging of each invoice and "spread" them by 30, 60, 90, and 120 days. A percentage of each aging is calculated at the bottom. If you need an aging for your banker or investors, then this detail report should be adequate. But if you need individual customer totals for collections and management decisions, continue with the instructions to create the two customer reports.

Figure 5-3. Accounts Receivable Detailed Aging Summary

	A	B	C	D	E	F	G	H	I
1				Accounts Receivable Detailed Aging Summary					
2				As of:		4/22/90			
3									
4									
5	Inv#	Date	Customer	Total	Current	30 days	60 days	90 days	120 days
6									
7	1015	04/15/90	Gift Co.	$44.73	$44.73	$0.00	$0.00	$0.00	$0.00
8	1014	04/15/90	Sam Toy	$71.57	$71.57	$0.00	$0.00	$0.00	$0.00
9	1013	03/21/90	Sam Toy	$178.92	$0.00	$178.92	$0.00	$0.00	$0.00
10	1012	03/21/90	Try Inc.	$71.57	$0.00	$71.57	$0.00	$0.00	$0.00
11	1011	03/21/90	Gift Co.	$35.78	$0.00	$35.78	$0.00	$0.00	$0.00
12	1010	03/21/90	Sam Toy	$13.42	$0.00	$13.42	$0.00	$0.00	$0.00
13	1005	02/11/90	Sam Toy	$54.32	$0.00	$0.00	$54.32	$0.00	$0.00
14	1004	02/11/90	Try Inc.	$408.96	$0.00	$0.00	$408.96	$0.00	$0.00
15	1003	02/11/90	Sam Toy	$14.38	$0.00	$0.00	$14.38	$0.00	$0.00
16	1002	02/11/90	Gift Co.	$36.74	$0.00	$0.00	$36.74	$0.00	$0.00
17	1001	02/11/90	Sam Toy	$401.51	$0.00	$0.00	$401.51	$0.00	$0.00
18									
19			=======	=======	=======	=======	=======	=====	=======
20			Totals	$1,331.89	$116.30	$299.69	$915.90	$0.00	$0.00
21									
22			Percent	100%	9%	23%	69%	0%	0%
23	32985								

Creating the Accounts Receivable Data Transfer File

What follows is a brief review of the material from Chapter 2. If you're a *1-2-3* newcomer, you should read Chapter 2. Bring up the spreadsheet screen by typing *123* at the DOS prompt. The startup screen will have columns lettered A–H across the top of the screen and numbers for the rows going down the left side. The intersection of these columns and rows are called *cells*, where information is stored. For example, cell B4 is the intersection of the second column over (B) and the fourth row down (4). Cell D3 is the intersection of the fourth column over (D) and the third row down (3). The cursor will start in cell A1 and you can move it down or across with the arrow keys. What you type on the keyboard will appear on the line above the columns and then move into the cell on which the cursor is resting when you press the Enter key.

Entering a Menu Command

When you press the slash key (/), different menu options such as Worksheet, Range, Copy, File, Print, Graph, Data, System, and Quit appear across the top of the screen. To select a command, press the first letter of the option, then the first letter of the next submenu item until you're finished. You can also select a menu item by moving the right- and left-arrow keys until the option is highlighted and then pressing Enter. All the instructions in this chapter will be done by entering the first letter.

Cancel or Erase
Esc

The Esc key normally cancels a command and takes you back to the previous menu or status. If you make an error and want to erase what you've typed so far, press the Esc key. If you've already pressed the Enter key and want to erase the contents of a cell, move the cursor to the cell you want to clear. Enter

/Range Erase

and press Enter to accept the range as the current cell.

Moving the Cursor

Use the arrow keys to move from cell to cell. Other helpful keys to know are:

F5 (Goto)   Moves to any cell location
Home   Moves to upper left corner (A1)
PageUp   Moves up one page
PageDown Moves down one page

Retrieving a Spreadsheet File
/File Retrieve

To retrieve the Invoice spreadsheet you created in Chapter 4, enter

/File Retrieve

then type in

Invoice

and press Enter.

Press the Home key and enter some practice invoices for March and April as shown in Figure 5-4. The accounts receivable spreadsheet ages the invoices and you'll need some sample data with different months. Use the Alt-S macro each time to save the invoice to the summary area.

Figure 5-4. Xtract Invoice Data from Invoice File

```
D1018: (C2) 401.51
Enter xtract range: A1008..D1018
```

	A	B	C	D
1004			Easy Company	
1005			Sales Summary	
1006		========	========	===============	=========
1007		Inv#	Date	Customer	Total
1008		1015	04/15/90	Gift Co.	$44.73
1009		1014	04/15/90	Sam Toy	$71.57
1010		1013	03/21/90	Sam Toy	$178.92
1011		1012	03/21/90	Try Inc.	$71.57
1012		1011	03/21/90	Gift Co.	$35.78
1013		1010	03/21/90	Sam Toy	$13.42
1014		1005	02/11/90	Sam Toy	$54.32
1015		1004	02/11/90	Try Inc.	$408.96
1016		1003	02/11/90	Sam Toy	$14.38
1017		1002	02/11/90	Gift Co.	$36.74
1018		1001	02/11/90	Sam Toy	$401.51
1019					
1020			Range to xtract	
			To File ARDATA	

To move to the invoice sales summary portion of the spreadsheet, press the F5 function key, respond to the prompt *Enter address to go to:* with

A1008

and press Enter. If this isn't a practice file, save your file before continuing.

If you compare this spreadsheet with Figure 5-4, you'll notice that some of the columns won't be used in the new accounts receivable spreadsheet. To delete these columns, enter

/Worksheet **D**elete **C**olumn

Respond to the prompt *Enter column delete range:* with

D1007.F1007

and press Enter. You need only specify row 1007 since the command deletes the whole column. Don't save at this point or you'll change the good Invoice file. If you make a mistake and delete the wrong columns, just retrieve the file Invoice and try again.

Extracting a Portion of a File
/File Xtract Value

Only the range shown in Figure 5-4 containing the Inv#, Date, Customer, and Total will be saved to a new file. To save only this portion, enter

/File Xtract Value

and respond to the prompt *Enter name of file to extract to:* with

ARdata

Press Enter. Respond to the prompt *Enter xtract range:* with

A1008.D1018

and press Enter.

Clearing the Spreadsheet

Don't save the changed Invoice file. To clear the screen to start working on the accounts receivable file, enter

/Worksheet Erase Yes

and a fresh screen will appear.

Bringing In the Accounts Receivable Data
/File Combine Copy

Move the cursor to A7 and enter

/File Combine Copy Entire-File

Respond to the prompt *Enter name of file to combine:* with

ARdata

and press Enter. The screen should look like cells A7 though D17 in Figure 5-3. Enter the headings in cell D1 and E2 from Figure 5-3 and the heading line on row 5. Enter the headings in cell C20 and C22.

Widening the Column
/Worksheet Column Set-Width

To increase column D, move the cursor to D1 and enter

/Worksheet Column Set-Width

Then respond to the prompt *Enter column width:* with

11

and press Enter.

Entering Dates

1-2-3 has the capacity to make calculations with dates entered in the proper format. Move the cursor to F2, type

'4/22/90

and press Enter. Move the cursor to A23 and type

@DATEVALUE(F2)

The date at the top of the page enables you to change the date easily each time you create a new aging summary. The formula in A23 converts the date to a serial date for calculations later. The result of 32985 is the number of days from 1/1/1900 to 4/22/90.

Entering Formulas

Columns E through I hold formulas that subtract the date of the invoice from the serial date in cell A23, and they use an @IF function to compare with the 30–60–90–120 day range. The formula in row 20 totals each column, and the formula in row 22 divides each column by column D to figure a percentage of the total. To enter the formulas, type the following into the cells shown and press Enter.

```
E7     @IF($A$23-B7<30,D7,0)
F7     @IF($A$23-B7>=30#AND#$A$23-B7<60,D7,0)
G7     @IF($A$23-B7>=60#AND#$A$23-B7<90,D7,0)
H7     @IF($A$23-B7>=90#AND#$A$23-B7<120,D7,0)
I7     @IF($A$23-B7>=120,D7,0)
D20    @SUM(D7.D18)
D22    +D20/$D$20
```

Entering the Repeating Underline
\ =

Cell D19 contains a double underline created with the equal sign.
To enter the repeating underline, move the cursor to D19 and enter

\ =

Saving the Spreadsheet
/File Save

After entering headings and formulas, it's best to save the file
before executing copying and formatting commands. To save the
file, enter

/File Save

1-2-3 will then ask for a filename; type

AR

and press Enter. If you saved the spreadsheet earlier, press Enter
when the filename *AR* automatically displays. The software will
check to see if you want to write over your previous file, so enter

Replace

to replace the file.

Copying Formulas
/Copy

Copy the formulas in row 7 down to eliminate the need for entering the formula again. To copy, enter

/Copy

and respond to the prompt *Enter range to copy FROM:* with

E7.I7

Press Enter. Respond to the prompt *Enter range to copy TO:* with

E8. .I17

and press Enter. Continue copying the formulas and underscores as follows:

D20	to	E20.I20
D19	to	E19.I19
D22	to	E22.I22

Formatting the Spreadsheet
/Range Format Currency

You need to format Columns D through I to currency. Since you only want these columns to be in currency, use the Range command instead of the Worksheet Global Format command. Enter

/Range Format Currency

and respond to the prompt *Enter number of decimal places:* with

2

Press Enter. Respond to the prompt *Enter range to format:* with

D7.I20

and press Enter. To format the percentage row, enter

/Range Format Percent

and respond to the prompt *Enter number of decimal places:* with

0

Press Enter. Respond to the prompt *Enter range to format:* with

D22.I22

and press Enter.

Printing the Worksheet
/Print Printer Range Align Go Quit

You can print the accounts receivable summary now. The print command allows printing to a file or printer. Roll the paper to the perforation or top of form, enter

/Print Printer Range

and respond to the prompt *Enter print range:* with

A1.I22

Press Enter. To begin the printing job, enter

Align Go Quit

Saving the Worksheet with Replace
/File Save Replace

After printing the summary, save this spreadsheet one more time to keep the print instructions in the file. Enter

/File Save

and press Enter when the filename *AR* automatically displays. The software will check to see if you want to write over your previous file, so enter

Replace

to replace the file.

Figure 5-5. Accounts Receivable Detail by Customer and Macros

	K	L	M	N	O	P	Q	R	S
1	Inv#	Date	Customer	Total	Current	30 days	60 days	90 days	120 days
2			Sam Toy						
3				Accounts Receivable Detail by Customer					
4									
5	Inv#	Date	Customer	Total	Current	30 days	60 days	90 days	120 days
6	1014	04/15/90	Sam Toy	$71.57	$71.57	$0.00	$0.00	$0.00	$0.00
7	1013	03/21/90	Sam Toy	$178.92	$0.00	$178.92	$0.00	$0.00	$0.00
8	1010	03/21/90	Sam Toy	$13.42	$0.00	$13.42	$0.00	$0.00	$0.00
9	1005	02/11/90	Sam Toy	$54.32	$0.00	$0.00	$54.32	$0.00	$0.00
10	1003	02/11/90	Sam Toy	$14.38	$0.00	$0.00	$14.38	$0.00	$0.00
11	1001	02/11/90	Sam Toy	$401.51	$0.00	$0.00	$401.51	$0.00	$0.00
12									
13									
14									
15									
16									
17									
18									
19									
20									
21				=======	=====	=======	========	========	========
22			Sam Toy	$734.10	$71.57	$192.34	$470.20	$0.00	$0.00
23									
24									
25	Alt T	Transfer to Customer Summary					{goto}end~/wir~/rvM22.S22~~		
26									
27	Alt A	Print Accounts Rec. Detailed Aging Summary					/pprA1.I22~agq		
28									
29	Alt C	Print Accounts Rec. Detail by Customer					/pprK1.S22~agq		
30									
31	Alt S	Print Accounts Rec. Aging Summary by Customer				/pprSUMMARY~agq			

Creating the Accounts Receivable Customer Search

To move to an unused portion of the spreadsheet, press the F5 function key. Respond to the prompt *Enter address to go to:* with

K1

and press Enter. To copy the headings from the main summary to the criterion and output area, enter

/Copy

and respond to the prompt *Enter range to copy FROM:* with

A5.I5

Press Enter. Respond to the prompt *Enter range to copy TO:* with

K1

and press Enter. To repeat for row 5, enter

/Copy

and respond to the prompt *Enter range to copy FROM:* with

A5.I5

Press Enter. Respond to the prompt *Enter range to copy TO:* with

K5

and press Enter. Move the cursor to N3, type

Accounts Receivable Detail by Customer

and press Enter.

Decreasing the Column Width
/Worksheet Column Set-Width

To decrease column K, move the cursor to K1 and enter

/Worksheet Column Set-Width

Then respond to the prompt *Enter column width:* with

7

and press Enter.

Entering the Repeating Underline
\ =

Cell N21 contains an accented underline created with the equal sign. To enter the repeating underline, move the cursor to N21 and enter

\ =

Entering Formulas

Move the cursor to M22 and type

+M2

Move the cursor to N22, type

@SUM(N6.N20)

and press Enter. Copy the formula and underscore in rows 21 and 22 across to eliminate the need for entering the formula again. To copy, enter

/Copy

and respond to the prompt *Enter range to copy FROM:* with

N21.N22

Press Enter. Respond to the prompt *Enter range to copy TO:* with

O21.S22

and press Enter.

Formatting the Area to Currency
/Range Format Currency

Enter

/Range Format Currency

and respond to the prompt *Enter number of decimal places:* with

2

Press Enter. Respond to the prompt *Enter range to format:* with

N22.S22

and press Enter.

Entering the Customer Name to Be Searched

Cell M2 will hold the customer name you search for each time. You can search for Sam Toy in this first example. Move the cursor to M2, enter

Sam Toy

and press Enter. You need to type the name exactly as it appears in the customer section of the accounts receivable summary.

Setting the Input, Criteria, and Output Ranges

You need to let *1-2-3* know three things before it can perform a search:

- The input range
- The criteria range
- The output range

The input range is the accounts receivable summary and includes the heading line. The titles from this heading line (Inv#, Date, Customer, Total, and 30–60–90–120 days) become the field names. When running a search, it's easy to forget to include this line in the input, criteria, and output ranges.

The criteria range is the field name, Customer, and any customer name for which you want to search.

The output range is where you want the results of the search to list or the accounts receivable detail by customer area. Again, the output range must include the heading line that becomes the field names.

To do the search, enter

/Data Query Input

Respond to the prompt *Enter Input range:* with

A5.I17

and press Enter. Enter

Criteria

and respond to the prompt *Enter Criteria range:* with

K1.S2

and press Enter. Enter

Output

and respond to the prompt *Enter Output range:* with

K5.S20

Press Enter. To begin the search, enter

Extract Quit

All invoices charged to the customer Sam Toy are listed in the range of K6.S20.

Using the Query Key
F7

Use the F7 function key any time you change the customer for whom you want to search. You'll search for customer name *Gift Co.* next. Move the cursor to M2, type

Gift Co.

and press Enter. You don't need to enter the input, criterion, and output ranges again. Press F7 and the search will restart.

Saving the Worksheet with Replace
/File Save Replace

It's best to save the spreadsheet often. Enter

/File **S**ave

and press Enter when the filename *AR* automatically displays. The software will check to see if you want to write over your previous file, so enter

Replace

to replace the file.

Figure 5-6. Accounts Receivable Aging Summary by Customer

	M	N	O	P	Q	R	S
32			Accounts Receivable Aging Summary by Customer				
33	Date	4/22/90					
34							
35	Customer	Total	Current	30 days	60 days	90 days	120 days
36							
37	Gift Co.	$80.51	$44.73	$35.78	$0.00	$0.00	$0.00
38	Sam Toy	$332.60	$71.57	$192.34	$68.69	$0.00	$0.00
39	Try Inc.	$71.57	$0.00	$71.57	$0.00	$0.00	$0.00
40							
41		======	=======	=======	======	=======	=======
42		$484.68	$116.30	$299.69	$68.69	$0.00	$0.00
43							

Creating an Aging Summary by Customer

You can copy each total line for a customer to an unused area of the spreadsheet to create an aging summary by customer. To prepare the area where the total line will copy, move to the area below the search output. To copy the heading line, enter

/**C**opy

and respond to the prompt *Enter range to copy FROM:* with

C5.I5

Press Enter. Respond to the prompt *Enter range to copy TO:* with

M35

and press Enter. Move the cursor to O32, type

Accounts Receivable Aging Summary by Customer

and press Enter. Move to M33, type

Date

and press Enter. Move to N33, type

+F2

and press Enter.

Entering the Repeating Underline
\ =

Cell N41 contains an accented underline created with the equal sign. To enter the repeating underline, move the cursor to N41 and enter

\ =

Entering Formulas
Move the cursor to N42, type

@SUM(N36.N40)

and press Enter. Copy the formula and underscore in rows 41 and 42 across to eliminate the need for entering the formula again. To copy, enter

/Copy

and respond to the prompt *Enter range to copy FROM:* with

N41.N42

Press Enter. Respond to the prompt *Enter range to copy TO:* with

O41.S42

and press Enter.

Formatting the Area to Currency
/Range Format Currency

Enter

/Range Format Currency

and respond to the prompt *Enter number of decimal places:* with

2

Press Enter. Respond to the prompt *Enter range to format:* with

N42.S42

and press Enter.

Widening the Column
/Worksheet Column Set-Width

To increase column N, move the cursor to N32 and enter

/Worksheet Column Set-Width

Then respond to the prompt *Enter column width:* with

11

and press Enter.

To Create a Range Name
/Range Name Create

You need to name the line in the report area that will be the last
line of the range, to simplify transferring the data. To name a
range, enter

/Range Name Create

and respond to the prompt *Enter name:* with

End

Press Enter. Respond to the prompt *Enter range:* with

M37.S37

and press Enter. To name the range in the *Summary by Customer* area (to simplify printing macros), enter

/Range Name Create

and respond to the prompt *Enter name:* with

Summary

Press Enter. Respond to the prompt *Enter range:* with

M32.S42

and press Enter.

Entering Macros to Transfer Total Line and Print Reports

To avoid entering the commands to transfer the summary line every time a customer is searched, you can save the instructions in a macro, which you execute with the combination of the Alt key and a letter. Additionally, each time you want to print a different report, you'd have to enter the new range. You can create four macros to execute the transfer and printing jobs:

Alt-T   Transfer Total Line to Customer Summary
Alt-A   Print Accounts Receivable Detailed Aging Summary
Alt-C   Print Accounts Receivable Detail by Customer
Alt-S   Print Accounts Receivable Aging Summary by Customer

Type the information in rows 25 through 31 from Figure 5-5. Be sure to type the word *Alt* and letter *T—don't press the Alt-T key combination.* When entering information in a cell that begins with the slash, such as the entry in Q27, precede it with a single quotation mark (') prefix.

To Create a Macro
/Range Name Create

You need to name each macro range before you can execute it. To name the search and print macros, enter

/Range Name Create

and respond to the prompt *Enter name:* with

\T

Press Enter. Respond to the prompt *Enter range:* with

Q25

and press Enter. Repeat for the other macros:

/Range Name Create

and respond to the prompt *Enter name:* with the following entries and then press Enter:

Name	Range
\A	Q27
\C	Q29
\S	Q31

To execute the print macro, press Alt-A. The macro in cell Q27 will execute the Print Printer Range command. The range A1 through I22 is typed after the prompt to enter the print range, and the tilde symbol (~) activates the Enter key. Next the macro issues the Align, Go, and Quit commands.

Saving the Worksheet with Replace
/File Save Replace

After printing the report, save this spreadsheet one more time to keep the macro instructions in the file. Enter

/File Save

and press Enter when the filename *AR* automatically displays. The software will check to see if you want to write over your previous file, so enter

Replace

to replace the file.

How to Use the Accounts Receivable Spreadsheet

Move the cursor to M2 and type

Sam Toy

(or your first customer name) and press Enter. Press F7 and the invoices for Sam Toy will list. Press Alt-T; the total line for Sam Toy will transfer to the area shown in Figure 5-6. Move to M2, type

Gift Co.

or your next customer, and press Enter. Press F7 and the invoices for Gift Co. will list. Press Alt-T. Move to M2, type *Try Inc.* or your remaining customers, and repeat the steps above. Hold down the Alt key and press either *A, C,* or *S,* depending on which report you want to print.

Preparing the Spreadsheet for Your Accounts Receivable

Use the Range Erase command to clear the invoices in cells A7 through D17. Don't erase the formulas in columns E through I. Use the Worksheet Insert Row command to expand the area for your invoices if necessary. Either enter the invoice number, date, and customer name from your sales information, or use the File Xtract and File Combine Copy commands to bring your invoices in from your Invoice file, as explained earlier in the chapter. To clear the Accounts Receivable Aging Summary by Customer area, press F5 and type as the address to go to

End

Press Enter. Move the cursor up one row with the up arrow. Enter

/Worksheet Delete Row

and continue moving the arrow up until all unwanted invoices are highlighted; press Enter. The file is now ready for you to follow the steps in the section above, "How to Use the Accounts Receivable Spreadsheet."

Saving the Completed Worksheet
/File Save

If you want, save the new worksheet containing this period's data in a new file separate from the previous AR file. Enter

/File Save

Then type in

AR490

for *accounts receivable April 1990* (or any name that will be easy for you to remember) and press Enter.

The Accounts Payable Listing and Checkwriter

The accounts payable spreadsheet allows you to enter the invoice number, date, vendor name, and amount for your accounts payable invoices. You can sort this list by vendor before printing. The checkwriter portion of the spreadsheet totals the invoices for a selected vendor and lists the invoice numbers and dates for the invoices you're paying. It might take some time to line up the date, address, amount, and remittance advice information to your check format. Make some photocopies of your checks to use for practice. Use the Move command to move each cell as necessary. The address information for each vendor is kept in a table in a separate portion of the spreadsheet.

Figure 5-7. Accounts Payable Listing and Macros

	A	B	C	D
1		Accounts Payable Listing		
2				
3		Month	April 1990	
4				
5				
6	Inv#	Date	Vendor	Amount
7	354	4/30/90	City Utility	$1,209.54
8	3754	4/30/90	Current Inc.	$67.42
9	26590	4/7/90	Current Inc.	$93.00
10	26545	4/2/90	Current Inc.	$575.40
11	398	4/9/90	Current Inc.	$349.00
12	23	4/12/90	Dry Chem In	$67.00
13	64	4/28/90	Dry Chem In	$92.54
14	47	4/19/90	Dry Chem In	$43.00
15	59	4/25/90	Dry Chem In	$54.00
16	60087	4/30/90	State Bell	$798.45
17	56743	4/3/90	Sun Plastic	$4,954.40
18	27520	4/29/90	Sun Plastic	$3,749.80
19				
20				=========
21			Total	$12,053.55
22				
23				
24				
25				
26	Print Macros			
27				
28	Alt P	Print Payables Listing		{goto}a7~/dsrd.{end}{r}{end}{d}~
29		in Vendor Order		p{r}{r}~a~g/ppra1.D21~agq
30				
31	Alt C	Print Checks		/pprg7.k30~agq
32				

Creating the Accounts Payable Listing

What follows is a brief review of the material from Chapter 2. If you're a *1-2-3* newcomer, you should read Chapter 2. Bring up the spreadsheet screen by typing *123* at the DOS prompt. The startup screen will have columns lettered A–H across the top of the screen and numbers for the rows going down the left side. The intersection of these columns and rows are called *cells,* where information is stored. For example, cell B4 is the intersection of the second column over (B) and the fourth row down (4). Cell D3 is the intersection of the fourth column over (D) and the third row down (3). The cursor will start in cell A1 and you can move it down or across with the arrow keys. What you type on the keyboard will appear on the line above the columns. It will move into the cell on which the cursor is resting when you press the Enter key.

Entering a Menu Command

When you press the slash key (/), different menu options such as Worksheet, Range, Copy, File, Print, Graph, Data, System, and Quit appear across the top of the screen. To select a command, press the first letter of the option, then the first letter of the next submenu item until you're finished. You can also select a menu item by moving the right- and left-arrow keys until the option is highlighted and then pressing Enter. All the instructions in this chapter will be done by entering the first letter.

Cancel or Erase
Esc

The Esc key normally cancels a command and takes you back to the previous menu or status. If you make an error and want to erase what you've typed so far, press the Esc key. If you've already pressed the Enter key and want to erase the contents of a cell, move the cursor to the cell you want to clear. Enter

/Range Erase

and press Enter to accept the range as the current cell.

Moving the Cursor

Use the arrow keys to move from cell to cell. Other helpful keys to know are:

F5 (Goto)   Moves to any cell location
Home   Moves to upper left corner (A1)
PageUp   Moves up one page
PageDown   Moves down one page

Quitting and Saving the Spreadsheet

If you need to quit before completing the spreadsheet and want to save the file, enter

/File Save

1-2-3 will then ask for a filename; type

AP

and press Enter. A filename can be up to eight characters, but you should stick to letters and numbers. Don't include any symbols such as + = . * / ? (> % or leave any blank spaces. To quit without saving, enter

/Quit Yes

and you should be back at the DOS prompt. Just enter *123* to return to the spreadsheet.

Widening the Column
/Worksheet Column Set-Width

Since columns C, D, I, and J must be wide enough to hold long vendor names and balances, use the Set-Column Width command. To increase column C, move the cursor to C1 and enter

/Worksheet Column Set-Width

Then respond to the prompt *Enter column width:* with

15

and press Enter. To increase column D, move the cursor to D1 and enter

/Worksheet Column Set-Width

Then respond to the prompt *Enter column width:* with

15

and press Enter. To increase column I, move the cursor to I1 and enter

/**W**orksheet **C**olumn **S**et-Width

Then respond to the prompt *Enter column width:* with

11

and press Enter. Move the cursor to J1 and enter

/**W**orksheet **C**olumn **S**et-Width

Then respond to the prompt *Enter column width:* with

11

and press Enter.

Entering the Headings

Move the cursor to B1, type

Accounts Payable Listing

and press Enter. Move the cursor to B3, type

Month

and press Enter. Type the following into the cells below and press Enter:

C3   April 1990
A6   Inv#
B6   Date
C6   Vendor
D6   Amount
C21 Total

Entering Formulas

Cell D21 holds a formula that totals the invoices. Move the cursor to D21, type

@SUM(D7.D18)

and press Enter.

Formatting the Spreadsheet
/Range Format Currency

You need to format column D to currency. Since you only want this column to be in currency, use the Range command instead of the Worksheet Global Format command. Enter

/Range Format Currency

and respond to the prompt *Enter number of decimal places:* with

2

Press Enter. Respond to the prompt *Enter range to format:* with

D1.D50

and press Enter.

Saving the Worksheet with Replace
/File Save Replace

It's best to save the spreadsheet often. Enter

/File Save

and press Enter when the filename *AP* automatically displays. The software will check to see if you want to write over your previous file, so enter

Replace

to replace the file.

Entering the Repeating Underline
\ =

Cell D20 contains a double underline created with the equal sign. To enter the repeating underline, move the cursor to D20 and enter

\ =

Entering the Data

Enter the invoices in columns A, B, C, and D from Figure 5-7 or your accounts payable. When entering amounts, don't enter the comma or dollar sign. Enter the date in date format or '4/30/90 for April 30, 1990. If you see a row of asterisks instead of the amount you entered, the column isn't wide enough to hold that amount. Use the Worksheet Column-Set command, /WCS, to increase the size of the column.

Saving the Worksheet with Replace
/File Save Replace

It's best to save the spreadsheet often. Enter

/File Save

and press Enter when the filename *AP* automatically displays. The software will check to see if you want to write over your previous file, so enter

Replace

to replace the file.

Printing the Worksheet
/Print Printer Range Align Go Quit

You can print the accounts payable listing now. The print command allows printing to a file or printer. Roll the paper to the perforation or top of form and enter

/Print Printer Range

Respond to the prompt *Enter print range:* with

A1.D21

and press Enter. To begin the printing job, enter

Align **G**o **Q**uit

To sort the list before printing, enter the macro explained at the end of the checkwriter section.

Figure 5-8. Checkwriter

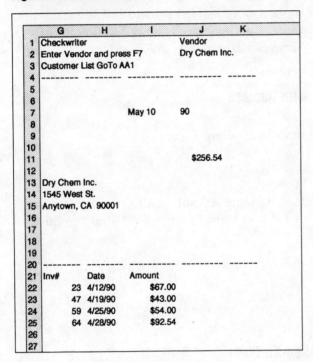

	G	H	I	J	K
1	Checkwriter			Vendor	
2	Enter Vendor and press F7			Dry Chem Inc.	
3	Customer List GoTo AA1				
4	_____	_____	_____	_____	_____
5					
6					
7			May 10	90	
8					
9					
10					
11				$256.54	
12					
13	Dry Chem Inc.				
14	1545 West St.				
15	Anytown, CA 90001				
16					
17					
18					
19					
20	_____	_____	_____	_____	_____
21	Inv#	Date	Amount		
22	23	4/12/90	$67.00		
23	47	4/19/90	$43.00		
24	59	4/25/90	$54.00		
25	64	4/28/90	$92.54		
26					
27					

The Checkwriter

1-2-3 has the ability to search though all the invoices and total them for a certain vendor. You can use the database feature of *1-2-3* if you need to print checks or a sample from which someone will type checks. You can create this checkwriter to the right of the listing. To move quickly to the database area, press the F5 function key and respond to the prompt *Enter address to go to:* with

G1

Press Enter. In this cell type

Checkwriter

and press Enter. Type the following into the cells below and press Enter:

G2   Enter Vendor and press F7
J1   Vendor
G3   Customer list GoTo AA1
I7   May 10
J7   '90
G21   Inv#
H21   Date
I21   Amount

Figure 5-9. Customer Database

	AA	AB	AC
1	Vendor	Address	CSZ
2	Dry Chem Inc.	1545 West St.	Anytown, CA 90001
3	Sun Plastics	329 North St.	Anytown, CA 90001
4	Current Inc.	12 South St.	Anytown, CA 90001
5	State Bell	P.O. Box 99	Anytown, CA 90001
6	City Utility	P.O. Box 999	Anytown, CA 90001
7			

Creating the Customer Database

To move to an unused portion of the spreadsheet, press the F5 function key and respond to the prompt *Enter address to go to:* with

AA1

Press Enter.

Widening the Column
/Worksheet Column Set-Width

To increase columns AA, AB, and AC, move the cursor to AA1 and enter

/Worksheet Column Set-Width

Then respond to the prompt *Enter column width:* with

15

and press Enter. Repeat for columns AB and AC. Type the headings *Vendor, Address*, and *CSZ* on row 1 from Figure 5-9. Enter the vendors and addresses from Figure 5-9 (or use your own files). Remember that addresses beginning with a number need to start with a single quotation mark prefix.

To Create a Range Name
/Range Name Create

You need to name the range in the address listing to simplify entering the formulas. To name a range, enter

/Range Name Create

and respond to the prompt *Enter name:* with

Address

Press Enter. Respond to the prompt *Enter range:* with

AA1.AC6

and press Enter. Press the Home and Tab right keys to return to the Checkwriter area.

Entering the Criterion to Search

Cell J2 will hold the vendor that's the criterion for your first search. Move the cursor to J2, enter

Dry Chem In

and press Enter.

Setting the Input, Criteria, and Output Ranges

You need to let *1-2-3* know three things before it can perform a search:

• The input range
• The criteria range
• The output range

The input range is where you enter the invoices and includes the heading line. The titles from this heading line—Inv#, Date, Vendor, and Amount—become the field names. When performing a search, it's easy to forget to include this line in the input, criteria, and output ranges.

The criteria range consists of the field names, and any certain field for which you want to search.

The output range is where you want the result of the search to be listed. Again, the output range must include the heading line, which becomes the field names.

To perform the search, enter

/Data Query Input

and respond to the prompt *Enter Input range:* with

A6.D18

Press Enter. Enter

Criteria

and respond to the prompt *Enter Criteria range:* with

J1.J2

Press Enter. Enter

Output

and respond to the prompt *Enter Output range:* with

G21.I37

and press Enter.
To begin the search, enter

Extract Quit

All invoices for Dry Chem In are listed in the output range of G22 though I37.

Using the Query Key
F7

Use the F7 function key any time you change the field and criterion searched. Search for vendor Sun Plastic next. Move the cursor to J2, type

Sun Plastic

and press Enter. You don't need to enter the input, criteria, and output ranges again. Press F7 and the search restarts. Everything you've purchased from the vendor Sun Plastic will list.

Using a Lookup Table and @DSUM Function

The formula in G13 displays the vendor selected in cell J2. The formulas in G14 and G15 look up the vendor's address in the table at cell AA1. The formula in J11 totals the invoices for the vendor in J2. Move the cursor to the following cells, type these entries, and press Enter:

```
J11    @DSUM(A6.D18,3,J1.J2)
G13    +J2
G14    @VLOOKUP(J2,ADDRESS,1)
G15    @VLOOKUP(J2,ADDRESS,2)
```

Formatting the Area to Currency
/Range Format Currency

Enter

/Range Format Currency

and respond to the prompt *Enter number of decimal places:* with

2

Press Enter. Respond to the prompt *Enter range to format:* with

J11

and press Enter.

Entering the Repeating Dash
\ —

Cells G4 and G20 contain a dashed line created with the minus sign. To enter the repeating dash, move the cursor to G4 and G20 and enter

\ —

and enter

/Copy

and respond to the prompt *Enter range to copy FROM:* with

G4

Press Enter. Respond to the prompt *Enter range to copy TO:* with

H4.L4

and press Enter. Copy cell G20 to H20 through L20.

Entering Macros to Print Reports

Each time you save the spreadsheet, only the latest printing instructions are saved. To print the checks you would have to reenter the range, since the range for the payables listing is now saved. You can save the printing instructions in macros, which you execute with the combination of the Alt key and a letter. A *macro* is simply a range of cells in the spreadsheet that holds the keystrokes necessary to execute commands. You can create two macros to print the following reports:

Alt-P Print Accounts Payable Listing in Vendor Order
Alt-C Print Accounts Payable Checks

To move to an unused portion of the spreadsheet, press the F5 function key and respond to the prompt *Enter address to go to:* with

A26

Press Enter. Type the heading,

Print Macros

and press Enter. Move the cursor to A28, type

Alt P

and press Enter. Be sure to type the word *Alt* and letter *P—don't press the Alt-P key combination.* Move to B28 and B29, type

**Print Payables Listing
in Vendor Order**

and press Enter. Type the information shown at the bottom of Figure 5-7 in the remaining cells through row 31. When entering information in a cell that begins with a slash, such as the text in D31, add a single quotation mark (') prefix.

To Create a Macro
/Range Name Create

You need to name each macro range before you can execute it. To name the print payables listing macro, enter

/Range Name Create

and respond to the prompt *Enter name:* with

\P

Press Enter. Respond to the prompt *Enter range:* with

D28.D29

and press Enter. Repeat this process for the other macro.

Name   Range
\C   D31

To execute the print payables listing macro, hold down the Alt key and simultaneously press the letter *P*. The macro in cell D28 will enter a data sort command to put the listing in vendor name order and then execute the Print Printer Range command. The range of A1.D21 will be typed after the prompt to enter the print range, and the tilde symbol (˜) will activate the Enter key. Next the macro issues the Align, Go, and Quit commands.

Saving the Worksheet with Replace
/File Save Replace

After entering the macros, enter

/File Save

and press Enter when the filename *AP* automatically displays. The software will check to see if you want to write over your previous file, so enter

Replace

to replace the file.

Preparing the Spreadsheet for Your Accounts Payable

Make a few photocopies of your checks and use the Alt-C macro to
test printing the checks. Use the Move command to change the location of the amount, date, and address cells as necessary. With the
Range Erase command, clear the invoices in cells A7 through D18.
Use the Worksheet Insert Row command to expand the area for
your invoices if necessary. Enter the invoice number, date, and
vendor name from your invoices to be paid. Press the GoTo key
(F5) to move to cell AA1, and enter the names and addresses of
your vendors.

How to Use the Accounts Payable Spreadsheet

After entering the vendors and invoices, press the Alt-P key combination to print a payables listing for approval. Move the cursor to
J2 and type the name of the first vendor you want to pay. Press F7
and PageDown to check if the invoices to be paid are correct. Align
the check in the printer and press Alt-C to print the check. Type a
new vendor in J2, press F7, and align the check; then press Alt-C
for the next vendor. Continue until all desired vendors are paid.

Fixed Assets and Depreciation

Fixed assets is the term for all the property you use to run your
business, from buildings to computers. Accounting for such property is difficult, since most of it must to be written off as it loses value. This has been further complicated by the past tax law changes,
which make depreciation calculations complex. *1-2-3* provides functions that calculate depreciation based on straight-line, sum of the
years' digits, and double-declining methods, but the new law has
added ACRS and MACRS methods. Additionally, new half-year,
midquarter, and midmonth conventions have been added to com-
plicate calculating the first year depreciation for most assets.

For these reasons, it's suggested you have your tax accountant
calculate the depreciation for each new asset you acquire. Get the
depreciation figure for each year of the asset's life and use this for
the first spreadsheet. If you have Release 3, you can use the new
function @VDB to calculate depreciation using the double-declining
200 percent method with a half-year convention and automatic
switch to straight-line when it exceeds the double-declining
amount. For nonresidential real and residential rental property this
doesn't apply, and you'll need to use a midquarter convention. If

you acquired over 40 percent of your assets in the last three months, you'll need to use a midquarter convention. Your tax accountant can calculate both of these situations for you.

Figure 5-10. Fixed Asset Depreciation Record

	A	B	C	D	E	F	G
1	Fixed Asset Record						
2						Release 3 Only	
3	Item	Desk				0	
4	ID#	26				0.5	$213
5	Method	200%				1.5	$365
6	Life	7				2.5	$261
7	Salvage	0				3.5	$186
8	Cost	$1,490				4.5	$133
9	Convention	0.5				5.5	$133
10						6.5	$133
11						7	$66
12	Date	Desc	Amount	Depr	Balance		$1,490
13	==========	======	======	=====	======		
14	05/08/88	Purchase	$1,490		$1,490		
15	12/31/88	Depr 1 Yr		$213	$1,277		
16	12/31/89	Depr 2 Yr		$365	$912		
17		Depr 3 Yr		$261	$652		
18		Depr 4 Yr		$186	$465		
19		Depr 5 Yr		$133	$332	* Switch to SL	
20		Depr 6 Yr		$133	$199		
21		Depr 7 Yr		$133	$66		
22				$66	$0		
23							

Creating the Fixed Asset Depreciation Record

The fixed asset depreciation record is similar to an equipment record that keeps a detailed listing of the cost, accumulated depreciation, and net balance of each asset you own.

What follows is a brief review of the material from Chapter 2. If you're a *1-2-3* newcomer, you should read Chapter 2. Bring up the spreadsheet screen by typing *123* at the DOS prompt. The startup screen will have columns lettered A–H across the top of the screen and numbers for the rows going down the left side. The intersection of these columns and rows are called *cells*, where information is stored. For example, cell B4 is the intersection of the second column over (B) and the fourth row down (4). Cell D3 is the intersection of the fourth column over (D) and the third row down (3). The cursor will start in cell A1 and you can move it down or across with the arrow keys. What you type on the keyboard will appear on the line above the columns. It will move into the cell on which the cursor is resting when you press the Enter key.

Entering a Menu Command

When you press the slash key (/), different menu options such as Worksheet, Range, Copy, File, Print, Graph, Data, System, and Quit appear across the top of the screen. To select a command, press the first letter of the option, then the first letter of the next submenu item until you've finished. You can also select a menu item by moving the right- and left-arrow keys until the option is highlighted and then pressing Enter. All the instructions in this chapter will be done by entering the first letter.

Cancel or Erase
Esc

The Esc key normally cancels a command and takes you back to the previous menu or status. If you make an error and want to erase what you've typed so far, press the Esc key. If you've already pressed the Enter key and want to erase the contents of a cell, move the cursor to the cell you want to clear. Enter

/Range Erase

and press Enter to accept the range as the current cell.

Moving the Cursor

Use the arrow keys to move from cell to cell. Other helpful keys to know are:

F5 (Goto)	Moves to any cell location
Home	Moves to upper left corner (A1)
PageUp	Moves up one page
PageDown	Moves down one page

Quitting and Saving the Spreadsheet

If you need to quit before completing the spreadsheet and want to save the file, enter

/**F**ile **S**ave

1-2-3 will then ask for a filename; type

Fixrec

and press Enter. A filename can be up to eight characters, but you should stick to letters and numbers. Don't include any symbols such as + = . * / ? (> % or leave any blank spaces. To quit without saving, enter

/**Q**uit **Y**es

and you should be back at the DOS prompt. Just enter *123* to return to the spreadsheet.

Widening the Column
/Worksheet Column Set-Width

Since column A must be wide enough to hold dates, use the Set-Column Width command. To increase column A, move the cursor to A1 and enter

/**W**orksheet **C**olumn **S**et-Width

Then respond to the prompt *Enter column width:* with

11

and press Enter.

Entering the Headings

Move the cursor to A1, type

Fixed Asset Record

and press Enter. Move the cursor to A3, type

Item

and press Enter. Enter the remaining headings in column A from Figure 5-10. Move the cursor to A12 and type

Date

Press Enter. Continue entering the headings in row 12 from Figure 5-10.

Entering Formulas

Cell E15 holds a formula that subtracts the depreciation in column D from the cost. Move the cursor to E15, type

+E14−D15

and press Enter.

Formatting the Spreadsheet
/Range Format Currency

You need to format columns C through E to currency. Since you only want these columns to be in currency, use the Range command instead of the Worksheet Global Format command. Enter

/Range Format Currency

and respond to the prompt *Enter number of decimal places:* with

0

Press Enter. Respond to the prompt *Enter range to format:* with

C14.E22
and press Enter. Repeat for cells B7 and B8.

To format the depreciation percentage, enter

/**R**ange **F**ormat **P**ercent

and respond to the prompt *Enter number of decimal places:* with

0

and press Enter. Respond to the prompt *Enter range to format:* with

B5

and press Enter.
To format column A to date format, enter

/**R**ange **F**ormat **D**ate **4**

and respond to the prompt *Enter range to format:* with

A14.A22

Press Enter.

Saving the Worksheet with Replace
/File Save Replace

It's best to save the spreadsheet often. Enter

/**F**ile **S**ave

and press Enter when the filename *Fixrec* automatically displays. The software will check to see if you want to write over your previous file, so enter

Replace

to replace the file.

Entering the Repeating Underline
\=

Cell A13 contains a double underline created with the equal sign.
To enter the repeating underline, move the cursor to A13 and enter

\=

Copying Formulas
/Copy

Copy the formula in E14 down to eliminate the need for reentering
the formula. To copy, enter

/Copy

and respond to the prompt *Enter range to copy FROM:* with

E15

Press Enter. Respond to the prompt *Enter range to copy TO:* with

E16.E22

and press Enter. Continue copying the underscore as follows:

A13   to   B13.E13

Saving the Worksheet with Replace
/File Save Replace

It's best to save the spreadsheet before entering any data. You can
use this fixed asset record file as a blank for each of your fixed assets. Enter

/File Save

and press Enter when the filename *Fixrec* automatically displays.
The software will check to see if you want to write over your previous file, so enter

Replace

to replace the file.

How to Use the Fixed Asset Depreciation Record

Type the entries in column B from Figure 5-10 or your fixed assets records. The Item entry can be any description, including serial numbers, model, and location. ID# is optional for those companies that tag all assets. Method can be SL, ACRS, 200 percent, 150 percent, or any depreciation method you use. *Life* is the asset's estimated life of usage from IRS guidelines. *Salvage* is the value remaining after fully depreciating the asset. *Cost* is the price you paid for it plus any additional expenses to get it ready for use (your accountant can supply this amount); the convention is .5 for half a year or 1.0 for a full year. Move the cursor to A14 and enter the date when the item was purchased as follows:

@DATE(88,5,8)

Press Enter. For a description, enter purchase or the check number. Enter the amount in both cell C14 and E14.

The description for each depreciation amount can show the year or possibly the journal voucher number that recorded the depreciation. You can obtain the depreciation in column D from your accountant. When entering amounts, don't enter the comma or dollar sign. If you see a row of asterisks instead of the amount you entered, the column isn't wide enough to hold that amount. Use the Worksheet Column-Set command, /WCS, to increase the size of the column. The balance in column E will be calculated automatically. You can now save this fixed asset record.

Saving the Worksheet
/File Save

Enter

/File Save

and when the filename *Fixrec* automatically displays, type

Desk26

or any name that will help you remember the item and press Enter.

Printing the Worksheet
/Print Printer Range Align Go Quit

You can print the fixed asset record now. The print command allows printing to a file or printer. Roll the paper to the perforation or top of form and enter

/Print Printer Range

and respond to the prompt *Enter print range:* with

A1.E23

and press Enter. To begin the printing job, enter

Align Go Quit

Saving the Worksheet with Replace
/File Save Replace

After printing the fixed asset record, save this spreadsheet one more time to keep the printing instructions in the file. Enter

/File Save

and press Enter when the filename *Desk26* automatically displays. The software will check to see if you want to write over your previous file, so enter

Replace

to replace the file.

Using the @VDB Function with Release 3

The @VDB function calculates depreciation using the double-declining method. The function automatically switches to straight-line when it exceeds the double-declining amount. Using the fixed asset record file, move the cursor to F3 and type

0

Press Enter. The amount in F3 should be a zero, not the letter *O*.

Move the cursor to F4, type

+F3+$B$9

and press Enter. The result should be .5, which is the result of adding the convention amount in B9 to zero. Move the cursor to G4, type

@VDB($B$8,$B$7,$B$6,F3,F4)

and press Enter. Then move the cursor to F5, type

+F4+1

and press Enter.

Copying Formulas
/Copy

Copy the formulas in cells F5 and G4 down. To copy, enter

/Copy

and respond to the prompt *Enter range to copy FROM:* with

F5

Press Enter. Respond to the prompt *Enter range to copy TO:* with

F6.F11

and press Enter. Enter

/Copy

and respond to the prompt *Enter range to copy FROM:* with

G4

Press Enter. Respond to the prompt *Enter range to copy TO:* with

G5.G11

and press Enter. The results should look similar to the table under

Release 3 Only in Figure 5-10. The @VDB function structure is as follows:

@VDB(Cost,Salvage,Life,Start-period,End-Period)

You can add two variables:

• The depreciation factor
• Disable straight-line depreciation switch

The following formula would use 150 percent instead of 200 percent, with no switch to straight-line:

@VDB(B8,B7,B6,F3,F4,150%,1)

The last two variables are optional; the default is 200 percent with an automatic switch to straight-line.

Figure 5-11. Fixed Assets Listing

	A	B	C	D	E	F	G	H	I
1			Easy Company						
2			Fixed Assets		Date	12/31/89			
3									
4	Date	ID	DESC	Method	Life	Cost	1989 Depr.	Accum. Depr.	Balance
5	========	=====	========	=====	====	=======	=======	=========	======
6	02/23/89	28	Truck	DDB	5	$9,850	$1,970		$7,880
7	02/06/89	33	Photocopier	DDB	7	$3,300	$660		$2,640
8	01/04/89	32	Computer	DDB	5	$4,300	$860		$3,440
9	05/03/88	26	Desk	DDB	7	$1,490	$365	$213	$912
10	04/03/87	23	Scope	DDBSL	5	$1,859	$357	$967	$535
11	08/04/85	20	Cabinets	ACRS	5	$2,370	$498	$1,872	$0
12	03/01/85	16	Forklift	ACRS	5	$5,700	$855	$4,845	$0
13	04/02/79	3	Building	SL	20	$55,000	$2,750	$24,750	$27,500
14									
15									
16									
17									
18									
19									
20									
21	========	=====	========	=====	====	=======	=======	=========	======
22			Totals			$83,869	$8,315	$32,647	$42,907
23									

The Fixed Assets Listing

You can use the fixed asset listing as a summary each year for income tax purposes and reconciliation of the asset and accumulated depreciation accounts. You can sort the items by depreciation method, date purchased, ID numbers, or description. After saving any previous spreadsheet, to clear the screen enter

/Worksheet Erase Yes

and you'll have a fresh screen.

Widening the Columns
/Worksheet Global Column-Width

Since all the columns must be wide enough to hold long amounts, use the Worksheet Global Column-Width command. To increase the columns, enter

/Worksheet Global Column-Width

Then respond to the prompt *Enter column width:* with

11

and press Enter.

Widening a Column
/Worksheet Column Set-Width

Since column C must be wide enough to hold long descriptions, use the Set-Column Width command. To increase column C, move the cursor to C1 and enter

/Worksheet Column Set-Width

Then respond to the prompt *Enter column width:* with

15

and press Enter. To decrease columns B and E, move to B1 and enter

/Worksheet Column Set-Width

Then respond to the prompt *Enter column width:* with

5

and press Enter. Move the cursor to E1, enter

/**W**orksheet **C**olumn **S**et-Width

and respond to the prompt *Enter column width:* with

5

Press Enter.

Entering the Headings

Move the cursor to C1, type

Easy Company

(or your company name) and press Enter. Move the cursor to C2, type

Fixed Assets

and press Enter. Move the cursor to E2, type

Date

and press Enter. Move the cursor to F2, type

"12/31/89

and press Enter. Enter the remaining headings on row 4 from Figure 5-11. Move the cursor to C22, type

Totals

and press Enter.

Entering Formulas

Cell I6 holds a formula that subtracts the total of 1989 depreciation and accumulated depreciation from the cost. Move the cursor to I6, type

+F6−(G6+H6)

and press Enter.

To total the cost column, move the cursor to F22 and type

@SUM(F6.F20)

Press Enter.

Formatting the Spreadsheet
/Range Format Currency

You need to format columns F through I to currency. Since you only want these columns to be in currency, use the Range command instead of the Worksheet Global Format command. Enter

/Range Format Currency

and respond to the prompt *Enter number of decimal places:* with

0

Press Enter. Respond to the prompt *Enter range to format:* with

F6.I22

and press Enter. To format column A to date format, enter

/Range Format Date 4

and respond to the prompt *Enter range to format:* with

A6.A20

Press Enter.

Saving the Spreadsheet
/File Save

To save the file, enter

/File Save

1-2-3 will then ask for a filename; type

Fixed

and press Enter. If you saved the spreadsheet earlier, press Enter when the filename *Fixed* automatically displays. The software will check to see if you want to write over your previous file, so enter

Replace

to replace the file.

Entering the Repeating Underline
\ =

Cells A5 and A21 contain a double underline created with the equal sign. To enter the repeating underline, move the cursor to A5 and enter

\ =

Repeat for A21.

Copying Formulas
/Copy

Copy the formula in cell I6 to eliminate the need for entering the formula again. To copy, enter

/Copy

and respond to the prompt *Enter range to copy FROM:* with

I6

Press Enter. Respond to the prompt *Enter range to copy TO:* with

I7.I20

and press Enter. Continue copying the totals formula and under-scores as follows:

A5   to   B5.I5
A21 to   B21.I21
F22 to   G22.I22

Saving the Worksheet with Replace
/File Save Replace

Now save this spreadsheet without data to use for other companies or years. Enter

/File Save

and press Enter when the filename *Fixed* automatically displays. The software will check to see if you want to write over your previous file, so enter

Replace

to replace the file.

How to Use the Fixed Asset Listing

Enter the fixed assets in columns A through H from Figure 5-11 or your own books. Enter the dates as follows:

@DATE(89,2,23)

The balance in column I and totals on row 22 will calculate automatically. When entering amounts, don't enter the comma or dollar sign. If you see a row of asterisks instead of the amount you entered, the column isn't wide enough to hold that amount. Use the Worksheet Column-Set command, /WCS, to increase the size of the column.

Saving the Completed Worksheet

Enter

/File Save

When the filename *Fixed* automatically displays, type

Fixed89

to save this data separate from the master Fixed file.

Suppress Zero Display
/Worksheet Global Zero Yes

It might be difficult to see the amounts in the listing due to the display of zeros. To eliminate them, enter

/Worksheet Global Zero Yes

and the zeros will be suppressed.

Printing the Worksheet
/Print Printer Range Align Go Quit

You can print the fixed assets listing now. The print command allows printing to a file or printer. Roll the paper to the perforation or top of form and enter

/Print Printer Range

Respond to the prompt *Enter print range:* with

A1.I22

and press Enter. To begin the printing job, enter

Align Go Quit

Use instructions given earlier for setting your printer for condensed mode.

Saving the Worksheet with Replace
/File Save Replace

After printing the fixed assets listing, save this spreadsheet one more time to keep the printing instructions in the file. Enter

/File Save

and press Enter when the filename *Fixed89* automatically displays. The software will check to see if you want to write over your previous file, so enter

Replace

to replace the file.

Sorting the Listing

Often you'll need to sort the listing in another order for tax purposes or for easier identification of the items. Make sure you save your file before doing any sort. To sort the listing by description, enter

/Data Sort Data-Range

and respond to the prompt *Enter data range:* with

A6.I13

Press Enter. Enter

Primary-Key

and respond to the prompt *Primary sort key:* with

C6

and press Enter. Enter

A

for the ascending sort order and press Enter.

To begin the sort, enter

Go

When doing a sort, it's best to limit the range to the last item in the list or row 13 in Figure 5-11. Also be sure to include all the columns through column I in the range to keep the data together. Try a few more sorts changing the primary key to column A, B, or column D. To get a fixed asset listing in ID number order, sort on column B and follow the print instructions above. The following chart lists the various sort options:

Report	Primary Key	Secondary Key
Fixed Assets in ID# order for physical inventory	B	
Fixed Assets in Date order for journal	A	
Fixed Assets in Description order	C	
Fixed Assets in Date and Method order for tax accountant	A	D

6
Payroll

In this chapter, you can create two spreadsheets that are helpful in calculating and summarizing payroll. Each one will provide you with different reports for your business. From the payroll calculation and payroll summary spreadsheets you'll be able to produce these reports:

• Payroll Register
• Employee Listing
• QTD and YTD Payroll Summary
• Employee Earnings Report

The payroll calculation and payroll summary are two of the most difficult spreadsheets in this book. You should pay careful attention to the formulas that calculate the payroll and continue to keep your manual payroll system for the first few pay periods. You'll need a current copy of Circular E, Employer's Tax Guide from the IRS, to build the tax tables. If all you want is to summarize for tax reports only, skip the payroll calculation spreadsheet and just create the payroll summary spreadsheet. Since these spreadsheets are complicated, you should enter the sample data from the figures in this chapter first to learn how the spreadsheet works before adding your own employees and payroll data.

The Payroll Calculation Spreadsheet

The payroll calculation spreadsheet allows you to enter the employee number, regular hours, and overtime hours. The spreadsheet calculates gross wages, FICA, federal withholding and net pay. If you pay your employees salary or commission, you can use the rate rather than the total hours. You can add up to three deductions for state taxes and insurance deductions. After learning how to set up the federal withholding tables, you should be able to add your state withholding tables if necessary. The totals for all employees are then calculated for a payroll register. After completing the payroll register, you can save the information in a payroll summary file and use the spreadsheet for the next payroll. There are three areas in the payroll calculation spreadsheet:

• Payroll register
• Tax tables
• Employee table

Figure 6-1. Payroll Calculation

	A	B	C	D	E	F	G	H	I	J	K	L
1				Key:	Tax Tables goto AA1							
2					Employee List goto BA1							
3												
4												
5				Easy Company		Payroll ending date						
6				Payroll Register		2/15/90						
7												
8												
9	Emp#	R Hr	OT	Name	Gross	FICA	Fed W/H	Ded 1	Ded 2	Ded 3	Net Pay	Date
10												
11	50	40		Jim West	$900.00	$67.59	$0.00	$7.40	$5.00	$0.00	$820.01	02/15/90
12	20	40	3	Joe First	$267.00	$20.05	$31.13	$3.40	$5.00	$0.00	$207.42	02/15/90
13	10	39		Sue Smith	$273.00	$20.50	$14.34	$3.40	$5.00	$0.00	$229.75	02/15/90
14	40	40	6	Sara Jones	$294.00	$22.08	$40.95	$2.50	$2.00	$0.00	$226.47	02/15/90
15	30	40		Sam Easy	$1,000.00	$0.00	$131.45	$6.00	$20.00	$0.00	$842.55	02/15/90
16				===========	=======	======	======	=====	=====	====	=======	======
17					$2,734.00	$130.22	$217.87	$22.70	$37.00	$0.00	$2,326.21	
18												
19												
20	Alt X			/fxvpaytemp~ {name} payroll ~r	Xtract and save payroll to Paytemp							

Creating the Payroll Calculation Spreadsheet

What follows is a brief review of the material from Chapter 2. If you're a 1-2-3 newcomer, you should read Chapter 2. Bring up the spreadsheet screen by typing 123 at the DOS prompt. The startup screen will have columns lettered A–H across the top of the screen and numbers for the rows going down the left side. The intersection of these columns and rows are called *cells*, where information is stored. For example, cell B4 is the intersection of the second column over (B) and the fourth row down (4). Cell D3 is the intersection of the fourth column over (D) and the third row down (3). The cursor will start in cell A1, and you can move it down or across with the arrow keys. What you type on the keyboard will appear on the line above the columns. It will move into the cell on which the cursor is resting when you press the Enter key.

Entering a Menu Command

When you press the slash key (/), different menu options such as Worksheet, Range, Copy, File, Print, Graph, Data, System, and Quit appear across the top of the screen. To select a command, press the first letter of the option, then the first letter of the next submenu item until you're finished. You can also select a menu item by moving the right- and left-arrow keys until the option is highlighted and then pressing Enter. All the instructions in this chapter will be done by entering the first letter.

Cancel or Erase
Esc

The Esc key normally cancels a command and takes you back to the previous menu or status. If you make an error and want to erase what you've typed so far, press the Esc key. If you've already pressed the Enter key and want to erase the contents of a cell, move the cursor to the cell you want to clear. Enter

/**R**ange Erase

and press Enter to accept the range as the current cell.

Moving the Cursor

Use the arrow keys to move from cell to cell. Other helpful keys to know are:

F5 (Goto)	Moves to any cell location
Home	Moves to upper left corner (A1)
PageUp	Moves up one page
PageDown	Moves down one page

Quitting and Saving the Spreadsheet

If you need to quit before completing the spreadsheet and want to save the file, enter

/**F**ile **S**ave

1-2-3 will then ask for a filename; type

Paycalc

and press Enter. A filename can be up to eight characters, but you should stick to letters and numbers. Don't include any symbols such as + = . * / ? (> % or leave any blank spaces. To quit without saving, enter

/Quit Yes

and you should be back at the DOS prompt. Just enter *123* to return to the spreadsheet.

Widening the Column
/Worksheet Column Set-Width

Since columns D, E, and K must be wide enough to hold long employee names and balances, and columns A, B, and C should be shorter for employee numbers and hours, use the Set-Column Width command. To increase column D, move the cursor to D1 and enter

/Worksheet Column Set-Width

Then respond to the prompt *Enter column width:* with

15

and press Enter. To increase column E, move the cursor to E1 and enter

/Worksheet Column Set-Width

Then respond to the prompt *Enter column width:* with

11

and press Enter. To increase column K, move the cursor to K1, enter

/**W**orksheet **C**olumn **S**et-Width

and respond to the prompt *Enter column width:* with

11

Press Enter. Move the cursor to the following columns and use the /Worksheet Column Set-Width command to decrease them to:

A1   5
B1   5
C1   5

Entering the Headings

The key in D1 through E2 is a guide to where the other sections of the spreadsheet are located. Move the cursor to D1, type

Key:

and press Enter. Move to E1 and E2, type

Tax Tables goto AA1
Employee List goto BA1

and press Enter. Move the cursor to D5, type

^Easy Company

(or your company name) and press Enter. The ^ key centers the text in the cell. Move the cursor to D6, type

^Payroll Register

and press Enter. Move the cursor to F5, type

Payroll ending date

and press Enter—you don't need to center this heading. Type the following headings across row 9 in the cells below and then press Enter:

A9   Emp#
B9   R Hr
C9   ^OT
D9   Name
E9   Gross
F9   FICA
G9   Fed W/H
H9   Ded 1
I9   Ded 2
J9   Ded 3
K9   Net Pay
L9   Date

To Create a Range Name
/Range Name Create

You need to name the range of the employee table to simplify entering the formulas later. To name the table, enter

/Range Name Create

and respond to the prompt *Enter name:* with

EMP

Press Enter. Respond to the prompt *Enter range:* with

BA3.BJ7

and press Enter.

Entering Formulas

The formulas in columns E, F, and G are complicated and depend on the withholding and employee tables, which you haven't completed yet. Move the cursor to E11, type

@IF(@ISERR(@IF(BM3="S",BP3,(B11*BP3)+C11*BP3*1.5)),
  0,@IF(BM3="S",BP3,(B11*BP3+C11*BP3*1.5)))

and press Enter. The main formula above means: If BM3 equals S (for Salary), then place the rate amount in the cell. If BM3 doesn't equal salary (an hourly employee), then take the hours in B11 times the rate in BP3, and add the overtime hours in C11 times the rate multiplied by 1.5; if your overtime rate is other than 1.5, replace both amounts in the formula above. Since cells BM3 and BP3 are in the employee table you haven't created yet, the payroll calculation won't work properly.

The remaining part of the formula is to convert an error (ERR) to zero. In simple terms it means that if the main formula creates an error, then enter a zero; if not, continue with the main formula.

Move the cursor to F11, type

@IF(@VLOOKUP(A11,$EMP,9)<1,0,E11*$AB$8)

and press Enter. The formula above looks up the employee number in A11 of the $EMP table and finds the FICA code in column 9. If this code is zero, then the FICA amount is zero. If you have an employee who is exempt from FICA, such as a son or daughter of the owner or someone who has reached the FICA maximum wages, then a code of zero will be entered in their employee setup in the employee table. If the code is 1, then the gross wages in E11 are multiplied by the FICA rate in the tax tables. Move the cursor to G11, type

@IF(@ISERR(BL3),0,BL3)

and press Enter.

The main formula to calculate federal withholding is much too large to combine with the error prevention formula above; it's in cell BL3. The formulas in columns D, H, I, and J look up the employee name and preset deductions in the employee table. Move to each cell, type the following entries, and press Enter:

```
D11   @VLOOKUP(A11,$EMP,1)
H11   @VLOOKUP(A11,$EMP,6)
I11   @VLOOKUP(A11,$EMP,7)
J11   @VLOOKUP(A11,$EMP,8)
```

The formula in column K calculates net pay by subtracting the total of the deductions from gross wages. Move the cursor to K11, type

+E11−@SUM(F11.J11)

and press Enter.

There's no formula to prevent a negative pay check; rather the negative amount will display in the net pay column. You'll need to manually reduce one of the deductions by this negative amount.

Move the cursor to E17, type

@SUM(E11.E15)

and press Enter. If you have five employees the totals line will be row 17. If not, adjust the total line to your maximum number of employees in one pay period. For example, if you have seven employees, your totals line is line 19. Change the formula to @SUM(E11.E17).

Entering Dates

1-2-3 has the capacity to make calculations with dates entered in the proper format. Later you'll need this feature to separate the payrolls by quarter and year-to-date amounts. To enter a date, move the cursor to F6, type

'2/15/90

and press Enter.

You need the dates in column L to convert the payroll ending date to a date value. Move the cursor to L11, type

@DATEVALUE($F$6)

and press Enter. The result of 32919 is the number of days from 1/1/1900 to 2/15/1990.

Entering the Repeating Underline

\ =

Cell D16 contains a double underline created with the equal sign. To enter the repeating underline, move the cursor to D16 and enter

\ =

Copying Formulas
/Copy

Copy the formulas from row 11 down to eliminate the need for re-entering the formulas. To copy, enter

/Copy

and respond to the prompt *Enter range to copy FROM:* with

D11.L11

Press Enter. Respond to the prompt *Enter range to copy TO:* with

D12.L15

and press Enter. Continue copying the formulas and underscores as follows:

```
D16   to   E16.L16
E17   to   F17.K17
```

Formatting the Spreadsheet
/Range Format

You need to format Columns E through K to currency. Since you only want these columns to be in currency, use the Range command instead of the Worksheet Global Format command. Enter

/Range Format Currency

and respond to the prompt *Enter number of decimal places:* with

2

and press Enter. Respond to the prompt *Enter range to format:* with

E11.K17

and press Enter.
     To format the dates, enter

/Range Format Date 4

and respond to the prompt *Enter range to format:* with

L11.L15

Press Enter.

Unprotect a Range
/Range Unprotect

When you've completed the spreadsheet, you can turn on the protection to prevent losing the formulas and employee tables. The only area that will change every payroll is the employee number, hours, overtime hours, and date cells. To keep them unprotected, enter

/Range Unprotect

and respond to the prompt *Enter range to unprotect:* with

A11.C15

Press Enter. Enter

/**R**ange Unprotect

and respond to the prompt *Enter range to unprotect:* with

F6

Press Enter. The unprotected cells are highlighted or change colors, depending on your monitor type.

To Create a Range Name
/Range Name Create

You need to name the range in the table that contains the payroll data to simplify transferring the data to the payroll summary spreadsheet. To name a range, enter

/**R**ange Name Create

and respond to the prompt *Enter name:* with

Payroll

Press Enter. Respond to the prompt *Enter range:* with

A11.L15

and press Enter.

Entering a Macro

A *macro* is simply a range of cells in the spreadsheet that holds the keystrokes necessary to execute commands. You can create a macro to save the payroll data in a temporary file for transfer to the payroll summary later. Move the cursor to A20, type the heading

Alt X

and press Enter. Be sure to type the word *Alt* and letter *X—not the Alt-X key combination.* Move the cursor to F20, type

Xtract and save payroll to Paytemp

and press Enter. Move the cursor to C20, type

'/fxvpaytemp˜{name}payroll˜r

and press Enter. It's important to remember when entering information in a cell that begins with a slash to precede the information
with a single quotation mark (') prefix.

To Create a Macro
/Range Name Create

You need to name each macro range before it can be executed. To
name the Alt-X macro, enter

/Range Name Create

and respond to the prompt *Enter name:* with

\X

Press Enter. Respond to the prompt *Enter range:* with

C20

and press Enter. Don't execute the macro now, since there's no
data to save and you haven't created the paytemp file yet.

Saving the Worksheet with Replace
/File Save Replace

It's best to save the spreadsheet often. Enter

/File Save

and either type *Paycalc* if this if your first time saving the file or
press Enter when the filename *Paycalc* automatically displays. The
software will check to see if you want to write over your previous
file, so enter

Replace

to replace the file.

Figure 6-2. Tax Table

	Z	AA	AB	AC	AD	AE	AF	AG
1	Single:	Over	Percent	Plus	Married:	Over	Percent	Plus
2	Weekly	0	0	0		0	0	0
3		21	0.15	0		62	0.15	0
4		378	0.28	53.55		657	0.28	89.25
5		885	0.33	195.51		1501	0.33	325.57
6		2028	0.28	572.7		3695	0.28	1049.59
7					Withholding allowance			38.46
8		FICA rate	0.0751					
9								
10								

Creating a Lookup Table

You can create a lookup table in cells AA1 through AG8 that will hold the withholding tax tables, withholding allowance, and FICA rates from Circular E, Employer's Tax Guide. The formulas in the employee table will take the gross wages calculated in the previous section and subtract the amount of withholding allowances in the employee setup. The tax gross will be compared to the amounts in columns AA or AE, depending on the married or single code in the employee setup. The corresponding tax percentage and base tax amount will be found and used in the federal tax calculating cell in column BL in the employee table.

To move to the tax tables, press the F5 key, respond to the prompt *Enter address to go to:* with

Z1

and press Enter. Use Figure 6-2 to create the table for weekly salary or use the appropriate table in Circular E under the instructions for the percentage method of withholding. Enter the FICA rate, which is usually on the front of Circular E. It isn't necessary to format the table to currency or percentage since you won't use this table as a report.

To Create a Range Name
/Range Name Create

You need to name the ranges in the table for single and married to simplify formulas later. To name the single tax table, enter

/Range **N**ame **C**reate

and respond to the prompt *Enter name:* with

Single

Press Enter. Respond to the prompt *Enter range:* with

AA2.AC6

and press Enter. To name the married table, enter

/Range **N**ame **C**reate

and respond to the prompt *Enter name:* with

Married

Press Enter. Respond to the prompt *Enter range:* with

AE2.AG6

and press Enter. To enter the employee lookup table and formulas for the lookup function, press the F5 function key and respond to the prompt *Enter address to go to:* with

BB1

and press Enter.

Figure 6-3. Employee Table

	BA	BB	BC	BD	BE	BF	BG	BH	BI	BJ	BK	BL	BM	BN	BO	BP
1	Emp#	Name	M/S	EXP	S/H	RATE	DED 1	DED 2	DED 3	FICA Y/N						
2						0	0	0	0	0		0				
3	10	Sue Smith	M	3	H	$7.00	$3.40	$5.00		1	$0.00	$0.00	S	M	99	$900.00
4	20	Joe First	S	1	H	$6.00	$3.40	$5.00		1	$228.54	$31.13	H	S	1	$6.00
5	30	Sam Easy	M	5	S	$1,000.00	$6.00	$20.00		0	$157.82	$14.34	H	M	3	$7.00
6	40	Sara Jones	S	0	H	$6.00	$2.50	$2.00		1	$294.00	$40.95	H	S	0	$6.00
7	50	Jim West	M	99	S	$900.00	$7.40	$5.00		1	$807.70	$131.45	S	M	5	$1,000.00
8																

Creating the Employee Table

Use the Worksheet Set-Column Width command to increase and decrease the columns in the table. Move to each cell and enter

/**W**orksheet **C**olumn **S**et-Width

Then respond to the prompt *Enter column width:* with the following entries and press Enter:

BB1   15
BC1   5
BD1   5
BE1   5
BF1   11
BM1   3
BN1   3
BO1   3
BP1   11

Enter the headings in row 1 from Figure 6-3. The formulas in columns BK through BP look up the filing status, deductions, rates, and gross wages and they calculate the withholding tax. Enter the formulas in the following cells:

BK3   @IF((E11−$AG$7*BO3)>0,E11−($AG$7*BO3),0)
BL3   @IF(BN3="S",(@VLOOKUP(BK3,$SINGLE,1)*(BK3−@VLOOKUP
      (BK3,$SINGLE,0)))+@VLOOKUP(BK3,$SINGLE,2),(@VLOOKUP
      (BK3,$MARRIED,1)*(BK3−@VLOOKUP(BK3,$MARRIED,0)))
      +@VLOOKUP(BK3,$MARRIED,2))
BM3   @VLOOKUP(A11,$EMP,4)
BN3   @VLOOKUP(A11,$EMP,2)
BO3   @VLOOKUP(A11,$EMP,3)
BP3   @VLOOKUP(A11,$EMP,5)

Enter cell BO3 as letter *B* and letter *O* instead of letter *B* and number 0. The first formula in cell BK3 takes the gross wages in cell E11 and subtracts the result of multiplying the withholding allowance in AG7 by the employee setup for exemptions that are looked up in BO3. If subtracting results in an amount less than zero, then zero is inserted.

The formula in BL3 is one of the most complex in the spreadsheet and will display an ERR until the spreadsheet is complete. It uses an @IF function to figure the withholding tax with either the single or married tax table. It looks up the withholding tax percentage and multiplies the taxable gross by that percentage and adds the base tax amount.

The next three formulas hold the code you could have incorporated into the previous two formulas if space would have allowed.

Copying Formulas
/Copy

Copy the formulas in cells BK3 through BP3 down the table. To copy, enter

/Copy

and respond to the prompt *Enter range to copy FROM:* with

BK3.BP3

Press Enter. Respond to the prompt *Enter range to copy TO:* with

BK4.BP7

and press Enter.

Formatting the Spreadsheet to Currency
/Range Format Currency

If you plan to print the employee table you'll need to format some of the columns to currency. Use the Range command instead of the Worksheet Global Format command. Enter

/Range Format Currency

and respond to the prompt *Enter number of decimal places:* with

2

Press Enter. Respond to the prompt *Enter range to format:* with

BF3.BI7

and press Enter. Repeat for the ranges BK3.BL7 and BP3.BP7.

How to Use the Payroll Calculation Spreadsheet

Move the cursor to BA3 and enter the first employee number from Figure 6-3 or your own files. Since this is a lookup table, keep all employee numbers in ascending order. Move the cursor to BB3 and enter the employee name. Enter the remaining information in the columns as follows:

BC   M for Married or S for Single
BD   Exemption allowances—enter 99 for exempt
BE   S for Salary or H or Hourly
BF   Hourly rate or pay period salary amount
BG   Fixed deduction per pay period
BH   Fixed deduction per pay period
BI   Fixed deduction per pay period
BJ   0 For FICA exempt, 1 for normal

You can enter up to five employees without changing the instructions. Enter the zeros on row 2 from Figure 6-3. It's normal to have an ERR or set of asterisks display in some of the columns until an employee number is entered. If you have more employees, change the copy instructions for the formulas.

Turn the protection on to prevent any further changes to the spreadsheet by entering

/Worksheet **G**lobal **P**rotection **E**nable

To turn it off, enter

/Worksheet **G**lobal **P**rotection **D**isable

After entering the employees, save the file again. Enter

/File Save

and press Enter when the filename *Paycalc* automatically displays. The software will check to see if you want to write over your previous file, so enter

Replace

to replace the file.

To calculate a payroll, press the Home key to return to the payroll register. Move the cursor to F6 and enter the payroll ending date in the following format:

'MM/DD/YY

or

'2/15/90

Move the cursor to A11 and enter any employee number. The name for that employee will display in cell C11. Enter the regular hours and overtime hours. The remaining amounts in columns E through K will calculate. Continue entering employee numbers and hours from Figure 6-1 or your own payroll data. When the payroll is complete, save the file again. Enter

/File Save

then type in

Pay21590

for the 2/15/90 payroll file. After getting the next payroll summary spreadsheet working properly, you might not want to save every payroll file.

Printing the Spreadsheet
/Print Printer Range Align Go Quit

To print the payroll register, enter

/Print Printer Range

Respond to the prompt *Enter print range:* with

A5.K17

and press Enter. To begin the printing job, enter

Align Go Quit

This spreadsheet is too wide to print on most 80-column printers without going to a second page. If you have a condensed print switch available on your printer, set it to condensed and from the print menu enter

Options Margins Right

for options, margins, right, and enter

135

for the new right margin. If your printer doesn't have a switch but accepts a condensed print code, enter from the options menu

Setup

for the setup string. For Epson printers, the string for condensed is \015. Look in the *Lotus 1-2-3* appendix for your specific printer code.

To quit the options menu, enter

Quit

and then to start the print job enter

Align Go Quit

To print the employee list, enter

/Print Printer Range

and respond to the prompt *Enter print range:* with

BA3.BP7

Press Enter. To begin the printing job, enter

Align Go Quit

This spreadsheet is also too wide to print on most 80-column printers. Use the condensed instructions above to print.

The Payroll Summary

The payroll summary spreadsheet stores the payroll data for each pay period and creates the YTD and QTD summary for completing tax reports. From the payroll data, an employee earnings report can be generated for any period. The spreadsheet has three sections:

• The summary section
• The database of payroll data
• The output area for the employee earnings reports

Creating the Payroll Summary

If you have Release 3 of *1-2-3* and want to use the 3-D spreadsheet functions, go to the section at the end of this chapter. For prior release users, before you can transfer data into the summary, you must create a temporary file to hold the data. From the payroll calculation spreadsheet enter

/File Xtract Values

and respond to the prompt *Enter xtract file name:* with

Paytemp

Press Enter. Respond to the prompt *Enter the xtract range:* with

Payroll

and press Enter. To bring up a fresh spreadsheet screen, enter

/Worksheet Erase Yes

To move to an the area that will hold the payroll data in a database spreadsheet, press the F5 function key and respond to the prompt *Enter address to go to:* with

A200

Press Enter. Type the headings across row 200 from Figure 6-4.

Figure 6-4. Payroll Summary Database

	A	B	C	D	E	F	G	H	I	J	K	L
196					Combine payroll data from Paytemkp file							
197				Alt R	{goto}a201~ {end} {down} {down}/fccnpayroll~paytemp~							
198												
199												
200	EMP#	R Hr	OT	NAME	GROSS	FICA	W/H	DED1	DED2	DED3	NET	DATE
201	50	40	3	Jim West	$900.00	$67.59	$0.00	$7.40	$5.00	$0.00	$820.01	02/15/90
202	20	40	3	Joe First	$267.00	$20.05	$31.13	$3.40	$5.00	$0.00	$207.42	02/15/90
203	10	39		Sue Smith	$273.00	$20.50	$14.34	$3.40	$5.00	$0.00	$229.75	02/15/90
204	40	40	6	Sara Jones	$294.00	$22.08	$40.95	$2.50	$2.00	$0.00	$226.47	02/15/90
205	30	40		Sam Easy	$1,000.00	$0.00	$131.45	$6.00	$20.00	$0.00	$842.55	02/15/90
206	50	40	3	Jim West	$900.00	$67.59	$0.00	$7.40	$5.00	$0.00	$820.01	02/28/90
207	20	40	2	Joe First	$258.00	$19.38	$29.78	$3.40	$5.00	$0.00	$200.44	02/28/90
208	10	39		Sue Smith	$273.00	$20.50	$14.34	$3.40	$5.00	$0.00	$229.75	02/28/90
209	40	40	5	Sara Jones	$285.00	$21.40	$39.60	$2.50	$2.00	$0.00	$219.50	02/28/90
210	30	40		Sam Easy	$1,000.00	$0.00	$131.45	$6.00	$20.00	$0.00	$842.55	02/28/90
211	50	40	3	Jim West	$900.00	$67.59	$0.00	$7.40	$5.00	$0.00	$820.01	03/15/90
212	20	40	6	Joe First	$294.00	$22.08	$35.18	$3.40	$5.00	$0.00	$228.34	03/15/90
213	10	39	5	Sue Smith	$325.50	$24.45	$22.22	$3.40	$5.00	$0.00	$270.44	03/15/90
214	40	40	7	Sara Jones	$303.00	$22.76	$42.30	$2.50	$2.00	$0.00	$233.44	03/15/90
215	30	40		Sam Easy	$1,000.00	$0.00	$131.45	$6.00	$20.00	$0.00	$842.55	03/15/90
216	50	40		Jim West	$900.00	$67.59	$0.00	$7.40	$5.00	$0.00	$820.01	03/30/90
217	20	40	1	Joe First	$249.00	$18.70	$28.43	$3.40	$5.00	$0.00	$193.47	03/30/90
218	10	39	3	Sue Smith	$304.50	$22.87	$19.07	$3.40	$5.00	$0.00	$254.16	03/30/90
219	40	40	6	Sara Jones	$294.00	$22.08	$40.95	$2.50	$2.00	$0.00	$226.47	03/30/90
220	30	40		Sam Easy	$1,000.00	$0.00	$131.45	$6.00	$20.00	$0.00	$842.55	03/30/90
221	50	40	1	Jim West	$900.00	$67.59	$0.00	$7.40	$5.00	$0.00	$820.01	04/15/90
222	20	40	6	Joe First	$294.00	$22.08	$35.18	$3.40	$5.00	$0.00	$228.34	04/15/90

Decreasing the Column Width
/Worksheet Column Set-Width

Since columns A, B, and C must be shorter for employee numbers and hours, use the Set-Column Width command. Move to A200 and enter

/Worksheet Column Set-Width

Then respond to the prompt *Enter column width:* with

5

and press Enter. To decrease column B, move the cursor to B200 and enter

/Worksheet Column Set-Width

Then respond to the prompt *Enter column width:* with

5

and press Enter. To decrease column C, move the cursor to C200 and enter

/Worksheet Column Set-Width

Then respond to the prompt *Enter column width:* with

5

and press Enter.

Widening the Column
/Worksheet Column Set-Width

Since columns D, E and K must be wide enough to hold long balances, use the Set-Column Width command. To increase column E, move the cursor to E1 and enter

/Worksheet Column Set-Width

Then respond to the prompt *Enter column width:* with

11

and press Enter. To increase column K, move the cursor to K1 and enter

/Worksheet **C**olumn **S**et-Width

Then respond to the prompt *Enter column width:* with

11

and press Enter. Repeat these steps to widen column D to 15.

Retrieving the Data
/File Combine Copy Named/Specified Range

To bring in the payroll data from the Paytemp file created earlier, move to A201, enter

/File **C**ombine **C**opy **N**amed/Specified-Range

and respond to the prompt *Enter range name or address:* with

Payroll

Press Enter. Respond to the prompt *Name of file to combine:* with

Paytemp

and press Enter. Your data should match the headings in row 200 and look similar to Figure 6-4. To make enough data to work with, create a macro to simplify the steps above.

Entering a Macro

A *macro* is simply a range of cells on the spreadsheet that holds the keystrokes necessary to execute commands. You can create a macro to retrieve the payroll data from the temporary payroll file. Move the cursor to D197, type the heading

Alt R

and press Enter. Be sure to type the word *Alt* and letter *R—don't enter the Alt-R key combination.* Move the cursor to E196, type

Combine payroll data from Paytemp file

and press Enter. Move the cursor to E197, type

'{goto}A201˜{end}{down}{down}/fccnpayroll˜paytemp˜

and press Enter.

It's important to remember when entering a cell that begins with a bracket to precede it with a single quotation mark (') prefix.

To Create a Macro
/Range Name Create

You need to name each macro range before you execute it. To name the Alt-R macro, enter

/Range Name Create

and respond to the prompt *Enter name:* with

\R

Press Enter. Respond to the prompt *Enter range:* with

E197

and press Enter. Don't execute the macro now since there's no new data to save and the file paytemp has already been brought into this file.

To Create a Range Name
/Range Name Create

You need to name the database range of payroll data to simplify formulas later. To name the database, enter

/Range **N**ame **C**reate

and respond to the prompt *Enter name:* with

Summary

Press Enter. Respond to the prompt *Enter range:* with

A200.L500

and press Enter.

Saving the Spreadsheet
/File Save

To save the file, enter

/File **S**ave

1-2-3 will then ask for a filename; type

Paysum

and press Enter. If you saved the spreadsheet earlier, press Enter when the filename *Paysum* automatically displays. The software will check to see if you want to write over your previous file, so enter

Replace

to replace the file.

To Create Sample Data

The following steps will create some sample data for you to use:

/FR Pay21590	Retrieve the previous payroll calculation file. Change the date in cell F6. Change some overtime hours to create new gross and net amount.
Alt-X	Execute macro to save the payroll data to the temporary file.
/FR Paysum	Retrieve the payroll summary file.
Alt-R	Execute macro to move to the last record and retrieve the payroll data from the paytemp file.
/File **S**ave	Save-replace with new data. Repeat steps above.

Repeat these steps until you have at least four or five pay periods with different dates and gross amounts in the database section.

Saving the Worksheet with Replace
/File Save Replace

It's best to save the spreadsheet often. Enter

/File **S**ave

and press Enter when the filename *Paysum* automatically displays. The software will check to see if you want to write over your previous file, so enter

Replace

to replace the file.

Figure 6-5. Payroll Summary with Macros

	A	B	C	D	E	F	G	H	I	J
1					Payroll YTD and QTD Summary					
2										
3					YTD GROSS	QTD GROSS	YTD FICA	QTD FICA	YTD W/H	QTD W/H
4										
5										
6			10	Sue Smith	$1,774.50	$294.00	$133.26	$22.08	$106.53	$17.49
7			20	Joe First	$1,602.00	$249.00	$120.31	$18.70	$186.79	$28.43
8			30	Sam Easy	$6,000.00	$1,000.00	$0.00	$0.00	$788.68	$131.45
9			40	Sara Jones	$1,728.00	$303.00	$129.77	$22.76	$240.30	$42.30
10			50	Jim West	$6,000.00	$1,000.00	$405.54	$67.59	$0.00	$0.00
11										
12				Totals	$17,104.50	$2,846.00	$788.89	$131.12	$1,322.30	$219.67
13										
14										
15										
16					Printing Macros					
17	Emp#	Date		Alt E						
18	10	1		/pprA100.L132~omr135~s\015~qagq		Print Employee Earnings Record				
19	Emp#	Date								
20	20	1		Alt S						
21	Emp#	Date		/pprC1.J12~omr135~s\015~qagq		Print Payroll Summary				
22	30	1								
23	Emp#	Date		Alt D						
24	40	1		/pprA200.L300~omr135~s\015~qagq		Print Payroll Database				
25	Emp#	Date								
26	50	1								
27										

Creating the YTD and QTD Summary

Press the HOME key to return to the top of the spreadsheet. Move the cursor to D1, type

Payroll YTD and QTD Summary

and press Enter. Type the headings in row 3 from Figure 6-5 and enter the employee numbers and names in columns C and D, starting in row 6. Also type the heading *Emp#* and each employee number in column A starting at row 17. Move the cursor to B17, type

Date

and press Enter. Move the cursor to B18, type

+L201>@DATE(90,4,1)

and press Enter.

The display in B18 will either be a 0 or 1. This cell will be a criterion cell for all payrolls in the second quarter. If the date of payroll is after 4/1/90 then totals will appear in the QTD columns in the summary above. As each quarter ends, you'll need to edit these cells to change the date to the first day of the current quarter:

• 1/1/YY
• 4/1/YY
• 7/1/YY
• 10/1/YY

All payrolls will total in the YTD columns since this cell won't be in the criteria range of the formula. Enter the heading, Date, and the formula in B18 into the remaining cells in column B through row 26.

Widening the Column
/Worksheet Column Set-Width

Since columns D through J must be wide enough to hold names and balances, use the Set-Column Width command. To increase column D, move the cursor to D1 and enter

/Worksheet Column Set-Width

Then respond to the prompt *Enter column width:* with

11

and press Enter. Repeat these steps and widen columns E through J.

Entering Formulas

The following formulas use the @DSUM function to accumulate YTD and QTD formulas. Enter the formulas into the following cells and press Enter:

E6   @DSUM($SUMMARY,4,A17.A18)
F6   @DSUM($SUMMARY,4,A17.B18)
G6   @DSUM($SUMMARY,5,A17.A18)
H6   @DSUM($SUMMARY,5,A17.B18)
I6   @DSUM($SUMMARY,6,A17.A18)
J6   @DSUM($SUMMARY,6,A17.B18)

The formula in E6 means to sum the fourth column of the database named SUMMARY for the employee number in cells A17 and A18. The formula in E7 is the same except the criteria range is extended to include B17 and B18. This narrows the database sum to the payrolls for employee number 10 after 4/1/90.

Copying Formulas
/Copy

Copy the formulas in row 6 down to eliminate the need for entering the formulas again. To copy, enter

/Copy

and respond to the prompt *Enter range to copy FROM:* with

E6. .J6

Press Enter. Respond to the prompt *Enter range to copy TO:* with

E7.J10

and press Enter.

Move the cursor to E7 and you'll see that the formula reads *@DSUM($SUMMARY,4,A18.A19)* instead of *@DSUM($SUMMARY,4, A19.A20)*. This is because the copy command copies cells relative to their new destination. Since you only copied one row down, the criteria range was adjusted just one row. To correct this problem, use the F2 key to edit the criteria range of the formula in cells D7 through J10 to the following criteria ranges:

E7,G7,I7	,A19.A20)
F7,H7,J7	,A19.B20)
E8,G8,I8	,A21.A22)
F8,H8,J8	,A21.B22)
E9,G9,I9	,A23.A24)
F9,H9,J9	,A23,B24)
E10,G10,I10	,A25.A26)
F10,H10,J10	,A25.B26)

Saving the Worksheet with Replace
/File Save Replace

It's best to save the spreadsheet often. Enter

/File Save

and press Enter when the filename *Paysum* automatically displays.
The software will check to see if you want to write over your previous file, so enter

Replace

to replace the file.

Entering Totals

To enter the formula for the totals on row 12, move the cursor to
D12, type

Totals

and press Enter. Move the cursor to E12, type

@SUM(E6.E10)

and press Enter.

Copying Formulas
/Copy

Copy the formula in cell E12 across the row to eliminate the need
for entering the formula again. To copy, enter

/Copy

and respond to the prompt *Enter range to copy FROM:* with

E12

Press Enter. Respond to the prompt *Enter range to copy TO:* with

F12.J12

and press Enter.

Formatting the Spreadsheet to Currency
/Range Format Currency

Before printing the summary, format some of the columns to currency. Use the Range command instead of the Worksheet Global Format command. Enter

/Range Format Currency

and respond to the prompt *Enter number of decimal places:* with

2

Press Enter. Respond to the prompt *Enter range to format:* with

E6.J12

and press Enter.

Printing the Spreadsheet
/Print Printer Range Align Go Quit

To print the payroll summary, enter

/Print Printer Range

and respond to the prompt *Enter print range:* with

C1.J12

Press Enter. To begin the printing job, enter

Align Go Quit

This spreadsheet is too wide to print on most 80-column printers without going to a second page. If you have a condensed print switch available on your printer, set it to condensed and from the print menu enter

Options Margins Right

for options, margins, right. Then enter

135

for the new right margin.

If your printer doesn't have a switch but accepts a condensed print code, enter from the options menu

Setup

for the setup string. For Epson printers, the string for condensed is ＼*015*. Look in the *Lotus 1-2-3* appendix for your specific printer code.

To quit the options menu, enter

Quit

and then enter

Align **G**o **Q**uit

to start the print job. To print the employee database, enter

/Print **P**rinter **R**ange

and respond to the prompt *Enter print range:* with

Summary

Press Enter. To begin the printing job, enter

Align **G**o **Q**uit

This spreadsheet is also too wide to print on most 80-column printers. Use the instructions above to print in condensed mode.

Saving the Worksheet with Replace
/File Save Replace

To save the spreadsheet with the print instructions, enter

/File **S**ave

and press Enter when the filename *Paysum* automatically displays.

The software will check to see if you want to write over your previous file, so enter

Replace

to replace the file.

Figure 6-6. Employee Earnings Record

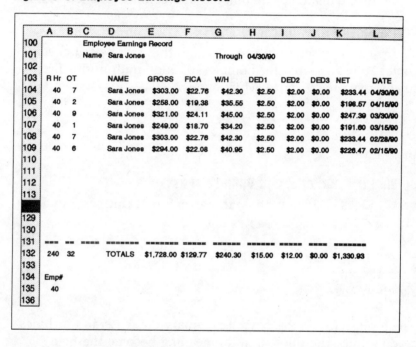

	A	B	C	D	E	F	G	H	I	J	K	L
100				Employee Earnings Record								
101			Name	Sara Jones			Through 04/30/90					
102												
103	R Hr	OT		NAME	GROSS	FICA	W/H	DED1	DED2	DED3	NET	DATE
104	40	7		Sara Jones	$303.00	$22.76	$42.30	$2.50	$2.00	$0.00	$233.44	04/30/90
105	40	2		Sara Jones	$258.00	$19.38	$35.55	$2.50	$2.00	$0.00	$198.57	04/15/90
106	40	9		Sara Jones	$321.00	$24.11	$45.00	$2.50	$2.00	$0.00	$247.39	03/30/90
107	40	1		Sara Jones	$249.00	$18.70	$34.20	$2.50	$2.00	$0.00	$191.60	03/15/90
108	40	7		Sara Jones	$303.00	$22.76	$42.30	$2.50	$2.00	$0.00	$233.44	02/28/90
109	40	6		Sara Jones	$294.00	$22.08	$40.95	$2.50	$2.00	$0.00	$226.47	02/15/90
110												
111												
112												
113												
129												
130												
131	====	==	====	=======	=======	=====	======	======	=====	====	=======	
132	240	32		TOTALS	$1,728.00	$129.77	$240.30	$15.00	$12.00	$0.00	$1,330.93	
133												
134	Emp#											
135	40											
136												

The Employee Earnings Record

The employee earnings record section of the database can produce many different searches by changing the criterion. The following instructions will print all payroll for employee number 10. To move to an unused portion of the spreadsheet, press the F5 function key and respond to the prompt *Enter address to go to:* with

A100

Press Enter. Move the cursor to C100, type

Employee Earnings Record

and press Enter. Type the following headings and press Enter:

C101   Name
G101   Through
A134   Emp#

Carefully type the headings in row 103 from Figure 6-6. They must match the corresponding headings in the database section in row 200. Some of the headings are omitted and column C is left blank.

Entering the Employee Number to Search

Cell A135 will hold the Employee number that will be searched each time. You can search for number 10, Sue Smith in this first example. Move the cursor to A135, enter

10

and press Enter.

Setting the Input, Criteria, and Output Ranges

You need to let *1-2-3* know three things before it can perform a search:

• The input range
• The criteria range
• The output range

The input range is the payroll summary database and includes the heading line. The titles from the heading become the field names. When performing a search, it's easy to forget to include this line in the input, criteria, and output ranges.

The criteria range is the field name, Emp#, and any employee number for which you want to search.

The output range is where you want the result of the search to display. Again, the output range must include the heading line that becomes the field names.

To initiate the search, enter

/Data Query Input

and respond to the prompt *Enter Input range:* with

Summary

Press Enter. Enter

Criteria

and respond to the prompt *Enter Criteria range:* with

A134.D135

and press Enter. Enter

Output

and respond to the prompt *Enter Output range:* with

A103.L130

and press Enter. Enter

Extract Quit

to begin the search. Press the PageUp key. All payroll data for employee number 10 are listed in the output range of A103 through L130.

Using the Query Key
F7

Use the F7 function key any time you change the employee for whom you want to search. Search for employee number 40 next. Move the cursor to A135, type

40

and press Enter. You don't need to enter the input, criteria, and output ranges again. Press F7 and the search will restart. Press the PageUp key and Sara Jones' payroll is displayed. To add additional criterion to limit the search, add a field name and criterion next to the employee number. Move the cursor to B134, enter

DATE

and press Enter. Move the cursor to B135, enter

+L201>@DATE(90,4,1)

and press Enter. Press the F7 key and the search will restart. Now only payroll data for dates later than 4/1/90 for employee number 40 will display.

    If you want only payroll data for periods that contain more than five hours of overtime, then move the cursor to C134, type

OT

and press Enter. Move the cursor to C135, type

+C201>5

and press Enter. Press F7 and the search will restart. Now only payroll data for employee number 40 from this quarter that includes more than five hours of overtime will print.

    If you want to review all employees who have over five hours of overtime for the quarter, use the Range Erase /RE command to erase cell A135 and press F7 again.

Entering Totals

To enter the formula for the totals on row 132, move the cursor to A132, enter

@SUM(A104.A130)

and press Enter.

Entering the Repeating Underline

\ =

Cell A131 contains a double underline created with the equal sign. To enter the repeating underline, move the cursor to A131 and enter

\ =

Copying Formulas and Underline
/Copy

Copy the formulas in cells A131 and A132 across the row to eliminate the need for entering the formulas again. To copy, enter

/Copy

and respond to the prompt *Enter range to copy FROM:* with

A131.A132

Press Enter. Respond to the prompt *Enter range to copy TO:* with

B131.K132

and press Enter. Move the cursor to D132, type

Totals

and press Enter.

Entering Name and Date Formula

Move the cursor to D101, type

+D104

and press Enter. Move the cursor to H101, type

@DMAX(Summary,11,A134.D135)

and press Enter. This formula finds the maximum date in the database, based on your search criterion.

Formatting the Spreadsheet
/Range Format

You need to format row 132 of columns E through K to currency. Since you only want this row in these columns to be in currency, use the Range command instead of the Worksheet Global Format command. Enter

/Range Format Currency

and respond to the prompt *Enter number of decimal places:* with

2

Press Enter. Respond to the prompt *Enter range to format:* with

E132.K132

and press Enter. To format the date, enter

/Range Format Date 4

and respond to the prompt *Enter range to format:* with

H101

Press Enter.

Saving the Worksheet with Replace
/File Save Replace

Save the spreadsheet, now that it contains the search information. Enter

/File Save

and press Enter when the filename *Paysum* automatically displays. The software will check to see if you want to write over your previous file, so enter

Replace

to replace the file.

Printing the Worksheet
/Print Printer Range Align Go Quit

To print the employee earnings record, enter

/Print Printer Range

and respond to the prompt *Enter print range:* with

A100.L132

Press Enter. To begin the printing job, enter

Align Go Quit

This spreadsheet is too wide to print on most 80-column print-ers without going to a second page. If you have a condensed print switch available on your printer, set it to condensed and from the print menu enter

Options Margin Right

Enter

135

for the new right margin. If your printer doesn't have a switch but accepts a condensed print code, from the options menu enter

Setup

for the setup string. For Epson printers, the string for condensed is \ *015*. Look in the *Lotus 1-2-3* appendix for your specific printer code. Enter

Quit

to quit the options menu; then to start the print job, enter

Align Go Quit

Entering Macros to Print Reports

Each time you save the spreadsheet only the latest printing instructions are saved. To print the payroll summary, you have to enter the range again since only the range for the employee earnings report is now saved. You can save the printing instructions in macros, which you execute with the combination of the Alt key and a letter. A *macro* is simply a range of cells on the spreadsheet that holds the keystrokes necessary to execute commands. You can create three macros to print the following reports:

Alt-E   Employee Earnings Record
Alt-S   Payroll Summary
Alt-D   Payroll Database

To move to an unused portion of the spreadsheet, press the F5 function key and respond to the prompt *Enter address to go to:* with

E16

Press Enter. Type the heading

Printing Macros

and press Enter. Move the cursor to D17, type

Alt E

and press Enter. Be sure to type the word *Alt* and letter *E—don't enter the Alt-E key combination.* Move to D18, type

'/pprA100.L132~OMR135~S \ 015~qagq

and press Enter. When entering a macro that begins with a slash, precede it with single quote (') prefix. Move the cursor to G18, type

Print employee earnings record

and press Enter. Enter the remaining macros and titles from Figure 6-5.

To Create a Macro
/Range Name Create

You need to name each macro range before you can execute it. To name the employee earnings record printing macros, enter

/Range Name Create

and respond to the prompt *Enter name:* with

\E

Press Enter. Respond to the prompt *Enter range:* with

D18

and press Enter. Repeat for the other two macros:

Name	Range
\S	D21
\D	D24

To execute the employee earnings record print macro, hold down the Alt key and simultaneously press the letter *E*. The macro will execute the Print Printer Range command. The range A100 through L132 is typed after the prompt to enter the print range, and the tilde symbol (~) activates the Enter key. Next the macro adjusts the margins and issues an Epson condensed print code. Finally it executes the Align, Go, and Quit commands. You'll need to adjust the range in the Alt-D macro as the summary database grows.

Saving the Worksheet with Replace
/File Save Replace

After printing the statement, now save this spreadsheet one more time to keep the macro instructions in the file. Enter

/File Save

and press Enter when the filename *Paysum* automatically displays.

The software will check to see if you want to write over your previous file, so enter

Replace

to replace the file.

Getting the Files Ready for Your Payroll

To get the Paycalc file you created in this chapter ready for your payroll, enter your employees into the employee table (BA3) and enter this payroll period's date (F6), the employees' hours, and overtime hours (A11). In the Paysum file, use the Range Erase command to erase A201.L250 in the database section. Go to C6 and enter your employee numbers and names in cells C6 through D10. In cells A17 through B26, enter your criterion date for this quarter and your employee numbers.

If you want to enter previous quarter totals, enter a total for each employee starting in cell A201. Use a quarter ending date such as 3/31/90 for the quarter total. If you need to adjust the files to hold more employees, use the Worksheet Insert Row command. Be sure to copy formulas into the new rows and format any additional cells.

The first time an employee exceeds the FICA maximum or needs a special amount of income tax withheld, you'll need to manually insert the FICA or Federal W/H amount. To override the normal deductions, disable the protection and enter the amount for the employee in columns F and G.

Complete the payroll and save the data to the summary database. Copy the formula back into the cell from the row above the changed cell and enable the protection.

Figure 6-7. Multiple 3-D Spreadsheets

Sheet D

D	A	B	C	D	E
1			Employee Earnings Record		
2			Name	Sara Jones	
3					
4	R Hr	OT		NAME	GROSS
5	40	5		Sara Jones	$285.00
6	40	4		Sara Jones	$276.00
7	40	3		Sara Jones	$267.00

Sheet C

C	A	B	C	D	E	F
1				Payroll YTD and QTD Summary		
2						
3					YTD GROSS	QTD GROSS
4						
5						
6			10	Sue Smith	$0.00	$0.00
7			20	Joe First	$0.00	$0.00

Sheet B

B	A	B	C	D	E	F	G
5							
6				Payroll Database			
7							
8							
9	Emp#	R Hr	OT	Name	Gross	FICA	Fed W/H
10	10	40	3	Sue Smith	$311.50	$23.39	$20.12
11	20	40	3	Joe First	$267.00	$20.05	$31.13
12	30	40		Sam Easy	$1,000.00	$0.00	$131.45
13	50	40		Jim West	$900.00	$67.59	$0.00

Sheet A

A	A	B	C	D	E	F	G	I
1				KEY:	SHEET A	PAYROLL CALCULATE/REGISTER		
2					SHEET B	DATABASE HOLDING PREVIOUS PAYROLL DATA		
3					SHEET C	YTD AND QTD SUMMARY		
4					SHEET D	EMPLOYEE EARNINGS RECORD		
5			Easy Company		Payroll ending date			
6			Payroll Register		4/30/90			
7								
8								
9	Emp#	R Hr	OT	Name	Gross	FICA	Fed W/H	Ded 1
10								
11	10	40	1	Sue Smit	$290.50	$21.82	$16.97	$3.40
12	20	40	6	Joe First	$294.00	$22.08	$35.18	$3.40

289

Creating the Payroll Summary with Release 3

You can keep the summary data in the separate worksheet in the same file with Release 3. Retrieve the Paycalc file and open three new worksheets behind the payroll calculation worksheet. Enter

/Worksheet Insert Sheet After 3

and press Enter. The paycalc worksheet will be sheet A and the summary will be sheet B. Sheet C will contain the QTD and YTD totals and sheet D the employee earnings record.

To view three of these as shown in Figure 6-7, enter

/Worksheet Window Perspective

and press Ctrl-PageDown and Ctrl-PageUp to move between the worksheets.

To change the column widths in sheets B, C, and D to match A, move the cursor to sheet A with the Ctrl-PageDown, enter

/Worksheet Global Group Enable

and the group command will make all the sheets in the file match sheet A.

To copy the headings in sheet A to sheet B, enter

/Copy

and respond to the prompt *Enter range to copy FROM:* with

A:A9.A:L9

and press Enter. Respond to the prompt *Enter range to copy TO:* with

B:A9

and press Enter.

Entering a Macro

A *macro* is simply a range of cells on the spreadsheet that holds the keystrokes necessary to execute commands. You can create a macro to post payroll data from sheet A to sheet B. Move the cursor to A:A20 and type the heading

Alt S

Be sure to type the word *Alt* and the letter *S—don't press the Alt-S key combination.* Move the cursor to A:F20, type

Save payroll data to summary sheet B

and press Enter. Move the cursor to A:C20, type

'{appendbelow summary, payroll}

press Enter. Appendbelow is a new macro for Release 3 only. The macro will append or add to the records in the summary range with the information in the payroll range.

To Create a Macro
/Range Name Create

You need to name each macro range before you can execute it. To name the Alt-S macro, enter

/Range Name Create

and respond to the prompt *Enter name:* with

\ S

Press Enter. Respond to the prompt *Enter range:* with

A:C20

and press Enter. Don't execute the macro now since there's no new data to save and you need to name the data range.

To Create a Range Name
/Range Name Create

You need to name the database range of payroll data. To name the database, enter

/Range Name Create

and respond to the prompt *Enter name:* with

Summary

Press Enter. Respond to the prompt *Enter range:* with

B:A9.B:L9

and press Enter.

Saving the Spreadsheet
/File Save

To save the file, enter

/File Save

1-2-3 will then ask for a filename; type

Paysum

and press Enter. You saved the spreadsheet earlier under the name *Paycalc,* but it's best to have two files for now. Paycalc will be your backup file if you have some difficulty with this release of *1-2-3.* When you save a file with multiple worksheets, all sheets are saved in the same file.

To Create Sample Data

The following steps will create some sample data for you to work with:

- Change the date in cell F6. Change some overtime hours to create new gross and net amounts.
- Execute Alt-S macro to save the payroll data to sheet B.

Repeat these steps until you have at least four or five pay periods with different dates and gross amounts in the database section.

Saving the Worksheet with Replace
/File Save Replace

It's best to save the spreadsheet often. Enter

/File Save

and press Enter when the filename *Paysum* automatically displays. The software will check to see if you want to write over your previous file, so enter

Replace

to replace the file.

Creating the YTD and QTD Summary

Press the Ctrl-PageUp key until you're on sheet C. Move the cursor to D1, type

Payroll YTD and QTD Summary

and press Enter. Type the headings in row 3 from Figure 6-5 and enter the employee numbers and names in columns C and D. Also type the heading *Emp#* and each employee number in column A starting at row 17. Move the cursor to C:B17, type

Date

and press Enter.
    Move the cursor to C:B18, type

+B:L10>@DATE(90,4,1)

and press Enter. The display in C:B18 will either be a 0 or 1. This cell will be a criterion cell for all payrolls in the second quarter. If the date of payroll is after 4/1/90, then it will total in the QTD columns in the summary above. As each quarter ends you'll need to edit these cells to change the date to the first day of the current quarter:

• 1/1/YY
• 4/1/YY
• 7/1/YY
• 10/1/YY

All payrolls will total in the YTD columns since this cell won't be in the criterion range of the formula. Enter the heading *Date* and the above formula into the remaining cells in column B through row 26.

Turning the Group Command Off

This worksheet will have different column widths. To turn off the group formatting, enter

/Worksheet **G**lobal **G**roup **D**isable

Widening the Column
/Worksheet Column Column-Range Set-Width

Since columns E through J of sheet C must be wide enough to hold long balances, use the Set-Column Range command. To increase a range of columns, enter

/Worksheet **C**olumn **C**olumn-Range **S**et-Width

then respond to the prompt *Enter range for column-width change:* with

E1.J1

Press Enter. Respond to the prompt *Enter column width:* with

11

and press Enter.

Entering Formulas

The following formulas use the @DSUM function to accumulate YTD and QTD formulas. Enter these formulas in the following cells and press Enter:

```
E6    @DSUM($SUMMARY,4,C:A17.C:A18)
F6    @DSUM($SUMMARY,4,C:A17.C:B18)
G6    @DSUM($SUMMARY,5,C:A17.C:A18)
H6    @DSUM($SUMMARY,5,C:A17.C:B18)
I6    @DSUM($SUMMARY,6,C:A17.C:A18)
J6    @DSUM($SUMMARY,6,C:A17.C:B18)
```

The formula in D6 sums the fourth column of the database named SUMMARY for the employee number in cells A17 and A18. The formula in E7 is the same, except the criteria range is extended to include B17 and B18. This narrows the database sum to the payrolls for employee number 10 after 4/1/90.

Copying Formulas
/Copy

Copy the formulas in row 6 down to eliminate the need for entering the formulas again. To copy, enter

/Copy

and respond to the prompt *Enter range to copy FROM:* with

E6.J6

Press Enter. Respond to the prompt *Enter range to copy TO:* with

E7.J10

and press Enter. Move the cursor to E7 and you'll see that the formula reads *@DSUM($SUMMARY,4,A18.A19)* instead of *@DSUM ($SUMMARY,4,A19.A20)*. This is because the copy command copies cells relative to their new destination. Since you only copied one row down, the criterion range was adjusted by just one row.

To correct this problem, use the F2 key to edit the criteria range of the formula in cells D7 through J10 to the following criteria ranges:

E7,G7,I7	,A19.A20)
F7,H7,J7	,A19.B20)
E8,G8,I8	,A21.A22)
F8,H8,J8	,A21.B22)
E9,G9,I9	,A23.A24)
F9,H9,J9	,A23.B24)
E10,G10,I10	,A25.A26)
F10,H10,J10	,A25.B26)

Saving the Worksheet with Replace
/File Save Replace

It's best to save the spreadsheet often. Enter

/File Save

and press Enter when the filename *Paysum* automatically displays. The software will check to see if you want to write over your previous file, so enter

Replace

to replace the file.

Entering Totals

To enter the formula for the totals on row 12, move the cursor to D12, type

Totals

and press Enter. Move the cursor to E12, type

@SUM(E6.E10)

and press Enter.

Copying Formulas
/Copy

Copy the formula in cell E12 across the row to eliminate the need for entering the formula again. To copy, enter

/Copy

and respond to the prompt *Enter range to copy FROM:* with

E12

Press Enter. Respond to the prompt *Enter range to copy TO:* with

F12.J12

and press Enter.

Formatting the Spreadsheet to Currency
/Range Format Currency

Before printing the summary you need to format some of the columns to currency. Use the Range command instead of the Worksheet Global Format command. Enter

/Range Format Currency

and respond to the prompt *Enter number of decimal places:* with

2

Press Enter. Respond to the prompt *Enter range to format:* with

E6.J12

and press Enter.

Printing the Spreadsheet
/Print Printer Range Align Go Quit

To print the payroll summary, enter

/Print Printer Range

and respond to the prompt *Enter print range:* with

A1.J12

Press Enter. To begin the printing job, enter

Align Go Quit

This spreadsheet is too wide to print on most 80 column printers without going to a second page. If you have a condensed print
switch available on your printer, set it to condensed and from the
print menu enter

Options Margins Right

for options, margins, right. Enter

135

for the new right margin. If your printer doesn't have a switch but
accepts a condensed print code, enter from the options menu

Setup

for the setup string. For Epson printers, the string for condensed is
\ *015*. Look in the *Lotus 1-2-3* appendix for your specific printer
code.

To quit the options menu, enter

Quit

Then to start the print job, enter

Align Go Quit

To print the employee database, enter

/Print **P**rinter **R**ange

and respond to the prompt *Enter print range:* with

Summary

Press Enter. To begin the printing job, enter

Align **G**o **Q**uit

This spreadsheet is also too wide to print on most 80-column printers. Use the condensed instructions above to print.

The Employee Earnings Record

The employee earnings record section of the database can produce many different searches by changing the criterion. The following instructions will print all payroll for employee number 10. To move to sheet D, press the F5 function key and respond to the prompt *Enter address to go to:* with

D:A1

Press Enter. Move the cursor to C1, type,

Employee Earnings Record

and press Enter. Type the following headings and then press Enter:

C2   Name
G2   Through
A34   Emp#

Carefully type the headings in row 4 from Figure 6-6 using row 103 from the figure. They must match the corresponding headings in the database section in sheet B. Some of the headings are omitted.

Entering the Employee Number to Search

Cell A35 will hold the Employee number that will be searched each time. You can search for number 10, Sue Smith, in this first example. Move the cursor to A35, enter

10

and press Enter.

Setting the Input, Criterion, and Output Ranges

You need to let *1-2-3* know three things before it can perform a search:

• The input range
• The criteria range
• The output range

The input range is the payroll summary database and includes the heading line. The titles from the heading become the field names. When performing a search, it's easy to forget to include this line in the input, criteria, and output ranges.

The criteria range is the field name Emp# and any employee number for which you want to search.

The output range is where you want the result of the search to list or the employee earnings record. Again, the output range must include the heading line that becomes the field names. To initiate the search, enter

/**D**ata **Q**uery **I**nput

and respond to the prompt *Enter Input range:* with

Summary

Press Enter. Enter

Criteria

and respond to the prompt *Enter Criterion range:* with

A34.D35

Press Enter. Enter

Output

and respond to the prompt **Enter Output range:** with

A4.L30

Press Enter. To begin the search, enter

Extract Quit

All payroll data lines for employee number 10 are listed in the range of A4 through K30.

Using the Query Key
F7

Use the F7 function key any time you change the employee for whom you want to search. Search for employee number 40 next. Move the cursor to A35, type

40

and press Enter. You don't need to enter the input, criterion, and output ranges again. Press F7 and the search will restart. To add additional criterion to limit the search, add a field name and criterion next to the employee number. Move the cursor to B34, enter

Date

and press Enter. Move to cursor to B35, enter

+B:L10>@DATE(90,4,1)

and press Enter. Press F7 and the search will restart. Now only payroll data for dates later than 4/1/90 for employee number 40 will display.

If you want only payroll data for periods that contain more than 5 hours of overtime, move the cursor to C34, type

OT

and press Enter. Move the cursor to C35, type

+B:C10>5

and press Enter. Press F7 and the search will start again. Now only payroll data for employee number 40 for this quarter that has more than five hours of overtime will print.

If you want all employees who have over five hours of over-time for the quarter, use the Range Erase /RE command to erase cell A35 and press F7 again.

Entering Totals

To enter the formula for the totals on row 32, move the cursor to A32, enter

@SUM(A5.A30)

and press Enter.

Entering the Repeating Underline
\ =

Cell A31 contains a double underline created with the equal sign. To enter the repeating underline, move the cursor to A31 and enter

\ =

Copying Formulas and Underline
/Copy

Copy the formulas in cells A31 and A32 across the row to elimi-nate the need for entering the formulas again. To copy, enter

/Copy

and respond to the prompt *Enter range to copy FROM:* with

A31.A32

Press Enter. Respond to the prompt *Enter range to copy TO:* with

B31.K32

and press Enter. Move the cursor to C32, type

Totals

and press Enter.

Entering Name and Date Formula
Move the cursor to D2, type

+D5

and press Enter. Move the cursor to H21, type

@DMAX(Summary,11,A34.D35)

and press Enter. This formula finds the maximum date in the database based on your search criterion.

Formatting the Spreadsheet
/Range Format
You need to format row 32 of columns E through K to currency. Since you only want these columns to be in currency, use the Range command instead of the Worksheet Global Format command. Enter

/Range Format Currency

and respond to the prompt *Enter number of decimal places:* with

2

Press Enter. Respond to the prompt *Enter range to format:* with

E32.K32

and press Enter. To format the date, enter

/Range Format Date 4

and respond to the prompt *Enter range to format:* with

H2

Press Enter.

Saving the Worksheet with Replace
/File Save Replace

Save the spreadsheet now that it contains the search information. Enter

/File Save

and press Enter when the filename *Paysum* automatically displays. The software will check to see if you want to write over your previous file, so enter

Replace

to replace the file.

Printing the Worksheet
/Print Printer Range Align Go Quit

To print the employee earnings record, enter

/Print Printer Range

and respond to the prompt *Enter print range:* with

A1.L32

Press Enter. To begin the printing job, enter

Align Go Quit

This spreadsheet is too wide to print on most 80-column printers without going to a second page. If you have a condensed print switch available on your printer, set it to condensed and from the print menu enter

Options **M**argins **R**ight

for options, margins, right. Enter

135

for the new right margin. If your printer doesn't have a switch but accepts a condensed print code, enter from the options menu

Setup

for the setup string. For Epson printers, the string for condensed is \ *015*. Look in the *Lotus 1-2-3* appendix for your specific printer code. Enter

Quit

to quit the options menu. Then to start the print job, enter

Align **G**o **Q**uit

Entering Macros to Print Reports

Each time you save the spreadsheet only the latest printing instructions are saved. To print the payroll summary, you have to enter the range again since only the range for the employee earnings report is now saved. You can save the printing instructions in macros, which you execute with the combination of the Alt key and a letter. A *macro* is simply a range of cells on the spreadsheet that holds the keystrokes necessary to execute commands. You can create three macros to print the following reports:

Alt-E   Employee Earnings Record
Alt-S   Payroll Summary
Alt-D   Payroll Database

To move to an unused portion of the spreadsheet, press the F5 function key, respond to the prompt *Enter address to go to:* with

C:E16

and press Enter. Type the heading

Printing Macros

and press Enter. Move the cursor to D17, type

Alt E

and press Enter. Be sure to type the word *Alt* and letter *E—don't press the Alt-E key combination.* Move to D18, type

'/pprD:A1.D:L32~OMR135 ~S \015~qagq

and press Enter.

When entering a macro that begins with a slash, precede it with a single quote (') prefix. Move the cursor to the following cells, type these entries, and press Enter:

C:G18   Print employee earnings record
C:D20   Alt S
C:D21   '/pprc:c1.c:j12~omr135~s \015~qagq
C:G21   Print Payroll Summary
C:D23   Alt D
C:D24   '/pprb:a1.b:L200~omr135~s \015~qagq
C:G24   Print Payroll Database

The macros are similar to the ones shown in Figure 6-5 earlier in the chapter, but adjusted for the 3-D spreadsheet locations. You'll need to adjust the range in the Alt-D macro as your summary database grows.

To Create a Macro
/Range Name Create

You need to name each macro range before you can execute it. To name the employee earnings record printing macros, enter

/Range Name Create

and respond to the prompt *Enter name:* with

\E

Press Enter. Respond to the prompt *Enter range:* with

D18

and press Enter. Repeat for the other two macros:

Name   Range
\S   D21
\D   D24

To execute the employee earnings record print macro, hold down the Alt key and simultaneously press the letter *E*. The macro will execute the Print Printer Range command. The range A1 through L32 is typed after the prompt to enter the print range, and the tilde symbol (˜) activates the Enter key. Next the macro adjusts the margins and issues an Epson condensed print code. Finally it executes the Align, Go, and Quit commands.

Saving the Worksheet with Replace
/File Save Replace

After printing the statement, save the spreadsheet one more time to keep the macro instructions in the file. Enter

/File Save

and press Enter when the filename *Paysum* automatically displays. The software will check to see if you want to write over your previous file, so enter

Replace

to replace the file.

Getting the Files Ready for Your Payroll

To get the Paysum file ready for your payroll, move to sheet A; enter your employees in the employee table and enter this payroll period's date, the employees' hours, and overtime hours. In sheet B use the Range Erase command to erase A10.L200 in the database section. If you want to enter previous quarter totals, enter a total for each employee in sheet B starting in cell A10. Use a quarter ending date such as 3/31/90 for the quarter total. Go to sheet C and enter your employee numbers and names in cells C6 through D10. In cells A17 through B26, enter your criterion date for this quarter and your employee numbers. If you need to adjust the files to hold more employees, use the Worksheet Insert Row command. Be sure to copy formulas into the new rows and format any added cells.

7
Other Management Applications

In this chapter, you can create spreadsheets that are helpful in managing your business. Each one will provide you with different reports or analyses for your business. From the various spreadsheets, you'll be able to produce:

• Tax Estimator for Tax Planning
• Loan Amortization
• Breakeven Analysis
• Forecasted Volume Profit Analysis
• Graphs of Breakeven and Profit Analysis
• Graphs and Profit Analysis with Allways (2.2 only)

The Tax Estimator

The basic tax estimator allows you to enter income, adjustments to income, credits, and taxes. The net tax due or refund is calculated at the bottom of the screen. This basic tax estimator might be all you need, but if you want to add the tax tables to calculate taxes, continue through all the instructions. You can update the tax tables for any year the tax rate changes. Since the tax recalculates after each entry, this spreadsheet is ideal for tax planning.

Creating the Tax Estimator

What follows is a brief review of the material from Chapter 2. If you're a *1-2-3* newcomer, you should read Chapter 2. Bring up the spreadsheet screen by typing *123* at the DOS prompt. The startup screen will have columns lettered A–H across the top of the screen and numbers for the rows going down the left side. The intersection of these columns and rows are called *cells*, where information is stored. For example, cell B4 is the intersection of the second column over (B) and the fourth row down (4). Cell D3 is the intersection of the fourth column over (D) and the third row down (3). The cursor will start in cell A1 and you can move it down or across with the arrow keys. What you type on the keyboard will appear on the line above the columns. It will move into the cell on which the cursor is resting when you press the Enter key.

Figure 7-1. Tax Estimator

	A	B	C
1	Tax Estimator for Tax Planning		
2			
3	Number of exemptions	3	
4	M for Married S for Single	M	
5			
6	Income		
7	Wages	$61,360.00	
8	Interest & Taxable Dividends	$130.00	
9	State/Local tax refunds		
10	Alimony		
11	Business Income		
12	Capital Gains/other gains	$3,472.00	
13	Taxable IRA,pensions		
14	Rents,royalities,partnerships,etc.		
15	Farm income		
16	Unemploy.,taxable social security		
17	Other income		
18	Total Income.................		$64,962.00
19			
20	Adjustments		
21	Reimbursed employee business exp.		
22	IRA deductions	$2,000.00	
23	Self-employed health insurance		
24	Keogh, SEP		
25	Penalty on savings withdrawal		
26	Alimony paid		
27	Total Adjustments............		$2,000.00
28			
29	Adjusted Gross Income		$62,962.00
30	Itemized Deductions	$2,642.00	
31	Standard Deduction		$5,200.00
32	Exemptions		$6,000.00
33	Taxable Income		$51,762.00
34	Tax	$10,289.86	$10,289.86
35			
36	Credits		
37	Other Taxes Due		
38			
39	Federal Income tax withheld	$9,880.00	
40	Estimated Tax Payments		
41			
42	Tax due (Refund)		$409.86
43			=========

Entering a Menu Command

When you press the slash key (/), different menu options such as Worksheet, Range, Copy, File, Print, Graph, Data, System, and Quit appear across the top of the screen. To select a command, press the first letter of the option, then the first letter of the next submenu item until you've finished. You can also select a menu item by moving the right- and left-arrow keys until the option is highlighted and then pressing Enter. All the instructions in this chapter will be done by entering the first letter.

Cancel or Erase
Esc

The Esc key normally cancels a command and takes you back to the previous menu or status. If you make an error and want to erase what you've typed so far, press the Esc key. If you've already pressed the Enter key and want to erase the contents of a cell, move the cursor to the cell you want to clear. Enter

/Range Erase

and press Enter to accept the range as the current cell.

Moving the Cursor

Use the arrow keys to move from cell to cell. Other helpful keys to know are:

F5 (Goto)	Moves to any cell location
Home	Moves to upper left corner (A1)
PageUp	Moves up one page
PageDown	Moves down one page

Quitting and Saving the Spreadsheet

If you need to quit before completing the spreadsheet and want to save the file, enter

/File Save

1-2-3 will then ask for a filename; type

TaxEst

and press Enter. A filename can be up to eight characters, but you should stick to letters and numbers. Don't include any symbols such as + = . * / ? (> % or leave any blank spaces. To quit without saving, enter

/Quit Yes

and you should be back at the DOS prompt. Just enter *123* to return to the spreadsheet.

Widening the Column
/Worksheet Column Set-Width

Since column A must be wide enough to hold long descriptions, use the Set-Column Width command. To increase column A, move the cursor to A1 and enter

/Worksheet Column Set-Width

Then respond to the prompt *Enter column width:* with

35

and press Enter. To increase the remaining columns, enter

/Worksheet Global Column-Width

Then respond to the prompt *Enter column width:* with

13

and press Enter.

Entering the Headings

Move the cursor to A1, type

^Tax Estimator for Tax Planning

and press Enter. The ^ key centers the text in the cell. Move the cursor to A6, type

^Income

and press Enter. Move the cursor to A20, type

^Adjustments

and press Enter. The remaining headings don't need to be centered. Type the headings from Figure 7-1 into column A.

Saving the Worksheet with Replace
/File Save Replace

It's best to save the spreadsheet often. Enter

/File Save

and press Enter when the filename *Taxest* automatically displays. The software will check to see if you want to write over your previous file, so enter

Replace

to replace the file.

Entering Formulas

Cell C18 holds a formula that adds the income entries in column B. Move the cursor to C18, type

@SUM(B7.B17)

and press Enter. The @SUM is a function that enables some time-saving. Instead of entering the formula B7+B8+B9 into C18, and so on though B17, the @SUM function totals every cell from B7 through B17. Enter the following formulas in the cells below:

```
C27   @SUM(B21.B26)
C29   +C18−C27
C31   @IF(B4="S",AE5,AE6)
C32   +B3*AE3
C33   +C29−@IF(B30>C31,B30+C32,C31+C32)
C34   +B34
C42   +C34−(B36+B39+B40)+B37
```

To enter the minimum amount of information in the tax tables, press F5, respond to the prompt *Enter address to go to:* with

AE3

and press Enter. Enter the amount for the exemptions and standard deductions in AE3, AE5, and AE6 from Figure 7-2 or the current tax publication for this year. These amounts are important for the formulas in C31 and C32 above. The formula in C31 looks for the *S* or *M* in B4. If it finds an *S*, then it places the single standard deduction in AE5 in the cell. If not, it places the married standard deduction from AE6 in the cell. C33 then compares the standard deduction to the itemized deductions in B30 and subtracts the greater one; it then subtracts the exemption amount in C32 from the adjusted gross income. Move the cursor to B4 and enter *M* for Married. Cell C31 should display 5200 and cell C33, −5200.

Formatting the Spreadsheet to Currency
/Range Format Currency

You need to format columns B and C from row 7 down to currency. Since you only want these columns to be in currency, use the Range command instead of the Worksheet Global Format command. Enter

/Range Format Currency

and respond to the prompt *Enter number of decimal places:* with

2

Press Enter. Respond to the prompt *Enter range to format:* with

B7.C42

and press Enter.

Entering the Repeating Underline
\ =

Cell C43 contains a double underline created with the equal sign. To enter the repeating underline, move the cursor to C43 and enter

\ =

Protecting and Unprotecting the Spreadsheet
When you complete the spreadsheet, you can turn the protection on to prevent losing the formulas and headings. The only entries that will change will be in column B. To keep that area unprotected, enter

/Range Unprotect

and respond to the prompt *Enter range to unprotect:* with

B3.B42

Press Enter. The spreadsheet is complete. Turn the protection on to prevent any further changes. Enter

/Worksheet Global Protection Enable

and if you need to make changes later, enter

/Worksheet Global Protection Disable

to turn it off.

Saving the Spreadsheet

/File Save
Since you can use this tax estimator for each year or person, save the spreadsheet without data. To save the file, enter

/File Save

and press Enter when the filename *Taxest* automatically displays.

The software will check to see if you want to write over your previous file, so enter

Replace

to replace the file.

How to Use the Tax Estimator

Check the exemption and standard deduction amounts in cells AE3 though AE6 to see if they match the current year tax publication. Enter the number of exemptions in B3. Enter an *M* for married filing jointly or *S* for single in B4. Enter your wages and other income in cells B7 through B17. When entering amounts, don't enter the comma or dollar sign. If you see a row of asterisks instead of the amount you entered, the column isn't wide enough to hold that amount. Use the Worksheet Column-Set command, /WCS, to increase the size of the column. Enter any adjustments to income in cells B21 through B26. Enter your itemized deductions in cell B30. Look up your taxable income in the current year tax publication and enter the tax in cell B34. Enter your federal tax withheld and estimated payments made in cells B39 and B40. Your estimated tax due or refund will calculate in cell C42.

Since it's difficult to include all tax law items in one spreadsheet, use this as an estimator for planning your taxes rather than as a complete tax preparation tool.

Saving the Completed Worksheet
/File Save

Save the new worksheet containing this year's tax information in a new file separate from the previous Taxest file. Enter

/File Save

Then type in

Taxest89

for Tax estimator 1989 (or any name that will be easy for you to remember) and press Enter. It's a good idea to save the file before printing.

Printing the Worksheet
/Print Printer Range Align Go Quit

You can print the tax estimator now. The print command allows printing to a file or printer. Roll the paper to the perforation or top of form and enter

/Print Printer Range

Respond to the prompt *Enter print range:* with

A1.C43

and press Enter. To begin the printing job, enter

Align Go Quit

Saving the Worksheet with Replace
/File Save Replace

After printing the balance sheet, save this spreadsheet one more time to keep the printing instructions in the file. Enter

/File Save

and press Enter when the filename *Taxest89* automatically displays. The software will check to see if you want to write over your previous file, so enter

Replace

to replace the file.

Figure 7-2. Tax Tables

	AA	AB	AC	AD	AE	AF	AG	AH	AI
1			Tax Tables 1989						
2									
3	Status	M		Exemptions	2000.00				
4	Taxable	51762.00		Standard Deductions:					
5	Tax 1	4462.50		Single	3100.00				
6	percent	0.28		Married	5200.00				
7	Tax 2	5827.36							
8	Total Tax	10289.86							
9		Single:	Over	Percent	Plus		Married:	Over	Percent	Plus
10									
11			0.00	0.15	0.00			0.00	0.15	0.00
12			18550.00	0.28	2677.50			30950.00	0.28	4462.50
13			44900.00	0.33	9761.50			74850.00	0.33	16264.50
14			93130.00	0.00	-13651.44			155320.00	0.00	-34174.14
15									
16									
17		Exemptions	3					Exemption	3
18	1		26076.40				1		43489.60
19	2	51762.00					2	51762.00	
20	3	93130.00					3	155320.00	
21	4		-41368.00				4		-103558.00
22	5		-11583.04				5		-28996.24
23	6		-2068.40				6		-5177.90
24	7		1680.00				7		1680.00
25	8		-2068.40				8		-5177.90
26	9		-13651.44				9		-34174.14
27									

Adding the Tax Tables

1-2-3 has the ability to look up tax amounts and rates from a table. You can create a lookup table in cells AC11 through AI14 that will hold the taxable income and corresponding tax rate percentage and base tax amount. When you enter amounts in column B, formulas in cells AB4 through AB7 will look up the taxable income from C33 in the table. If the protection is still enabled, use the command /WGPD to disable.

To enter the table, press the F5 function key, respond to the prompt *Enter address to go to:* with

AA1

and press Enter. Enter the headings in cell AC1, columns AA and AD, and row 9 from Figure 7-2. Move the cursor to AB3, type

+B4

and press Enter. Move the cursor to AB4, type

+C33

and press Enter.

There are two tax tables, one in cells AB9 through AE14 for single filers and the other in AF9 through AI14 for married filing jointly. Enter both tables from Figure 7-2 or your current tax publication. Don't enter cells AE14 and AI14, since they contain a formula you'll enter later.

To enter the formula for the lookup function, move the cursor to AB5, type

@IF($AB$3="S",@VLOOKUP($AB$4,$AC$11.$AE14,2),@VLOOKUP ($AB$4,$AG$11.$AI$14,2))

and press Enter. This formula means to vertically look up the taxable income in AB4 at the table located at AC11 through AE14, and to use the information in the second column after the taxable amount. Enter the location of the table with a dollar sign prefix for an absolute location. When you copy this formula down column AB, the location of AC11 through AE14 won't adjust to AC12.AE15.

Copying Formulas
/Copy

Copy the formula in cell AB5, which has the lookup formula, down the column to eliminate the need for entering the formula again. To copy, enter

/Copy

and respond to the prompt *Enter range to copy FROM:* with

AB5

Press Enter. Respond to the prompt *Enter range to copy TO:* with

AB6.AB7

and press Enter. Move the cursor to AB6 and press F2 to edit the formula to the following:

**@IF($AB$3="S",@VLOOKUP($AB$4,$AC$11.$AE14,1),@VLOOKUP
($AB$4,$AG$11.$AI$14,1))**

Move the cursor to AB7 and edit the formula to the following:

**(+AB4−@IF($AB$3="S",@VLOOKUP($AB$4,$AC$11.$AE14,0),
@VLOOKUP($AB$4,$AG$11.$AI$14,0)))*AB6**

Move the cursor to AB8, type

+AB5+AB7

and press Enter.

Creating the Worksheet for Incomes Exceeding Table Limits

The two tables starting at row 17 are for incomes that exceed $93,130 for single and $155,320 for married filing jointly. They recreate the worksheet that can be found at the bottom of the IRS Tax Rate Schedules. Be sure to check the percentages in cells AC22, AI22, AC23, and AI23; the exemption amount in cells AC24 and AI24; and the amounts in AC18 and AI18 each year. Enter headings in the following cells:

AB17 and AH17   Exemptions

Enter in column AA and AG the numbers 1 through 9 from Figure 7-2. These match the line numbers in the IRS Worksheet. Enter the following formulas in the cells below and press Enter:

AE14	+AC26
AI14	+AI26
AC17	+B3
AI17	+B3
AH19	+AB4
AB19	+AB4
AC21	+AB19−AB20
AI21	+AH19−AH20
AC22	+AC21*.28
AI22	+AI21*.28

AC23	+AC21*.05
AI23	+AI21*.05
AC24	+AC17*560
AI24	+AI17*560
AC25	@IF(AC23<AC24,AC23,AC24)
AI25	@IF(AI23<AI24,AI23,AI24)
AC26	+AC22+AC25
AI26	+AI22+AI25

Enter the following tax and limit amounts into the corresponding cells and press Enter:

AC18	26076.40
AI18	43489.60
AB20	93130
AH20	155320

Saving the Spreadsheet
/File Save

To save the completed file, enter

/File Save

1-2-3 will then ask for a filename; type

Taxest

and press Enter. If you saved the spreadsheet earlier, press Enter when the filename *Taxest* automatically displays. The software will check to see if you want to write over your previous file, so enter

Replace

to replace the file.

The Loan Amortization

The loan amortization spreadsheet allows you to enter the loan amount, rate, and number of months. The monthly payment, interest, principal, and current balance are calculated. The total interest paid is accumulated for tax purposes. The instructions include a loan up to 120 months, but you can extend the spreadsheet by copying the formulas to the desired limit.

Figure 7-3. Loan Amortization

	A	B	C	D	E	F
1	Loan Amortization					
2						
3	Loan Amt	$9,380.00				
4	Rate	16.25%				
5	Months	36				
6						
7	Payment	Interest	Principal	Balance	Total Int	Pmt#
8	$330.93	$127.02	$203.91	$9,176.09	$127.02	1
9	$330.93	$124.26	$206.67	$8,969.42	$251.28	2
10	$330.93	$121.46	$209.47	$8,759.95	$372.74	3
11	$330.93	$118.62	$212.31	$8,547.64	$491.37	4
12	$330.93	$115.75	$215.18	$8,332.46	$607.11	5
13	$330.93	$112.84	$218.10	$8,114.36	$719.95	6
14	$330.93	$109.88	$221.05	$7,893.31	$829.83	7
15	$330.93	$106.89	$224.04	$7,669.27	$936.72	8
16	$330.93	$103.85	$227.08	$7,442.19	$1,040.58	9
17	$330.93	$100.78	$230.15	$7,212.04	$1,141.35	10
18	$330.93	$97.66	$233.27	$6,978.77	$1,239.02	11
19	$330.93	$94.50	$236.43	$6,742.34	$1,333.52	12
20	$330.93	$91.30	$239.63	$6,502.71	$1,424.82	13
21	$330.93	$88.06	$242.87	$6,259.84	$1,512.88	14
22	$330.93	$84.77	$246.16	$6,013.67	$1,597.65	15
23	$330.93	$81.44	$249.50	$5,764.18	$1,679.09	16
24	$330.93	$78.06	$252.88	$5,511.30	$1,757.14	17
25	$330.93	$74.63	$256.30	$5,255.00	$1,831.77	18
26	$330.93	$71.16	$259.77	$4,995.23	$1,902.94	19
27	$330.93	$67.64	$263.29	$4,731.94	$1,970.58	20
28	$330.93	$64.08	$266.85	$4,465.09	$2,034.66	21
29	$330.93	$60.46	$270.47	$4,194.62	$2,095.12	22
30	$330.93	$56.80	$274.13	$3,920.49	$2,151.93	23
31	$330.93	$53.09	$277.84	$3,642.65	$2,205.02	24
32	$330.93	$49.33	$281.60	$3,361.05	$2,254.34	25
33	$330.93	$45.51	$285.42	$3,075.63	$2,299.86	26
34	$330.93	$41.65	$289.28	$2,786.35	$2,341.51	27
35	$330.93	$37.73	$293.20	$2,493.15	$2,379.24	28
36	$330.93	$33.76	$297.17	$2,195.97	$2,413.00	29
37	$330.93	$29.74	$301.19	$1,894.78	$2,442.74	30
38	$330.93	$25.66	$305.27	$1,589.51	$2,468.39	31
39	$330.93	$21.52	$309.41	$1,280.10	$2,489.92	32
40	$330.93	$17.33	$313.60	$966.50	$2,507.25	33
41	$330.93	$13.09	$317.84	$648.66	$2,520.34	34
42	$330.93	$8.78	$322.15	$326.51	$2,529.13	35
43	$330.93	$4.42	$326.51	($0.00)	$2,533.55	36
44					END	

Creating the Loan Amortization

What follows is a brief review of the material from Chapter 2. If you're a *1-2-3* newcomer, you should read Chapter 2. Bring up the spreadsheet screen by typing *123* at the DOS prompt. The startup screen will have columns lettered A–H across the top of the screen and numbers for the rows going down the left side. The intersection of these columns and rows are called *cells*, where information is stored. For example, cell B4 is the intersection of the second column over (B) and the fourth row down (4). Cell D3 is the intersection of the fourth column over (D) and the third row down (3). The cursor will start in cell A1, and you can move it down or across with the arrow keys. What you type on the keyboard will appear on the line above the columns. It will move into the cell on which the cursor is resting when you press the Enter key.

Entering a Menu Command

When you press the slash key (/), different menu options such as Worksheet, Range, Copy, File, Print, Graph, Data, System, and Quit appear across the top of the screen. To select a command, press the first letter of the option, then the first letter of the next submenu item until you've finished. You can also select a menu item by moving the right- and left-arrow keys until the option is highlighted and then pressing Enter. All the instructions in this chapter will be done by entering the first letter.

Cancel or Erase
Esc

The Esc key normally cancels a command and takes you back to the previous menu or status. If you make an error and want to erase what you've typed so far, press the Esc key. If you've already pressed the Enter key and want to erase the contents of a cell, move the cursor to the cell you want to clear. Enter

/Range Erase

and press Enter to accept the range as the current cell.

Moving the Cursor

Use the arrow keys to move from cell to cell. Other helpful keys to know are:

F5 (Goto)   Moves to any cell location
Home   Moves to upper left corner (A1)
PageUp   Moves up one page
PageDown   Moves down one page

Quitting and Saving the Spreadsheet

If you need to quit before completing the spreadsheet and want to save the file, enter

/File Save

1-2-3 will then ask for a filename; type

LoanAmor

and press Enter. A filename can be up to eight characters, but you should stick to letters and numbers. Don't include any symbols such as + = . * / ? (> % or leave any blank spaces. To quit without saving, enter

/Quit Yes

and you should be back at the DOS prompt. Just enter *123* to go back into the spreadsheet.

Widening the Columns
/Worksheet Global Column-Width

Since all the columns must be wide enough to hold long amounts, use the Worksheet Global Column-Width command. To increase the columns, enter

/Worksheet Global Column-Width

Then respond to the prompt *Enter column width:* with

11

and press Enter.

Entering the Headings

Move the cursor to A1, type

Loan Amortization

and press Enter. Move the cursor to A3, type

Loan Amt

and press Enter. Move the cursor to A4, type

Rate

and press Enter. Move the cursor to A5, type

Months

and press Enter. Type the headings on row 7 from Figure 7-3.

Creating a Named Range

To simplify entering formulas later, name the range in B3 though B5 with the names in column A. To name this range, move the cursor to A3, enter

/Range Name Labels Right

and respond to the prompt *Enter label range:* with

A3.A5

Press Enter. To check if the labels are properly named, press the F5 (goto) key, respond to the prompt *Enter address to go to:* with

Rate

and press Enter. The cursor should move to B4.

Saving the Worksheet with Replace
/File Save Replace

It's best to save the spreadsheet often. Enter

/File Save

and press Enter when the filename *Loanamor* automatically displays. The software will check to see if you want to write over your previous file, so enter

Replace

to replace the file.

Entering Formulas

Cell A8 holds the formula that calculates the monthly payment. The @PMT function structure is @PMT(Loan amount, interest rate, term of loan). Move the cursor to A8 and type

@PMT($Loan Amt,$Rate/12,$Months)

or, if you didn't name the ranges,

@PMT($B$3,$B$4/12,$B$5)

and press Enter. Enter the following formulas in the cells below:

```
B8    +Rate/12*Loan Amt
C8    +A8-B8
D8    +Loan Amt-C8
E8    +B8
F8    1
A9    @IF(F9<=$Months,$A$8,0)
B9    +$Rate/12*D8
C9    +A9-B9
D9    +D8-C9
E9    +E8+B9
F9    @IF(F8<$Months,F8+1,"END")
```

The formulas in A9 and F9 have @IF functions to stop at the number of months in B5. Since you'll be copying the formulas in row 9, the absolute ($) sign is necessary to prevent the range for Loan Amt, Months, and Rate from adjusting to the new cell location. It's normal to have an ERR display in some of the cells until you complete the spreadsheet.

Formatting the Spreadsheet to Currency
/Worksheet Global Format Currency

Since most of the spreadsheet will be in currency, use the Worksheet Global Format command. Enter

/Worksheet Global Format Currency

and respond to the prompt *Enter number of decimal places:* with

2

Press Enter.

You need to format column F to fixed format. Since you only want this column to be in fixed format, use the Range command instead of the Worksheet Global Format command. Enter

/Range Format Fixed

and respond to the prompt *Enter number of decimal places:* with

0

Press Enter. Respond to the prompt *Enter range to format:* with

F8.F150

and press Enter.

To format the percentage for interest rate, enter

/Range Format Percent 2

and respond to the prompt *Enter range to format:* with

Rate

Press Enter.

To format the number of months, enter

/Range Format Fixed 0

and respond to the prompt *Enter range to format:* with

Months

Press Enter.

Copying Formulas
/Copy

Copy the formula in row 9 down to eliminate the need for entering the formula again. To copy, enter

/Copy

and respond to the prompt *Enter range to copy FROM:* with

A9.F9

Press Enter. Respond to the prompt *Enter range to copy TO:* with

A10.F48

and press Enter.

Saving the Spreadsheet
/File Save

Since you can use this loan amortization spreadsheet for each loan, save the spreadsheet without data. To save the file, enter

/File Save

and press Enter when the filename *Loanamor* automatically displays. The software will check to see if you want to write over your previous file, so enter

Replace

to replace the file.

How to Use the Loan Amortization Spreadsheet

Move the cursor to B3 and enter the loan amount. Move the cursor to B4 and enter the interest rate in decimal form as .1625 for 16.25

percent, or 9.5% for 9.5 percent interest. Enter the number of months in B5. If you see a row of asterisks instead of the amount you entered, the column isn't wide enough to hold that amount. Use the Worksheet Column-Set command, /WCS, to increase the size of the column.

Saving the Completed Worksheet
/File Save

Save the new worksheet containing this loan information in a new file separate from the previous Loanamor file. Enter

/File Save

then type in

Carloan2

for Car loan number 2 (or any name that will be easy for you to remember) and press Enter. It's a good idea to save the file before printing.

Printing the Worksheet
/Print Printer Range Align Go Quit

You can print the loan amortization now. The print command allows printing to a file or printer. Roll the paper to the perforation or top of form, enter

/Print Printer Range

and respond to the prompt *Enter print range:* with

A1.F43

Press Enter. You need to adjust the range depending on the length of your loan. Move the cursor down the screen until you find the *END* in column F. The row before this will be your last row in the print range. To begin the printing job, enter

Align Go Quit

Saving the Worksheet with Replace
/File Save Replace

After printing the balance sheet, save this spreadsheet one more
time to keep the printing instructions in the file. Enter

/File Save

and press Enter when the filename *Carloan2* automatically displays.
The software will check to see if you want to write over your previous file, so enter

Replace

to replace the file.

Volume Profit Analysis

A volume profit analysis is a useful tool in setting prices and forecasting profit. The spreadsheet uses the given amounts for fixed
costs, sales price, variable cost, and forecasted units. The remaining
items are calculated based on formulas in the spreadsheet. If you
have Release 2.2, you can print the spreadsheet and graph with
Allways as in Figure 7-4. If not, you'll need to first print the spreadsheet and then use the PrintGraph program to print the graph.

Creating the Volume Profit Analysis

What follows is a brief review of the material from Chapter 2. If
you're a 1-2-3 newcomer, you should read Chapter 2. Bring up the
spreadsheet screen by typing *123* at the DOS prompt. The startup
screen will have columns lettered A–H across the top of the screen
and numbers for the rows going down the left side. The intersection of these columns and rows are called *cells*, where information
is stored. For example, cell B4 is the intersection of the second column over (B) and the fourth row down (4). Cell D3 is the intersection of the fourth column over (D) and the third row down (3). The
cursor will start in cell A1, and you can move it down or across
with the arrow keys. What you type on the keyboard will appear
on the line above the columns. It will move into the cell on which
the cursor is resting when you press the Enter key.

Figure 7-4. Printing Volume Profit Analysis with Allways

Volume Profit Analysis

Fixed Costs	$86,650
Sales Price	$175
Variable Cost	$63
Fixed and Variable Cost	$135,391
Profit per unit	$112
Breakeven Point	$135,391
Breakeven Point in Units	774
Forecasted Units	995
Forecasted Sales	$174,125
Forecasted Fixed and Variable Costs	$149,335
Forecasted Profit	$24,790

Forecasted
Breakeven and Profit Analysis

(Thousands)

△ Breakeven Point

□ Fixed costs   + Sales   ◇ Fixed and Variable

Entering a Menu Command

When you press the slash key (/), different menu options such as
Worksheet, Range, Copy, File, Print, Graph, Data, System, and
Quit appear across the top of the screen. To select a command,
press the first letter of the option, then the first letter of the next
submenu item until you've finished. You can also select a menu
item by moving the right- and left-arrow keys until the option is
highlighted and then pressing Enter. All the instructions in this
chapter will be done by entering the first letter.

Cancel or Erase
Esc

The Esc key normally cancels a command and takes you back to the previous menu or status. If you make an error and want to erase what you've typed so far, press the Esc key. If you've already pressed the Enter key and want to erase the contents of a cell, move the cursor to the cell you want to clear. Enter

/Range Erase

and press Enter to accept the range as the current cell.

Moving the Cursor

Use the arrow keys to move from cell to cell. Other helpful keys to know are:

F5 (Goto)   Moves to any cell location
Home   Moves to upper left corner (A1)
PageUp   Moves up one page
PageDown   Moves down one page

Quitting and Saving the Spreadsheet

If you need to quit before completing the spreadsheet and want to save the file, enter

/File Save

1-2-3 will then ask for a filename; type

Vlprofit

and press Enter. A filename can be up to eight characters, but you should stick to letters and numbers. Don't include any symbols such as + = . * / ? (> % or leave any blank spaces. To quit without saving, enter

/Quit Yes

and you should be back at the DOS prompt. Just enter 123 to go back into the spreadsheet.

Widening the Column
/Worksheet Column Set-Width

Since column B must be wide enough to hold long descriptions, use the Set-Column Width command. To increase column B, move the cursor to B1 and enter

/Worksheet Column Set-Width

Then respond to the prompt *Enter column width:* with

40

and press Enter.

Entering the Headings

Move the cursor to B2, type

^Volume Profit Analysis

and press Enter. The ^ prefix centers the heading in the cell. Type the following in the cells below and press Enter:

B5	Fixed Costs
B6	Sales Price
B7	Variable Cost
B11	Fixed and Variable Cost
B12	Profit per unit
B13	Breakeven Point
B14	Breakeven Point in Units
B17	Forecasted Units
B18	Forecasted Sales
B19	Forecasted Fixed and Variable Costs
B20	Forecasted Profit

Entering Formulas

Most of the cells in column D hold formulas. Type the following formulas into the cells below:

D11   +D5+D7*D14
D12   +D6−D7
D13   +D5/(D12/D6)
D14   +D5/D12
D18   +D17*D6
D19   +D17*D7+D5
D20   +D18−D19

Hidden Column for Graph

Column C, not shown in Figure 7-4, is a hidden column that holds some amounts that you can create later for the graph. Enter the following amounts in the cells below:

C5   +D5
C11 0
C13 0
C18 0
C19 +D5

To hide this column, move to C1, enter

/Worksheet Column Hide

and press Enter to hide the current column.

Formatting the Spreadsheet
/Range Format Currency

You need to format column D to currency. Since you only want this column to be in currency, use the Range command instead of the Worksheet Global Format command. Enter

/Range Format Currency

and respond to the prompt *Enter number of decimal places:* with

0

Press Enter. Respond to the prompt *Enter range to format:* with

D1.D20

and press Enter. To format the two cells containing units, enter

/Range Format Fixed

and respond to the prompt *Enter number of decimal places:* with

0

Press Enter. Respond to the prompt *Enter range to format:* with

D14

and press Enter. Repeat for D17.

Saving the Worksheet with Replace
/File Save Replace

It's best to save the spreadsheet often. Enter

/File Save

and press Enter when the filename *Vlprofit* automatically displays. The software will check to see if you want to write over your previous file, so enter

Replace

to replace the file.

Unprotect a Range
/Range Unprotect

When you've completed the spreadsheet you can turn the protection on to prevent losing the formulas. The only amounts that will change will be the fixed costs, sales price, variable cost, and forecasted units. Unprotecting also highlights the cells to make it easy to see what you need to enter. To keep them unprotected, enter

/Range Unprotect

and respond to the prompt *Enter range to unprotect:* with

D5.D7

Press Enter. Then enter

/Range Unprotect

and respond to the prompt *Enter range to unprotect:* with

D17

Press Enter.

How to Use the Volume Profit Analysis

Enter the fixed costs, sales price, variable cost, and forecasted units in cells D5 through D7 and D17 from Figure 7-4 or your books. The remaining amounts will calculate automatically. When entering amounts, don't enter the comma or dollar sign. If you see a row of asterisks instead of the amount you entered, the column isn't wide enough to hold that amount. Use the Worksheet Column-Set command, /WCS, to increase the size of the column.

Saving the Worksheet with Replace
/File Save Replace

It's best to save the spreadsheet often. Enter

/File **S**ave

and press Enter when the filename *Vlprofit* automatically displays. The software will check to see if you want to write over your previous file, so enter

Replace

to replace the file.

Printing the Worksheet
/Print Printer Range Align Go Quit

You can print the volume profit analysis now. The print command allows printing to a file or printer. Roll the paper to the perforation or top of form, enter

/Print Printer Range

and respond to the prompt *Enter print range:* with

A1.D20

Press Enter. To begin the printing job, enter

Align Go Quit

Saving the Worksheet with Replace
/File Save Replace

After printing the volume profit analysis, save this spreadsheet one more time to keep the printing instructions in the file. Enter

/File Save

and press Enter when the filename *Vlprofit* automatically displays. The software will check to see if you want to write over your previous file, so enter

Replace

to replace the file.

The Breakeven and Profit Analysis Graph

Sometimes a graph enables you to see changes much better than amounts listed side by side. You can create a breakeven point graph from this volume profit analysis that displays the fixed costs, fixed and variable costs, and forecasted sales. Your computer will need the ability to display graphics for you to view the graph on your monitor. If a graphic mode isn't possible, you'll still be able to print the graph you create if you have a graphics printer.

Creating the Graph

There are three basic steps involved in creating a graph:

• Select the graph type.
• Define the range.
• Enter View to display the graph.

There are more commands that create titles, legends, color display, grids, and custom scaling. To create a simple graph, load the file that created the volume profit analysis above.

Retrieving a Spreadsheet File
/File Retrieve

After entering *123* at the DOS prompt, to retrieve the previous volume profit analysis file enter

/File Retrieve

then type in

Vlprofit

and press Enter.

Creating the Graph
/Graph

Enter

/Graph Type Line A

for the *A* range. Respond to the prompt *Enter first data range:* with

C5.D5

and press Enter. Enter

B

to enter the *B* range. Respond to the prompt *Enter second data range:* with

C18.D18

and press Enter. Enter

C

to enter the *C* range. Respond to the prompt *Enter third data range:* with

C19.D19

and press Enter. Enter

D

to enter the *D* range. Respond to the prompt *Enter the fourth data range:* with

D13

and press Enter. Enter

Options Titles First

and type

Forecasted

and press Enter. Enter

Titles Second

and type

Breakeven and Profit Analysis

and press Enter. Enter

Legend **A**

and respond to the prompt *Enter legend for first data range:* with

Fixed costs

and press Enter. Enter

Legend B

and respond to the prompt *Enter legend for second data range:* with

Sales

and press Enter. Enter

Legend C

and respond to the prompt *Enter legend for third data range:* with

Fixed and Variable

and press Enter. Enter

Data-Labels D

and respond to the prompt *Enter data-label range for fourth data range:* with

B13

and press Enter. Enter

Right Quit Quit View

to place the Breakeven label to the right of the data point, quit the options menu, and view the graph. If you get a beep and a blank screen, then possibly your computer system or software setup isn't ready for graphics. After viewing the graph, press any key to bring back the graph menu.

To limit the size of the graph, enter

Options Scale Y-axis Manual Lower

and type

80000

Press Enter. Enter

Upper

and type

190000

and press Enter. To see the new graph, enter

Quit Quit View

and press any key to return to the spreadsheet. Enter

Quit

to quit the graph menu.

Viewing the Graph from the Spreadsheet
F10
It's possible to make changes to data in the spreadsheet and have
1-2-3 redraw the graph. Change the fixed costs and press F10; the
new graph will reflect the change. Press any key to bring back the
spreadsheet, change back to your original fixed cost, and press F10
again to see the original graph.

Saving the Spreadsheet with Replace
/File Save Replace
After finishing the graph settings, enter

Quit

to quit the graph menu. Now save this spreadsheet one more time
to keep the graph instructions in the file. Enter

/File Save

and press Enter when the filename *Vlprofit* automatically displays.

The software will check to see if you want to write over your previous file, so enter

Replace

to replace the file.

Printing the Graph

There's no option on the graph menu to print the graph. Sometimes you can produce a satisfactory graph with the Shift-PrintScreen keys but you can print a more sophisticated graph with the PrintGraph program. First save the graph in a graph picture file. Enter

/Graph **S**ave

When asked for a graph filename, type

Vlprofit

and press Enter. To quit the graph menu, enter

Quit

Then to exit *1-2-3*, enter

/Quit **Y**es

and at the DOS prompt type

LOTUS

Press Enter. This displays the Lotus Access System menu, which contains the PrintGraph program. Move the arrow key to highlight PrintGraph and press Enter. The PrintGraph menu displays the Image-Select and Settings options. Highlight the Settings option and press Enter. Check the printer type and directory setups, and make any necessary changes. If all are correct, press Esc, highlight Image-Select, and press Enter. After the available graph filenames are displayed, select Vlprofit and press Enter. Then enter

Align **G**o

and the graph will print. After printing, highlight the Exit option, press Enter, and answer Yes.

Printing with Allways with Release 2.2 Only

Allways is an add-in program included with Release 2.2 that enables you to create professional quality reports. Allways also has the feature to print graphs within *1-2-3* without using the PrintGraph program. To load Allways in Release 2.2, enter

/Add-in **A**ttach

and press Enter when Allways.ADN is highlighted. If no add-in files appear, you need to install Allways first. Use the instructions for setting up Allways in your *1-2-3* reference manual. After pressing the highlighted Allways.ADN file, you have the option to assign a key to load Allways each time you use it. Select 7 for Alt-F7 to load Allways. Enter Quit to exit the Add-in menu. If don't have the previous volume profit analysis file displayed, load the file. Enter

/File **R**etrieve

then type in

Vlprofit

and press Enter. Press Alt-F7 and Allways will load. Your spreadsheet might have a different appearance, depending on your monitor type. Press slash (/) to see the Allways commands. To load the graph at the bottom of the spreadsheet, enter

/Graph **A**dd

and respond to the prompt *Name of .PIC file:* with

Vlprofit

Press Enter. The next prompt is for the range to put the graph in; respond with

A23.E45

and press Enter. Enter

Quit

to quit the Allways graph menu. Move the cursor to B2, enter

/Format **F**ont

and highlight *Triumvirate 14 point* to put the heading *Volume Profit Analysis* in a larger print. Press Enter to accept the current cell. Enter

/Print **R**ange **S**et

and respond to the prompt *Enter print range:* with

A1.E45

Press Enter. Enter

Go

and the spreadsheet and graph will print. The result should be similar to Figure 7-4. You have many options:

• Draw boxes.
• Change fonts.
• Enter shades.

See Chapter 2 or the section in your *1-2-3* reference manual, "Publishing with Allways," for more features. Your Allways settings are saved when you save your *1-2-3* file. Press Alt-F7 to return to *1-2-3* and enter

/File **S**ave

Press Enter when the filename *Vlprofit* automatically displays. The software will check to see if you want to write over your previous file, so enter

Replace

to replace the file. You'll now have three Vlprofit files:

Vlprofit.wk1   *1-2-3 file*
Vlprofit.pic   Graph file
Vlprofit.all   Allways file

Changing from Forecasted to Actual with Release 2.2 and 3 Only

Both new releases of *1-2-3* have the search and replace feature. To easily change the volume profit analysis from a forecasted to actual spreadsheet, you can search for *forecasted* and replace with *actual*. With the file Vlprofit created earlier loaded, enter

/Range Search

and respond to the prompt *Enter range to search:* with

B1.B20

Press Enter. Respond to the prompt *Enter string to search for:* with

Forecasted

and press Enter. Enter

Labels Replace

and respond to the prompt *Enter replacement string:* with

Actual

Press Enter. Enter

All

to replace all matches. If you don't like the results of the command, press Alt-F4 to undo the replacement and try again.

    Press F5 to go to D17 to change forecasted units to actual, and follow the printing instructions given earlier to print the actual volume profit analysis.

Appendices

Appendices

Appendix A
Lotus 1-2-3 Commands

	WORKSHEET
Global	Format Label-Prefix Column-Width Recalculation Protection Default Zero
Insert	Column Row
Delete	Column Row
Column	Set-Width Reset-Width Reset Hide Display
Erase	Yes No
Titles	Both Horizontal Vertical Clear
Window	Horizontal Vertical Sync Unsync Clear
Status	
Page	

	RANGE
Format	Fixed Scientific Currency Comma General +/− Percent Date Text Hidden Reset
Label	Left Right Center
Erase	
Name	Create Delete Labels Reset Table
Justify	
Protect	
Unprotect	
Input	
Value	
Transpose	

COPY
MOVE
FILE

	FILE
Retrieve	
Save	
Combine	Copy Add Subtract
Xtract	Formulas Values
Erase	Worksheet Print Graph Other
List	Worksheet Print Graph Other
Import	Text Numbers
Directory	Disk

	PRINT
Printer	Range Line Page Options Clear Align Go Quit
File	Range Line Page Options Clear Align Go Quit

	GRAPH
Type	Line Bar XY Stack-Bar Pie
XABCDEF	
Reset	Graph X A B C D E F Quit
View	
Save	
Options	Legend Format Titles Grid Scale Color B&W Data-Labels Quit
Name	Use Create Delete Reset Table
Quit	

Appendix A

	DATA

Fill

Table   1 2 Reset

Sort   Data-Range Primary-Key Secondary-Key Reset Go Quit

Query   Input Criteria Output Find Extract Unique Delete Reset Quit

Distribution

Matrix   Invert Multiply

Regression   X-Range Y-Range Output-Range Intercept Reset Go Quit

Parse   Format-Line Input-Column Output-Range Reset Go Quit

SYSTEM
QUIT

350

Appendix B
Function Keys and Cursor Movements

F1	Help – Displays the help index
F2	Edit – Enables edit mode for current cell
F3	Name – Displays a list of range names
F4	Absolute – Inserts an absolute ($) reference
F5	GoTo – Quick movement to the specified cell
F6	Window – Moves back and forth between windows
F7	Query – Repeats a Data Query Extract or Find command
F8	Table – Repeats a Data Table command
F9	Calc – Recalculates the formulas
F10	Graph – Displays the current graph or redraws a graph

Cursor Movement

F5 (Go To)	Moves to any cell location
Home	Moves to upper left corner (A1)
End Right Arrow	Moves to bottom right corner
Page Up	Moves up one page
Page Down	Moves down one page
Ctrl-Right Arrow	Moves right one page
Ctrl Left Arrow	Moves left one page

Appendix C
New Commands for Release 2.2

	WORKSHEET

Global   Default
              Other   Clock Undo Beep Add-in
              Autoexec Yes No

Column   Column-Range
Learn   Range Cancel Erase

	RANGE

Search   Formulas Labels Both
              Find Replace

	FILE

List   Linked
Admin   Reservation Table Link-Refresh

	GRAPH

Reset   Ranges Options
Options   Legend
                   Range
              Format
                   Graph
              Data-Labels
                   Group
Group

	ADD-IN

Attach
Detach
Invoke
Clear
Quit

New Function Keys

Alt F2   Turns on and off step mode for macro debugging
Alt F4   Undo
Alt F5   Turns on and off macro learn feature

Appendix D
New Commands for Release 3

		WORKSHEET			
Global	Default				
	Other	Graph	Temp	Ext	Autoexec	Group
	Clock				Yes
	Undo				No
	Beep				
Column	Column–Range				
Hide	Enable	Disable			

		RANGE			
Search	Formulas Labels Both				
	Find Replace				

		FILE			
List	Active Linked				
New	Before After				
Open	Before After				
Admin	Reservation Table Seal Link–Refresh				

		PRINT			
Printer	Image	Sample	Hold		
Encoded					
Suspend					
Resume					
Cancel					
Quit					

GRAPH

Type	HLCO	Mixed	Feature			
Reset	Ranges Options					
Options	Legend	Format	Titles	Grid	Scale	Advanced	Data–Labels
	Range	Graph	2Y–Axis	Y–Axis	2Y Scale	Colors	Group
			Note			Text	
			Other Note			Hatches	

Group

DATA

External

New Function Keys

Alt F1   Compose characters that cannot be normally entered
Alt F2   Turns on and off record buffer and step mode
Alt F3   Selects a macro to run
Alt F4   Undo
Alt F6   Zoom in and out of current window in perspective mode

New Cursor Movements

Ctrl Page Up   Moves up one worksheet in perspective mode
Ctrl Page Down   Moves down one worksheet in perspective mode

Index